AICPA & CIMA

Worldwide leaders in public and management accounting

D1237313

Checklists and Illustrative Financial Statements

Not-for-Profit Entities

April 30, 2020

1910-75488

© 2020 Association of International Certified Professional Accountants. All rights reserved.

For information about the procedure for requesting permission to make copies of any part of this work, please email Copyright-Permissions@aicpa-cima.com with your request. Otherwise, requests should be written and mailed to Permissions Department, 220 Leigh Farm Road, Durham, NC 27707-8110 USA.

1 2 3 4 5 6 7 8 9 0 AAP 2 9 8 7 6 5 4 3 2 1 0

ISBN 978-1-95068-845-6

Notice to Readers

Dear Valued Customer,

The following checklists and illustrative financial statements have been developed by the AICPA Accounting and Auditing Publications staff to serve as nonauthoritative practice aids for use by preparers of financial statements and by practitioners who audit, review, or compile financial statements. The checklists address those requirements most likely to be encountered when reporting on financial statements of a not-for-profit entity prepared in conformity with U.S. generally accepted accounting principles.

Relevant financial statement reporting and disclosure guidance issued through April 30, 2020, has been considered in the development of this edition of the checklists. The accounting guidance in these checklists has been conformed to reflect reference to FASB *Accounting Standards Codification*® as it existed on April 30, 2020.

Any guidance issued subsequent to April 30, 2020, has not been included in these checklists; therefore, you need to consider the applicability of guidance issued after that date. In determining the applicability of newly issued guidance, its effective date also should be considered.

We hope you find these checklists helpful as you perform your audit and compilation and review engagements. We would greatly appreciate your feedback on these checklists. You may email your comments to a&apublications@aicpa.org or write to

A&A Publications
AICPA
220 Leigh Farm Road
Durham, NC 27707-8110

Applicability

.01 These checklists and illustrative financial statements are designed to be applied to nongovernmental not-for-profit entities (NFPs) except for providers of health care services that follow the AICPA Audit and Accounting Guide *Health Care Entities*. The term *not-for-profit entity* is defined in the glossary of FASB *Accounting Standards Codification* (ASC) as

[a]n entity that possesses the following characteristics, in varying degrees, that distinguish it from a business entity: (*a*) contributions of significant amounts of resources from resource providers who do not expect commensurate or proportionate pecuniary return, (*b*) operating purposes other than to provide goods or services at a profit, and (*c*) absence of ownership interests like those of business entities. Entities that clearly fall outside this definition include the following: (*a*) all investor-owned entities and (*b*) entities that provide dividends, lower costs, or other economic benefits directly and proportionately to their owners, members, or participants, such as mutual insurance entities, credit unions, farm and rural cooperatives, and employee benefit plans.

.02 The FASB ASC glossary defines a *nongovernmental entity* as an entity that is not required to issue financial reports in accordance with guidance promulgated by GASB or the Federal Accounting Standards Advisory Board. The description of a governmental organization is also found in paragraph 1.04 of the AICPA Audit and Accounting Guide *Not-for-Profit Entities* (guide). When an NFP meets the definition for a governmental entity in paragraph 1.04 of the guide, the appropriate generally accepted accounting principles (GAAP) for the financial statements of the NFP is promulgated by GASB. Therefore, other than the definition in the next paragraph, which quotes paragraph 1.04, the accounting and financial reporting guidance in these checklists does not constitute category (b) accounting and financial reporting guidance for NFPs that meet the definition for a governmental entity because the AICPA did not make these checklists applicable to such governmental NFPs, and GASB did not clear it.

.03 Paragraph 1.04 of the guide states that:

As noted in AICPA Audit and Accounting Guide *State and Local Governments*, public corporations and bodies corporate and politic are governmental organizations. Other organizations are governmental if they have one or more of the following characteristics:

- Popular election of officers or appointment (or approval) of a controlling majority of the members of the organization's governing body by officials of one or more state or local governments

- The potential for unilateral dissolution by a government with the net assets reverting to a government

- The power to enact and enforce a tax levy

Furthermore, organizations are presumed to be governmental if they have the ability to issue directly (rather than through a state or municipal authority) debt that pays interest exempt from federal taxation. However, organizations possessing only that ability (to issue tax-exempt debt) and none of the other governmental characteristics may rebut the presumption that they are governmental if their determination is supported by compelling, relevant evidence.

.04 Governmental not-for-profit organizations are under the jurisdiction of GASB. GASB Statement No. 35, *Basic Financial Statements—and Management's Discussion and Analysis—for Public Colleges and Universities—an amendment of GASB Statement No. 34*, and GASB Statement No. 34, *Basic Financial Statements—and Management's Discussion and Analysis—for State and Local Governments*, are the two major statements that describe the accounting and financial reporting models for governmental not-for-profit organizations.

.05 These checklists and disclosures are for annual financial statements of *nonpublic entities*, as that term is defined in accounting standards. If the NFP is a public entity — for example, because it makes a filing with a regulatory agency in preparation for the sale of debt securities in a public market or because it is a conduit bond obligor for conduit debt securities that are traded in a public market — additional reporting requirements apply. The questions in these checklists about the additional reporting requirements for public entities identify where those additional requirements can be found without including the detailed disclosure requirements.

.06 Most NFPs do not issue interim financial reports for external users. If they do, FASB ASC 270, *Interim Reporting*, and AU-C section 930, *Interim Financial Information*,[1] should be considered in addition to this checklist. Statements on Standards for Accounting and Review Services are applicable to reviews of interim financial information if conditions *a–c* in paragraph .02 of AR-C section 90A, *Review of Financial Statements*,[2] are not met. Accountants engaged to perform reviews of interim financial information when the conditions in *a–c* in paragraph .02 of AR-C section 90A are met should perform such reviews in accordance with AU-C section 930.

.07 These checklists and illustrative financial statements are for financial statements prepared in accordance with GAAP. If financial statements are presented in accordance with special purpose framework (SPF), the provisions of AU-C section 800B, *Special Considerations — Audits of Financial Statements Prepared in Accordance With Special Purpose Frameworks* (if the suite of new reporting standards has not yet been adopted), and AU-C section 800, *Special Considerations — Audits of Financial Statements Prepared in Accordance With Special Purpose Frameworks* (if the suite of new reporting standards has been adopted), should be considered. The interpretation applies to cash, modified cash, regulatory, income tax, and other basis presentations. It addresses the summary of significant accounting policies; disclosures for financial statement items that are the same as, or similar to, those in GAAP statements; issues relating to financial statement presentation; and disclosure of matters not specifically identified on the face of the statements. The interpretation contains examples of how SPF disclosures, including presentation, may differ from those in GAAP financial statements.

.08 These checklists are for audits conducted in accordance with generally accepted auditing standards (GAAS) and assurance standards for nonissuers. NFPs, including those that meet the accounting definition

---

[1] All AU-C sections can be found in AICPA *Professional Standards*
[2] All AR-C sections can be found in AICPA *Professional Standards*

of a public entity, are not issuers subject to oversight by the PCAOB; thus, auditing standards issued by the PCAOB do not apply to audits of NFPs.

.09 However, although uncommon, an auditor may be engaged to follow PCAOB auditing standards in the audit of an NFP. When the audit is not under the jurisdiction of the PCAOB but the entity desires, or is required by an agency, by a regulator, or by contractual agreement, to obtain an audit conducted under PCAOB standards, the AICPA Code of Professional Conduct requires the auditor to also conduct the audit in accordance with GAAS. AU-C section 700, *Forming an Opinion and Reporting on Financial Statements*, clarifies the format of the auditor's report that should be issued when the auditor conducts an audit in accordance the standards of the PCAOB, but the audit is not under the jurisdiction of the PCAOB. These checklists do not provide information about audits conducted in accordance with PCAOB standards.

.10 If the auditor is engaged to audit both an NFP's financial statements and management's assessment of the effectiveness of internal control over financial reporting in accordance with PCAOB auditing standards, refer to paragraphs 85–98 of PCAOB Auditing Standard No. 5, *An Audit of Internal Control Over Financial Reporting That Is Integrated with An Audit of Financial Statements*,[3] for the audit reports that should be used.

Introduction to the Not-for-Profit Entity Reporting Model

.11 FASB ASC 958-205-45 requires that all NFPs provide a statement of financial position, a statement of activities, and a statement of cash flows. These financial statements present the NFP's total assets, liabilities, and net assets; the balances of and changes in each of the classes of net assets; and the change in cash and cash equivalents.

.12 All NFPs are required to report expenses on a functional basis, although that information need not appear on the face of the statement of activities. For example, NFPs that receive little or no support from the general public, such as trade associations, may prefer to report expenses by natural classification (for example, salaries, employee benefits, supplies, and utilities) on the face of the statement of activities and report expenses by functional classification in the notes to financial statements.

.13 All NFPs are required to include an analysis of expenses by both natural and functional classes, which may be presented in the format of a separate statement of functional expenses (presenting information about their expenses by both functional and natural classifications) as part of their general-purpose external financial statements. Alternatively, the analysis may be presented on the face of the statement of activities or in notes to the financial statements.

.14 A wide variety of users are interested in the financial statements of NFPs. Among the principal users are (*a*) contributors and potential contributors to the NFP, (*b*) beneficiaries of the NFP, (*c*) the NFP's trustees or directors, (*d*) employees of the NFP, (*e*) governmental units, (*f*) the NFP's creditors and potential creditors, and (*g*) constituent entities.

.15 A principal purpose of an NFP's financial statements is to communicate the ways resources have been used to carry out the NFP's mission. Although adequate measures of program accomplishment generally are not available in the context of present financial statements, the financial statements should identify the NFP's major programs and their costs. The financial statements of an NFP should also help the user evaluate the NFP's ability to continue to carry out its mission in the future.

.16 Another important aspect of financial reporting for NFPs is disclosure of the limitations placed by donors on use of resources. Many NFPs receive resources restricted by donors for particular purposes. The nature and extent of those restrictions determine the classification of resources within the net asset classes. To facilitate observance of limitations, NFPs often maintain their accounts using fund accounting, by which resources are classified for internal purposes into funds associated with specific activities or objectives. Each fund is a separate accounting entity with a self-balancing set of accounts for recording assets, liabilities, fund

---

[3] All AS sections can be found in *PCAOB Standards and Related Rules*.

© 2020, Association of International Certified Professional Accountants

balance, and changes in the fund balance. Although separate accounts may be maintained for each fund for internal purposes, financial statements prepared in accordance with GAAP focus on the entity as a whole rather than on fund balances and changes in fund balances. Fund balances should be classified on a statement of financial position based on the existence and type of donor-imposed restrictions. As discussed in chapter 16, "Fund Accounting," of the guide, because of differences in the types of limitations a fund accounting system tracks, for external financial reporting purposes, a fund balance may have to be divided among more than one net asset class.

Acknowledgments

.17 The AICPA gratefully acknowledges those members of the AICPA Not-for-Profit Entities Expert Panel who reviewed this edition of the checklist: Paul Chobanian, Karen Miessner, Laura Roos, and Sibi Thomas. The AICPA also acknowledges the invaluable assistance Susan E. Budak, CPA, provided in updating and maintaining the guidance in these checklists.

TABLE OF CONTENTS

Part 1
Instructions

General

.01 This publication includes the following parts:

- **Part 2, "Financial Statements and Notes Checklist."** For use by preparers of financial statements and by practitioners who audit, review, or compile them as they evaluate the adequacy of disclosures.

- **Part 3, "Auditors' Reports Checklist."** For use by auditors in reporting on audited financial statements.

- **Part 4, "Auditors' Reports Checklist for Audits Performed in Accordance With *Government Auditing Standards* and the Uniform Guidance."** For use in preparing auditor's reports on financial statement audits performed in accordance with *Government Auditing Standards*, the Single Audit Act Amendments of 1996, and Office of Management and Budget *Uniform Administrative Requirements, Cost Principles, and Audit Requirements for Federal Awards*.

- **Part 5, "Accountants' Reports on Compiled Financial Statements or Information or Reviewed Financial Statements Checklist."** For use by accountants in reporting on compiled or reviewed financial statements.

- **Part 6, "Illustrative Financial Statements, Notes, and Auditor's Report."**

.02 The checklists and illustrative financial statements included in this publication have been developed by the AICPA Accounting and Auditing Publications Team to serve as nonauthoritative technical practice aids to be used by preparers of a not-for-profit entity's (NFP's) financial statements prepared in conformity with accounting principles generally accepted in the United States (U.S. GAAP) and by practitioners who audit, review, or compile those financial statements as they evaluate the financial statements and the adequacy of disclosures. The checklists do not include disclosures that are applicable only to NFPs with activities in specialized industries (such as broadcasting or insurance); nor does it include disclosures prescribed by guidance whose applicability to NFPs is considered to be unlikely. It is designed for NFPs that are going concerns; thus, it does not contain disclosures about the liquidation basis of accounting. The auditor's and accountant's report checklists address those requirements most likely to be encountered when reporting on financial statements of an NFP prepared in conformity with U.S. GAAP. They do not include reporting requirements relating to other matters such as internal control or agreed-upon procedures.

.03 Users of the financial statements and notes checklist should remember that it is a disclosure checklist only and not a comprehensive U.S. GAAP recognition or measurement checklist. Accordingly, recognition and measurement issues related to preparing financial statements in conformity with U.S. GAAP are not included in the checklist.

.04 The AICPA Accounting and Auditing Publications staff has included guidance from FASB *Accounting Standards Codification* (ASC) as it existed on April 30, 2020. Questions are derived primarily from the content of the "Presentation" (section 45) and "Disclosure" (section 50) sections of FASB ASC. Because the checklist contains only presentation and disclosure items deemed most likely to be encountered when reporting on the financial statements of an NFP prepared in conformity with U.S. GAAP, not all paragraphs of the "Presentation" and "Disclosure" sections of FASB ASC have been included. Users should evaluate whether circumstances exist for which the relevant presentation and disclosure guidance is not provided in these checklists and illustrative financial statements and refer directly to FASB ASC as appropriate.

.05 The checklists and illustrative financial statements should be used by, or under the supervision of, persons having adequate technical training and proficiency in the application of U.S. GAAP, generally accepted auditing standards (GAAS), and other relevant technical guidance.

Guidance Considered in This Edition

.06 Relevant financial statement reporting and disclosure guidance issued through April 30, 2020, has been considered in the development of this edition of the checklists. This includes relevant guidance issued up to and including the following:

- FASB Accounting Standards Update No. 2020-04, *Reference Rate Reform (Topic 848): Facilitation of the Effects of Reference Rate Reform on Financial Reporting*

- Statement on Auditing Standards (SAS) No. 141, *Amendment to the Effective Dates of SAS Nos. 134–140*

- Interpretation No. 5, "Communicating Critical Audit Matters When Reporting on Audits Conducted in Accordance With Auditing Standards Generally Accepted in the United States of America and the Standards of the PCAOB" (AU-C sec. 9700 par. .22–.26), of AU-C section 700, *Forming an Opinion and Reporting on Financial Statements*[1]

- Statement of Position 17-1, *Performing Agreed-Upon Procedures Related to Rated Exchange Act Asset-Backed Securities Third-Party Due Diligence Services as Defined by SEC Release No. 34-72936* (AUD sec. 60)[2]

- Statement on Standards for Accounting and Review Services No. 25, *Materiality in a Review of Financial Statements and Adverse Conclusions*[3]

.07 Any guidance issued subsequent to April 30, 2020, has not been included in these checklists; therefore, the checklists and illustrative financial statements should be modified, as appropriate, for subsequent pronouncements. In determining the applicability of a pronouncement, its effective date should also be considered.

Instructions

.08 The checklists consist of a number of questions or statements that are accompanied by references to the applicable authoritative guidance.

.09 The checklists provide for checking off or initialing each question or point to show that it has been considered. Carefully review the topics listed and consider whether they represent potential disclosure items for the reporting entity for which you are preparing or auditing financial statements. Users should check or initial the following as specified:

- *Yes* — If the item is required and has been made appropriately.

- *No* — If the item is required but has not been made.

- *N/A (Not Applicable)* — If the item is not required to be made.

.10 It is important that the effect of any "No" response be considered on the auditor's or accountant's report. For audited financial statements, a "No" response that is material to the financial statements may warrant a departure from an unqualified opinion as discussed in AU-C section 705B, *Modifications to the Opinion in the Independent Auditor's Report*.[4] For reviewed or compiled financial statements or information, a "No" response

---

[1] All AU-C sections can be found in AICPA *Professional Standards*.

[2] All Statements of Position can be found in AICPA *Professional Standards*.

[3] All AR-C sections can be found in AICPA *Professional Standards*.

[4] AU-C section 705, *Modifications to the Opinion in the Independent Auditor's Report*, is effective for audits of financial statements for periods ending on or after December 15, 2021. Early implementation is permitted.

that is material to the financial statements may warrant a departure from a standard report as discussed in AR-C sections 80A and 90A, *Compilation Engagements* and *Review of Financial Statements*, respectively.[5]

.11 Users may find it helpful to use the right margin for certain remarks and comments as appropriate, including the following:

a. For each disclosure for which a "Yes" is indicated, a notation regarding where the disclosure is located in the financial statements and a cross-reference to the applicable working papers where the support for a disclosure may be found.

b. For items marked as "N/A," the reasons for which the disclosure does not apply in the circumstances of the particular financial statements.

c. For each disclosure for which a "No" response is indicated, the AICPA Accounting and Auditing Publications staff recommend a notation regarding why the disclosure was not made (for example, because the item was not considered to be material to the financial statements).

.12 These checklists and illustrative financial statements have been prepared by AICPA staff. They have not been reviewed, approved, disapproved, or otherwise acted on by any senior technical committee of the AICPA and do not represent official positions or pronouncements of the AICPA.

.13 The use of these or any other checklists requires the exercise of individual professional judgment. These checklists are not substitutes for the original authoritative guidance. Users of these checklists and illustrative financial statements are urged to refer directly to applicable standards and requirements when appropriate. The checklists and illustrative materials may not include all disclosures and presentation items promulgated, nor do they represent minimum standards or requirements. Additionally, users of the checklists and illustrative materials are encouraged to tailor them as required to meet specific circumstances of each particular engagement. As an additional resource, users may call the AICPA Technical Hotline at 877.242.7212.

.14 We hope you find these checklists helpful and we would greatly appreciate your feedback on this edition. You may email your comments to a&apublications@aicpa.org.

---

[5] AR-C sections 80 and 90, *Compilation Engagements* and *Review of Financial Statements*, respectively, are effective for audits of financial statements for periods ending on or after December 15, 2021. Early implementation is permitted.

Part 2
Financial Statements and Notes Checklist

.01 This nonauthoritative checklist can be used by preparers of not-for-profit entity (NFP) financial statements prepared in conformity with accounting principles generally accepted in the United States (U.S. GAAP) and by practitioners who audit, review, or compile those financial statements as they evaluate the adequacy of disclosures made in the financial statements and notes to the financial statements.

.02 These checklists contain numerous references to accounting and auditing guidance. Abbreviations and acronyms used in such references include the following:

AAG = AICPA Audit and Accounting Guide *Not-for-Profit Entities* (as of March 1, 2020)

APB = Accounting Principles Board Opinion

AU-C = Reference to section number in AICPA *Professional Standards*

FASB ASC = Reference to a topic, subtopic, section, or paragraph in Financial Accounting Standards Board *Accounting Standards Codification*

Q&A = Reference to a section number in *Technical Questions and Answers*

SOP = AICPA Statement of Position

.03 A few questions in this checklist do not cite a specific authoritative reference but indicate that the disclosure is common practice. Most NFPs disclose that information even though a requirement to do so in the authoritative literature cannot be identified.

.04 Checklist Questionnaire:

This checklist is organized into the sections listed as follows. Carefully review the topics listed and consider whether they represent potential disclosure items for the NFP. Place a check mark by the topics or sections considered not applicable; these sections need not be completed. For example, if the NFP does not have a merger or acquisition, place a check by "Mergers and Acquisitions" and skip that section when completing the checklist.

			Place ✓ by Sections Applicable
I.		General	
	A.	Titles and References	_____
	B.	Accounting Policies and Other Disclosures	_____
	C.	Accounting Changes and Error Corrections	_____
	D.	Comparative Financial Statements	_____
	E.	Related Entities	_____
	F.	Mergers and Acquisitions	_____
	G.	Consolidated Financial Statements	_____
	H.	Nonmonetary Transactions Other Than Contributions	_____
	I.	Contingencies and Commitments	_____

Place ✓ by Sections
Applicable

J.	Risks and Uncertainties	_____
K.	Related Parties	_____
L.	Subsequent Events	_____
M.	Pension and Other Postretirement Benefit Plans	_____
N.	Liquidity	_____
O.	Advertising Costs	_____
P.	Website Development and Cloud Computing Costs	_____
Q.	Costs to Exit or Dispose of an Activity	_____
R.	Fair Value Measurements	_____
S.	Doubt About the NFP's Ability to Continue as a Going Concern	_____

II. Statement of Financial Position

A.	General	_____
B.	Cash and Cash Equivalents	_____
C.	Investments Other Than Derivative Instruments	_____
D.	Derivative Instruments and Hedging Activities	_____
E.	Financial Instruments	_____
F.	Accounts, Notes, Contributions, and Loans Receivable	_____
G.	Beneficial Interests in Assets Held by Others	_____
H.	Inventories	_____
I.	Property and Equipment	_____
J.	Collections of Works of Art and Similar Items	_____
K.	Goodwill and Other Intangible Assets	_____
L.	Other Assets and Deferred Charges	_____
M.	Current Liabilities	_____
N.	Notes Payable and Other Debt, Including Interfund Borrowing	_____
O.	Leases as Lessee	_____
P.	Other Liabilities and Deferred Credits	_____
Q.	Agency Transactions	_____
R.	Restricted Resources	_____
S.	Mandatorily Redeemable Interests	_____
T.	Discontinued Operations	_____

III. Statement of Activities

A.	General	_____
B.	Revenue Recognition (Other Than Contributions)	_____
C.	Taxes	_____
D.	Refunds Due To and Advances From Third Parties	_____
E.	Donated or Contributed Services	_____
F.	Donated Materials and Facilities	_____
G.	Fundraising	_____
H.	Contributions	_____
I.	Split-Interest Agreements	_____

          © 2020, Association of International Certified Professional Accountants

	Place ✓ *by Sections Applicable*
J. Expenses	_____
K. Investments and Endowments	_____
L. Discontinued Operations	_____
IV. Statement of Cash Flows	_____

I. General

	Yes	No	N/A

A. Titles and References

1. Are the financial statements suitably titled?

   [AU-C 700B.16]

2. Does each statement include a general reference that the notes are an integral part of the financial statement presentation?

   [Common Practice]

3. For each period, are the following financial statements presented:

   a. Statement of financial position?

   b. Statement of activities?

   c. Statement of cash flows?

4. If the primary component of the NFP's mission is to receive resources as an agent, has presentation of the statement of cash flows as the first financial statement been considered?

   [AAG 3.50]

B. Accounting Policies and Other Disclosures

1. Is a description of all significant accounting policies adopted and followed presented as an integral part of the financial statements?

   [FASB ASC 235-10-50-1]

2. If the NFP prepared its financial statements on a comprehensive basis of accounting other than generally accepted accounting principles (GAAP), was disclosure made of the basis of presentation and how that basis differs from GAAP?

   [AU-C 800.11]

3. Does disclosure of significant accounting policies encompass important judgments as to appropriateness of principles concerning recognition of revenue and allocation of asset costs to current and future periods?

   [FASB ASC 235-10-50-3]

4. Does the disclosure of significant accounting policies include appropriate reference to details presented elsewhere (in the statements and notes thereto) so duplication of details is avoided?

   [FASB ASC 235-10-50-5]

5. Is the need for disclosure of the impact of a new FASB standard issued but not yet effective where restatement of prior periods is required considered?

   [Common Practice]

	Yes	No	N/A

C.　Accounting Changes and Error Corrections

1.　If the NFP makes a change in an accounting principle, is the change reported through retrospective application of the new accounting principle to all prior periods, unless it is impracticable to do so?

　　[FASB ASC 250-10-45-5]

2.　If the NFP makes a change in an accounting principle, is the following information disclosed in the fiscal period in which the change is made:

　　a.　The nature of the change in accounting principle?

　　b.　The reason for the change in accounting principle, including an explanation of why the newly adopted accounting principle is preferable?

　　c.　The method of applying the change?

　　d.　A description of the prior-period information that has been retrospectively adjusted, if any?

　　e.　The effects, in total and by class, of the change on change in net assets, and on the operating measure (if any), as well as on any other affected financial statement line item (except subtotals) for the current period and any prior periods retrospectively adjusted?

　　f.　The cumulative effect of the change on total net assets and on each class of net assets in the statement of financial position, as of the beginning of the earliest period presented?

　　g.　If retrospective application to all prior periods is impracticable, disclosure of the reasons therefore, and a description of the alternative method used to report the change?

　　h.　If indirect effects of a change in accounting principle are recognized

　　　　i.　a description of the indirect effects of a change in accounting principle, including the amounts that have been recognized in the current period?

　　　　ii.　unless impracticable, the amount of the total recognized indirect effects of the accounting change that are attributable to each prior period presented?

　　　　[FASB ASC 250-10-50-1]

3.　If the change in accounting principle has no material effect in the period of change but is reasonably certain to have a material effect in later periods, are the disclosures required by questions 2*a*–*b* provided whenever the financial statements of the period of change are presented?

　　[FASB ASC 250-10-50-1]

4.　If the NFP makes a change in an accounting estimate, is the change accounted for in (*a*) the period of change if the change affects that period only or (*b*) the period of change and future periods if the change affects both? (**Note:** A change in accounting estimate cannot be accounted for by restating or retrospectively adjusting amounts reported in financial statements of prior periods or by reporting pro forma amounts for prior periods.)

　　[FASB ASC 250-10-45-17]

　　　　　　　　© **2020, Association of International Certified Professional Accountants**

	Yes	No	N/A

Note

The disclosure provisions for a change in accounting estimate are not required for revisions resulting from a change in a valuation technique used to measure fair value or its application when the resulting measurement is fair value in accordance with FASB ASC 820, *Fair Value Measurement.*

5. If the NFP makes a change in an accounting estimate that either (*a*) will affect several future periods or (*b*) is material and is made in the ordinary course of accounting for items such as uncollectible accounts, is the following information disclosed in the fiscal period in which the change is made:

   a. The effects, in total and by class, of the change on change in net assets, and on the operating measure (if any), for the current period?

   b. If the change in estimate is effected by changing an accounting principle, the information in the preceding question 2?

   [FASB ASC 250-10-50-4]

6. If a change in accounting estimate has no material effect in the period of change but is reasonably certain to have a material effect in later periods, is a description of the change in estimate provided whenever the financial statements of the period of change are presented?

   [FASB ASC 250-10-50-4]

7. If a change in the reporting entity occurs, is the change retrospectively applied to the financial statements of all prior periods presented to show financial information for the new reporting entity for those periods?

   [FASB ASC 250-10-45-21]

8. If a change in the reporting entity occurs, is the following information disclosed in the fiscal period in which the change is made:

   a. The nature of the change and the reason for it?

   b. The effects, in total and by class, of the change on change in net assets, on change in net assets from continuing operations (if there are discontinued operations), and on the operating measure (if any), for all the periods presented?

   [FASB ASC 250-10-50-6]

9. If a change in reporting entity has no material effect in the period of change but is reasonably certain to have a material effect in later periods, is the nature of the change and the reason for it disclosed whenever the financial statements of the period of change are presented?

   [FASB ASC 250-10-50-6]

	Yes	No	N/A

10. If an error in the financial statements of a prior period is discovered subsequent to their issuance, is the correction of the error reported as a prior-period adjustment by restating the prior-period financial statements? (*Note:* Q&A section 6140.23, "Changing Net Asset Classifications Reported in a Prior Year," states that "Individual net asset classes, rather than net assets in the aggregate (total net assets), are relevant in determining whether an NFP's correction of net asset classifications previously reported in prior years' financial statements is an error in previously issued financial statements.")
    [FASB ASC 250-10-45-23]

11. If the financial statements are restated to correct an error, is the following information disclosed:

    a. The fact that the previously issued financial statements have been corrected?
       [FASB ASC 250-10-50-7]

    b. The nature of the error?
       [FASB ASC 250-10-50-7]

    c. The effect of the correction on each financial statement line item for each prior period presented?
       [FASB ASC 250-10-50-7]

    d. The cumulative effect, in total and by class, of the correction on net assets as of the beginning of the earliest period presented?
       [FASB ASC 250-10-50-7]

    e. The effects, in total and by class, of the correction on change in net assets for each of the periods presented?
       [FASB ASC 250-10-50-8]

    f. For single period financial statements, the effects, in total and by class, of the correction on change in net assets of the preceding year?
       [FASB ASC 250-10-50-9]

D. Comparative Financial Statements

1. Has presentation of comparative statements been considered?
   [FASB ASC 205-10-45-2]

2. Are the disclosures included in the prior year's financial statements repeated, or at least referred to, to the extent that they continue to be of significance?
   [FASB ASC 205-10-45-4]

3. If changes have occurred in the manner of or basis for presenting corresponding items for two or more periods, are appropriate explanations of the changes disclosed?
   [FASB ASC 205-10-50-1]

4. If prior year information is summarized and does not include the minimum information required by FASB ASC 958, *Not-for-Profit Entities*, is the nature of the prior year information described by appropriate titles and in the notes?
   [FASB ASC 958-205-45-8; FASB ASC 958-205-50-4]

 © 2020, Association of International Certified Professional Accountants

	Yes	No	N/A

5. If prior year information is summarized and does not include the minimum information required by FASB ASC 958, does the NFP include all the disclosures required by GAAP for the prior year?

[FinREC recommendation in AAG 3.66]

6. *For public entities:* If the NFP is the new entity that resulted from a merger is a *public entity* (as defined in FASB ASC 958-805-20), has it disclosed the information in paragraphs 4–5 of FASB ASC 958-805-50?

[FASB ASC 958-805-50 par. 4–5]

7. *For public entities:* If the NFP is both the acquirer in an acquisition by an NFP and a *public entity* (as defined in FASB ASC 958-805-20), has it disclosed the information in FASB ASC 958-805-50-9?

[FASB ASC 958-805-50-9]

E. Related Entities

1. If the NFP has a relationship characterized by a controlling financial interest through (*a*) direct or indirect ownership of a majority voting interest in another NFP, (*b*) sole corporate membership in another NFP, (*c*) direct or indirect ownership of a majority voting interest in a for-profit entity, or (*d*) controlling financial interest by a general or limited partner of a limited partnership of similar entity, are consolidated financial statements presented unless control does not rest with the majority owner or sole corporate member? *Note:* Consolidation is not required if a limited partnership interest is an investment within the scope of FASB ASC 958-325 and the NFP has elected to report all other investments at fair value. (Refer to section I.G., "Consolidated Financial Statements.")

[FASB ASC 958-810-25 par. 2–2a; FASB ASC 958-810-15-4; FASB ASC 958-810-25, pars.1129]

2. If the NFP has a relationship characterized by both (*a*) control of a related but separate NFP through a majority voting interest in the board of the other NFP by means other than ownership or sole corporate membership and (*b*) an economic interest in that other NFP, are consolidated financial statements presented?

[FASB ASC 958-810-25-3]

3. If the NFP is a lessee in a transaction involving a special-purpose entity lessor, are consolidated financial statements presented if required by paragraphs 8–10 of FASB ASC 958-810-25? (Refer to section I.G.)

[FASB ASC 958-810-25 par. 8–10]

4. If the NFP has a relationship that is characterized by ownership of an investment in voting stock that gives one significant influence over the operating and financial policies of the other (generally 20% or more of the voting stock), is the investment accounted for under the equity method unless the NFP has elected to report it at fair value, where permitted? (Refer to section II.C., "Investments Other Than Derivative Instruments.")

[FASB ASC 958-810-15-4]

	Yes	No	N/A

5. If the NFP has a noncontrolling interest in a for-profit real estate partnership, LLC, or similar entity that constitutes more than a minor interest (as defined in FASB ASC 810-20-25), does the NFP apply the equity method of accounting unless it carries that investment at fair value, where permitted? (Refer to section II.C.)

   [FASB ASC 958-810-15-4]

6. If the NFP is using the proportional amortization method as an investor in a qualified affordable housing project through a limited liability entity, is the amortization of the investment in the limited liability entity recognized as a component of income tax expense (or benefit)?

   [FASB ASC 323-740-45-2]

7. If the NFP is an investor in a qualified affordable housing project, has it considered the items in FASB ASC 323-10-50-2 and disclosed information that enables users of its financial statements to understand the following:

   a. The nature of its investments in qualified affordable housing projects?

   b. The effect of the measurement of its investments in qualified affordable housing projects and the related tax credits on its financial position and results of operations?

   [FASB ASC 323-740-50-1]

8. Is the nature of a controlled relationship disclosed, even though there are no transactions between the entities, if the reporting entity and one or more other entities are under common ownership or management control, and the existence of the control could result in operating results or financial position of the reporting entity being significantly different from those that would have been obtained if the entity were autonomous?

   [FASB ASC 850-10-50-6]

9. If the NFP both (*a*) controls a related but separate NFP through a majority voting interest in the board of that NFP by means other than majority ownership interest, sole corporate membership, or majority voting interest and (*b*) has an economic interest in that other NFP, and consolidated financial statements are not presented, do disclosures include

   a. identification of the other NFP and the nature of its relationship with the reporting entity that results in control?

   b. summarized financial data of the other NFP including total assets, liabilities, net assets, revenue, and expenses, and resources that are held for the benefit of the reporting entity or that are under its control?

   c. disclosures required by FASB ASC 850, *Related Party Disclosures*, as described in question 8 and in section I.K., "Related Parties"?

   [FASB ASC 958-810-50-2]

© 2020, Association of International Certified Professional Accountants

	Yes	No	N/A

10. If either control or economic interest exists, but not both, are the disclosures required by FASB ASC 850 as described in question 8 and in section I.K. made and are the entities consolidated only if they were consolidated prior to the issuance of SOP 94-3, *Reporting of Related Entities by Not-for-Profit Organizations*, in conformity with the guidance in SOP 78-10, *Accounting Principles and Reporting Practices for Certain Nonprofit Organizations*?

    [FASB ASC 958-810-25-5; FASB ASC 958-810-50-3]

11. Are the nature and extent of leasing transactions with related parties appropriately disclosed?

    [FASB ASC 840-10-50-1]

12. If the NFP has an investment in an unincorporated legal entity, such as a partnership or a joint venture, is that investment accounted for using either full consolidation, the equity method, or cost, as appropriate, but not proportionate consolidation?

    [FASB ASC 810-10-45-14]

13. If the NFP transferred assets to a *financially interrelated entity* (as defined in FASB ASC 958-20-20) and specified itself or its affiliate as the beneficiary, has it disclosed the following for each period in which a statement of financial position is presented:

    a. The identity of the financially interrelated entity to which the transfer was made?

    b. Whether variance power was granted to the financially interrelated entity and, if so, a description of the terms of the variance power?

    c. The terms under which amounts will be distributed to the NFP or its affiliate?

    d. The aggregate amount recognized in the statement of financial position for those transfers and whether that amount is recorded as an interest in the net assets of the financially interrelated entity or as another asset (such as a beneficial interest in assets held by others or as a refundable advance)?

    [FASB ASC 958-20-50-1]

14. If the transfer in question 13 was made in a year presented in the financial statements, is it reported on a separate line in the statement of activities if it is an equity transaction (that is, it meets the 3 conditions in FASB ASC 958-20-25-4)?

    [FASB ASC 958-20-45 par. 1–2]

15. Are costs incurred and revenue generated from transactions with third parties (that is, parties that do not participate in the collaborative arrangement) reported in the NFP's statement of activities pursuant to the guidance in FASB ASC 605-45 or if FASB ASC 606, *Revenue from Contracts with Customers*, has been adopted, in accordance with principal versus agent considerations in paragraphs 36–40 of FASB ASC 606-10-55? *Note:* An NFP is precluded from presenting transactions in a collaborative arrangement together with revenue from contracts with customers unless the NFP applies the guidance in FASB ASC 606 to a unit of account that is within the scope of that topic.

    [FASB ASC 808-10-45-1]

	Yes	No	N/A

16. If the NFP is a participant to a collaborative arrangement, has it disclosed the following information (separately for any arrangement that is individually significant):

    a.   Information about the nature and purpose of its collaborative arrangements? ____ ____ ____

    b.   The NFP's rights and obligations under the collaborative arrangements? ____ ____ ____

    c.   The NFP's accounting policy for collaborative arrangements? ____ ____ ____

    d.   The classification in the statement of activities and amounts attributable to transactions arising from the collaborative arrangement between participants for each period a statement of activities is presented? ____ ____ ____

    [FASB ASC 808-10-50-1]

17. If the NFP prepares combined financial statements for a group of related entities, are intra-entity transactions and profits or losses eliminated, and are noncontrolling interests, foreign operations, different fiscal periods, or income taxes presented in the same manner as in consolidated financial statements? ____ ____ ____

    [FASB ASC 810-10-45-10]

F.　Mergers and Acquisitions

Note

FASB ASC 958-805 provides standards for the information an NFP provides in its financial reports about a combination with one or more other NFPs, businesses, or nonprofit activities. It requires the NFP to determine whether the combination is a merger or an acquisition.

Questions 1–11 should be completed for mergers.

Questions 12–39 should be completed for acquisitions.

Mergers

1. If the new entity formed by the merger presents a statement of financial position as of the beginning of the initial reporting period, does that statement present the combined assets, liabilities, and net assets of the merging entities as of the merger date? ____ ____ ____

    [FASB ASC 958-805-45-1]

2. Are assets and liabilities as of the beginning of the initial reporting period measured at the amounts reported in the financial statements prepared in accordance with GAAP of the merging entities as of that date? ____ ____ ____

    [FASB ASC 958-805-30-1]

3. Are amounts as of the beginning of the initial reporting period adjusted as necessary in accordance with paragraphs 2–4 of FASB ASC 958-805-30? ____ ____ ____

    [FASB ASC 958-805-30-1]

4. Does the statement of activities for the new entity include in the opening amounts (the reported amounts as of the beginning of the period), the combined amounts of the merging entities' net assets, in total and by classes of net assets, as of the merger date, and are any adjustments in accordance with FASB ASC 958-805-25-7 and paragraphs 2 and 4 of FASB ASC 958-805-30 reflected in the opening amounts? ____ ____ ____

    [FASB ASC 958-805-45-2]

 © 2020, Association of International Certified Professional Accountants

	Yes	No	N/A

5. Does the statement of activities reflect only activity from the merger date to the end of the reporting period?

   [FASB ASC 958-805-45-2]

6. Does the statement of cash flows for the new entity include in the reported amounts as of the beginning of the period (the opening amounts) of cash and cash equivalents at the beginning of the period as of the merger date and are any adjustments in accordance with FASB ASC 958-805-25-7 and paragraphs 2 and 4 of FASB ASC 958-805-30 reflected in the opening amounts?

   [FASB ASC 958-805-45-2]

7. Does the statement of cash flows reflect only activity from the merger date to the end of the reporting period?

   [FASB ASC 958-805-45-2]

8. Does the new entity disclose the following information for the merger that resulted in its formation:

   a. The name and a description of each merging entity?

   b. The merger date?

   c. The primary reasons for the merger?

   d. The nature and amount of any significant adjustments made to conform the individual accounting policies of the merging entities?

   e. The nature and amount of any significant adjustments made to eliminate intra-entity balances?

   [FASB ASC 958-805-50-2]

9. Does the new entity disclose the following information about each of the merging entities:

   a. The amounts recognized as of the merger date for each major class of assets and liabilities and each class of net assets?

   b. The nature and amounts, if applicable, of any significant assets (for example, conditional promises receivable or collections) or liabilities (for example, conditional promises payable) that GAAP does not require to be recognized?

   [FASB ASC 958-805-50-2]

10. If the disclosures made in questions 1–9 are insufficient to enable users of the financial statements to evaluate the nature and financial effect of the merger that resulted in the formation of the new entity, did the entity disclose whatever additional information is necessary to meet that objective?

    [FASB ASC 958-805-50-6]

11. *For public entities:* If the new entity is a *public entity* as defined in FASB ASC 958-805-20, have the additional disclosures in paragraphs 3–5 of FASB ASC 958-805-50 been included with the financial statements?

    [FASB ASC 958-805-50 par. 3–5]

	Yes	No	N/A

Acquisitions

12. If the operations of the acquiree as part of the combined entity are expected to be predominantly supported by contributions and returns on investments, does the NFP acquirer report a separate charge in its statement of activities as of the acquisition date, measured in accordance with FASB ASC 958-805-30-6 (rather than goodwill)?

    [FASB ASC 958-805-25-29; FASB ASC 958-805-45-4]

13. Does the NFP recognize an inherent contribution received, measured in accordance with FASB ASC 958-805-30-8, as a separate credit in its statement of activities as of the acquisition date?

    [FASB ASC 958-805-25-31; FASB ASC 958-805-45-5]

14. If an inherent contribution received is recognized (as described in question 13), does the classification of that contribution reflect the following types of restrictions:

    a. Restrictions imposed on the net assets of the acquiree by a donor before the acquisition?

    b. Restrictions imposed by the donor of the business or nonprofit activity acquired, if any?

    c. Report the contribution recognized as restricted support if restricted by the donor, even if the restrictions are met in the same reporting period in which the acquisition occurs? (That is, the acquirer shall not apply the reporting exception in FASB ASC 958-605-45-4 to restricted net assets acquired in an acquisition.)

        [FASB ASC 958-805-45-6]

15. Do the financial statements of the acquirer (the combined entity) report the acquisition as activity of the period in which the acquisition occurs?

    [FASB ASC 958-805-45-3]

16. If, by transferring consideration in the acquisition, the acquirer satisfied a donor-imposed restriction on its net assets, is the expiration of those restrictions either reported separately in the statement of activities or aggregated and reported with other similar expirations of donor-imposed restrictions during the period in which the acquisition occurs?

    [FASB ASC 958-805-45-9]

17. If other changes to the acquirer's net asset classifications occur during the period as a result of the acquisition, are those other changes reported separately from both any other reclassifications or any expiration of those restrictions during the period in which the acquisition occurs? (For example, an acquirer that transfers as consideration its assets with no associated donor restrictions and acquires assets from the acquiree that have associated donor restrictions shall recognize a reclassification of net assets in its statement of activities.)

    [FASB ASC 958-805-45-10]

          © 2020, Association of International Certified Professional Accountants

	Yes	No	N/A

18. Is the entire amount of any net cash flow resulting from the acquisition (cash paid as consideration, if any, less acquired cash of the acquiree) reported as an investing activity in the statement of cash flows? *Note*: NFPs that have adopted ASU No. 2016-15, *Statement of Cash Flows (Topic 230): Classification of Certain Cash Receipts and Cash Payments (a consensus of the Emerging Issues Task Force)*, should include cash payments made soon after the acquisition date to settle a contingent consideration liability.

    ["Pending Content" in FASB ASC 958-805-45-11]

19. Are noncash contributions received and any other noncash amounts received or transferred related to the acquisition reported as noncash activities in accordance with FASB ASC 230-10-50-3?

    [FASB ASC 958-805-50-15]

20. During the measurement period, are adjustments to the provisional amounts (amounts that were initially recognized for an identifiable asset or liability) recognized either

    a. as an increase or decrease in goodwill if goodwill was recognized for the acquisition?

    b. by a direct credit (charge) to the statement of activities if goodwill was not recognized as an asset? (Per FASB ASC 958-805-25-29, goodwill is not recognized as an asset if the operations of the acquiree as part of the combined entity are expected to be predominantly supported by contributions and returns on investments.)

    [FASB ASC 805-10-25-16]

21. Do the financial statements disclose the following information for each acquisition that occurs during the reporting period:

    a. The name and a description of the acquiree?

    b. The acquisition date?

    c. The percentage of ownership interests, such as voting equity instruments, acquired, if applicable?

    d. The primary reasons for the acquisition and a description of how the acquirer obtained control of the acquiree?

    [FASB ASC 805-10-50-2]

22. Do the financial statements disclose the following information for each acquisition that occurs during the reporting period:

    a. A qualitative description of the factors, such as expected synergies from combining operations of the acquiree and the acquirer, intangible assets that do not qualify for separate recognition, or other factors, such as the nonrecognition of collections, that make up either the goodwill recognized or the charge recognized in accordance with FASB ASC 958-805-25-29?

    b. The acquisition-date fair value of the total consideration transferred (or if no consideration was transferred, that fact?

    c. The acquisition-date fair value of each major class of consideration?

    d. The amounts recognized as of the acquisition date for each major class of assets acquired and liabilities assumed?

	Yes	No	N/A

e. The total amount of goodwill that is expected to be deductible for tax purposes? ____ ____ ____

f. The amount of collection items acquired that are recognized in the statement of activities as a decrease in the acquirer's net assets in accordance with FASB ASC 958-805-25-23? ____ ____ ____

g. The undiscounted amount of conditional promises to give acquired or assumed and a description and the amount of each group of promises with similar characteristics, such as amounts of promises conditioned on establishing new programs, completing a new building, or raising matching gifts by a specified date? ____ ____ ____

h. If the acquisition resulted in an inherent contribution received, a description of the reasons that the transaction resulted in a contribution received? ____ ____ ____

[FASB ASC 958-805-50 par. 11–12]

23. Do the financial statements disclose the following information about contingent consideration arrangements and indemnification assets:

a. The amount recognized as of the acquisition date? ____ ____ ____

b. A description of the arrangement and the basis for determining the amount of the payment? ____ ____ ____

c. An estimate of the range of outcomes (undiscounted) or, if a range cannot be estimated, that fact and the reasons why a range cannot be estimated? ____ ____ ____

d. If the maximum amount of the payment is unlimited, the acquirer shall disclose that fact? ____ ____ ____

[FASB ASC 958-805-50-11]

24. Do the financial statements disclose the following information about acquired receivables: (**Note:** This requirement does not apply if the disclosures required by FASB ASC 310-30 or FASB ASC 326-20 are made. See questions 25–28 in section II.F., "Accounts, Notes, Contributions, and Loans Receivable.")

a. The fair value of the receivables by major class of receivable? ____ ____ ____

b. The gross contractual amounts receivable by major class of receivable? ____ ____ ____

c. The best estimate at the acquisition date of the contractual cash flows not expected to be collected by major class of receivable? ____ ____ ____

[FASB ASC 805-20-50-1]

25. Does the note that describes the acquisition disclose the following information about assets and liabilities arising from contingencies recognized at the acquisition date:

a. The amounts recognized at the acquisition date and the measurement basis applied (that is, at fair value or at an amount recognized in accordance with FASB ASC 450, *Contingencies*)? ____ ____ ____

b. The nature of the contingencies? ____ ____ ____

[FASB ASC 805-20-50-1]

          © 2020, Association of International Certified Professional Accountants

	Yes	No	N/A

26. If contingencies have not been recognized at the acquisition date, are the disclosures required by FASB ASC 450, included in the note that describes the acquisition? See section I.I., "Contingencies and Commitments."   ____ ____ ____

[FASB ASC 805-20-50-1]

27. Do the financial statements disclose the following information about transactions that are recognized separately from the acquisition of assets and assumptions of liabilities in the acquisition (that is, a transaction entered into by or on behalf of the acquirer or primarily for the benefit of the acquirer or the combined entity, rather than primarily for the benefit of the acquiree [or its former owners] before the combination, as described in FASB ASC 805-10-25-20):

    a. A description of each transaction?   ____ ____ ____

    b. How the acquirer accounted for each transaction?   ____ ____ ____

    c. The amounts recognized for each transaction and the line item in the financial statements in which each amount is recognized?   ____ ____ ____

    d. If the transaction is the effective settlement of a preexisting relationship, the method used to determine the settlement amount?   ____ ____ ____

    [FASB ASC 805-10-50-2]

28. Does the disclosure required in question 27 include the following information about acquisition-related costs:

    a. The amount of acquisition-related costs?   ____ ____ ____

    b. The amount recognized as an expense?   ____ ____ ____

    c. The line item or items in the statement of activities in which that expense is recognized?   ____ ____ ____

    d. The amount of any debt issuance costs not recognized as an expense and how they were recognized?   ____ ____ ____

    [FASB ASC 805-10-50-2]

29. If the acquirer holds less than 100% of the equity interests in the acquiree at the acquisition date, do the financial statements disclose

    a. the fair value of the noncontrolling interest in the acquiree at the acquisition date?   ____ ____ ____

    b. the valuation technique(s) and significant inputs used to measure the fair value of the noncontrolling interest?   ____ ____ ____

    [FASB ASC 805-20-50-1]

30. For an acquisition achieved in stages

    a. is the gain or loss resulting from the acquirer remeasuring its previously held equity interest in the acquiree at its acquisition date fair value reported in the statement of activities?   ____ ____ ____

    b. is the amount of the gain or loss and the line item in the statement of activities in which that gain or loss is recognized disclosed?   ____ ____ ____

	Yes	No	N/A

c.   is the acquisition date fair value of the equity interest in the acquiree held by the acquirer immediately before the acquisition date disclosed?

[FASB ASC 805-10-25-10; FASB ASC 805-10-50-2]

31.   For individually immaterial acquisitions occurring during the reporting period that are material collectively, are the disclosures required by questions 22–30 made in the aggregate?

[FASB ASC 805-10-50-3]

32.   If the disclosures made in questions 12–31 are insufficient to enable users of the financial statements to evaluate the nature and financial effect of an acquisition, did the entity disclose whatever additional information is necessary to meet that objective?

[FASB ASC 805-10-50-7]

33.   *For public entities:* If the acquirer is a *public entity* as defined in FASB ASC 958-805-20, have the additional disclosures in paragraphs 8–10 of FASB ASC 958-805-50 been included with the financial statements?

[FASB ASC 958-805-50 par. 8–9; FASB ASC 958-805-50-10]

34.   If the initial accounting for an acquisition is incomplete for particular assets, liabilities, noncontrolling interests, or items of consideration and the amounts recognized in the financial statements for the acquisition thus have been determined only provisionally, are the following disclosures included in the financial statements:

a.   The reasons that the initial accounting is incomplete?

b.   The assets, liabilities, equity interests, or items of consideration for which the initial accounting is incomplete?

c.   The nature and amount of any measurement period adjustments recognized during the reporting period?

[FASB ASC 805–20–50–4A]

35.   Are the amounts that would have been recognized in previous periods if the adjustments to provisional amounts were recognized as of the acquisition date (rather than in the current period) disclosed separately for each line item of the statement of activities affected by the measurement period adjustments of provisional amounts? (*Note:* This requirement may be met by presenting those amounts separately on the face of the statement of activities.)

[FASB ASC 805-20-50-4A]

36.   If an acquisition included contingent consideration, is the following information disclosed if the NFP has not yet collected, sold, or otherwise lost the right to a contingent consideration asset, or settled or otherwise extinguished a contingent consideration liability:

a.   Any changes in the recognized amounts, including any differences arising upon settlement?

b.   Any changes in the range of outcomes (undiscounted) and the reasons for those changes?

c.   The disclosures required by FASB ASC 820-10-50 (section I.R., "Fair Value Measurements")?

[FASB ASC 958-805-50-16]

         © 2020, Association of International Certified Professional Accountants

	Yes	No	N/A

37. If the disclosures made in questions 34–36 are insufficient to enable users of the financial statements to evaluate the financial effects of adjustments recognized in the current reporting period that relate to acquisitions that occurred in the current or previous reporting periods, did the NFP disclose whatever additional information is necessary to meet that objective?

    [FASB ASC 805-10-50-7]

38. If, upon acquisition, a business or nonprofit activity meets the criteria in FASB ASC 205-20-45-1E to be classified as held for sale, are the results of operations of that discontinued operation, including any gain or loss recognized in accordance with FASB ASC 205-20-45-3C, reported as a discontinued operation for current and prior periods?

    [FASB ASC 205-20-45-1D]

39. If an NFP is an acquiree that elects the option to apply pushdown accounting in its separate financial statements, does it disclose the information in paragraphs 5–6 of FASB ASC 805-50-50 in the period in which the push-down accounting is applied?

    [FASB ASC 805-50-50, par. 5–6]

G. Consolidated Financial Statements

1. If consolidated financial statements are presented

   a. is the consolidation policy disclosed? (**Note:** In most cases this can be made apparent by the headings or other information in the financial statements, but in other cases a footnote is required.)

      [FASB ASC 810-10-50-1]

   b. in instances in which the financial reporting periods of subsidiaries differ from that of the parent, is recognition given to the effect of intervening events that materially affect financial position or the results of operations?

      [FASB ASC 810-10-45-12]

   c. are restrictions made by entities outside of the reporting entity on distributions from the controlled NFP (subsidiary) to the reporting entity (parent) and any resulting unavailability of the net assets of the subsidiary for use by the parent disclosed?

      [FASB ASC 958-810-50-1]

2. Has the parent properly presented its consolidated financial statements with intra-entity balances and transactions eliminated, including any intra-entity profit or loss on assets remaining within the consolidated group?

   [FASB ASC 810-10-45-1]

3. Has the parent properly presented its consolidated net assets *without* including retained earnings or deficit of a subsidiary at the date of acquisition?

   [FASB ASC 810-10-45-2]

4. If a subsidiary was initially consolidated during the year, has the parent included the subsidiary's revenues, expenses, gains, and losses only from the date the subsidiary was initially consolidated?

   [FASB ASC 810-10-45-4]

	Yes	No	N/A

5. If the parent properly has one or more less-than-wholly-owned subsidiaries, does it report on the face of the consolidated statement of activities both of the following:

   a. The amounts of change in net assets for the consolidated entity as a whole, as well as amounts for each of the three net asset classes? ____ ____ ____

   b. The related amounts attributable to the parent and the noncontrolling interest for each of the amounts in item *a* of this question? ____ ____ ____

   [FASB ASC 810-10-50-1A]

6. Are noncontrolling interests reported as a separate component of the appropriate class of net assets in the consolidated statement of financial position of the parent, and are the amounts clearly identified and described (for example, as noncontrolling ownership interest in subsidiaries) to distinguish it from the components of net assets of the parent? ____ ____ ____

   [FASB ASC 958-810-45-1]

7. Are the effects of donor-imposed restrictions, if any, on a partially owned subsidiary's net assets reported in accordance with FASB ASC 958-205 and FASB ASC 958-220? ____ ____ ____

   [FASB ASC 958-810-45-1]

8. Do the consolidated financial statements include a schedule that reconciles beginning and ending balances of the parent's controlling interest and the noncontrolling interests for each class of net assets for which a noncontrolling interest exists during the reporting period? ____ ____ ____

   [FASB ASC 958-810-50-4]

9. Does the schedule required in the preceding question, at a minimum, include the following:

   a. Amounts of discontinued operations? ____ ____ ____

   b. Changes in ownership interests in the subsidiary, including investments by and distributions to noncontrolling interests acting in their capacity as owners, which are reported separate from any revenues, expenses, gains, or losses and outside any measure of operations, if reported? ____ ____ ____

   c. An aggregate amount of all other changes in net assets without donor restrictions and net assets with donor restrictions? ____ ____ ____

   [FASB ASC 958-810-50-5]

10. Has the parent properly disclosed the information in FASB ASC 810-10-50-1B if a subsidiary has been deconsolidated or a group of assets is derecognized in accordance with FASB ASC 810-10-40-3A? ____ ____ ____

   [FASB ASC 810-10-50-1B]

11. Has the NFP considered financial statement and disclosure alternatives that may provide additional useful information about consolidated entities? (For example, an NFP may highlight the effects of consolidating a limited partnership by providing consolidating financial statements or separately classifying the assets and liabilities of the limited partnership(s) on the face of the statement of financial position.) ____ ____ ____

   [FASB ASC 958-810-45-2]

          © 2020, Association of International Certified Professional Accountants

	Yes	No	N/A

H. Nonmonetary Transactions Other Than Contributions

1. Do disclosures for nonmonetary transactions during the period include

    a. nature of the transactions? ____ ____ ____

    b. basis of accounting for the assets transferred? ____ ____ ____

    c. gains or losses recognized on the transfers? ____ ____ ____

    [FASB ASC 845-10-50-1]

I. Contingencies and Commitments

Note

The disclosures in section I.I. do not apply to an NFP's estimate of its allowance for credit losses (doubtful accounts).

1. Are the nature and amount of accrued loss contingencies disclosed as necessary to keep the financial statements from being misleading? ____ ____ ____

    [FASB ASC 450-20-50-1]

2. For loss contingencies not accrued, do disclosures indicate

    a. nature of the contingency? ____ ____ ____

    b. estimate of possible loss or range of loss, or a statement that such estimate cannot be made? ____ ____ ____

    [FASB ASC 450-20-50 par. 3–4]

3. If exposure to loss exists in excess of the amount accrued for a loss contingency, do disclosures include the excess amount or state that no estimate is possible? ____ ____ ____

    [FASB ASC 450-20-50 par. 3–4]

4. Are gain contingencies adequately disclosed to avoid any misleading implications about likelihood of realization? ____ ____ ____

    [FASB ASC 450-30-50-1]

5. Has the NFP disclosed the following commitments:

    a. Unused letters of credit? ____ ____ ____

    b. Commitments for plant acquisitions? ____ ____ ____

    c. Assets pledged as securities for loans? ____ ____ ____

    d. Commitments to reduce debts? ____ ____ ____

    e. Commitments to maintain working capital? ____ ____ ____

    f. Losses on inventory purchase commitments? ____ ____ ____

    [FASB ASC 440-10-50-1; FASB ASC 330-10-50-5]

6. If, after December 31, 2002, the NFP entered into or modified a guarantee, including a guarantee of the indebtedness of others, is the stand-ready obligation reported as a liability? ____ ____ ____

    [FASB ASC 460-10-25-4]

7. Do disclosures about guarantees, including guarantees of the indebtedness of others, include the following information:

© 2020, Association of International Certified Professional Accountants

	Yes	No	N/A

a.   The nature of the guarantee, including the approximate term, how the guarantee arose, the events or circumstances that would require the guarantor to perform under the guarantee, and the status of the payment/performance risk of the guarantee as of the date of the statement of financial position?

b.   The maximum potential amount of the future payments (undiscounted) that the NFP would be required to make, or if the guarantee provides no limitation on future payments, that fact?

c.   The reasons why the maximum future payments cannot be estimated, if the NFP is unable to estimate that amount?

d.   The current carrying amount of the liability?

e.   The nature of any recourse provisions that would enable the NFP to recover from third parties any amounts paid under the guarantee, and the extent to the proceeds are expected to cover the amount in the preceding question *7b*?

f.   A description of any assets (collateral) that can be liquidated to recover amounts paid under the guarantee, and the extent to which the proceeds from liquidation are expected to cover the amount in the preceding question *7b*?

g.   If the guarantee is a *credit derivative* as defined in FASB ASC 460-10-20, are the disclosures in FASB ASC 815-10-50-4K provided instead of the disclosures in this question?

[FASB ASC 460-10-50-4; FASB ASC 815-10-50-4K]

8.   Are environmental remediation obligations and related assets for third-party recoveries reported and disclosed in accordance with FASB ASC 410-30?

[FASB ASC 410-30]

9.   Are encumbrances, appropriations of fund balances, unspecified reserves, general or unspecified business risks, and other commitments not meeting the criteria of FASB ASC 450-20-25 *not* reported as expenses or liabilities? (***Note:*** These may be reported as segregations of net assets on the statement of financial position.)

[FASB ASC 450-20-25-2; FASB ASC 958-210-45-11]

10.   If the NFP has failed to maintain an appropriate composition of cash or other assets in amounts needed to comply with all donor restrictions, are the amounts and circumstances disclosed?

[FASB ASC 958-450-50-3]

11.   If there is a reasonable possibility that noncompliance with donor-imposed restrictions has resulted in a material contingent liability having been incurred at the financial statement date, could lead to a material loss of revenue, or could cause inability to continue as a going concern, are the amounts and circumstances disclosed?

[FASB ASC 958-450-50-2]

© 2020, Association of International Certified Professional Accountants

	Yes	No	N/A

12. If a long-term unconditional purchase obligation that has all of the characteristics described in FASB ASC 440-10-50-2 is not recorded in the statement of financial position, is the following information disclosed:

    a. Nature and term of the obligations?

    b. Amount of the fixed and determinable portion of the obligations as of the date of the most recent statement of financial position presented, in the aggregate and, if determinable, for each of the next five years?

    c. Nature of any variable components of the obligation?

    d. Amounts of purchases under the obligations for each year for which a statement of activities is presented?

    [FASB ASC 440-10-50-4]

13. If an unconditional purchase obligation is a derivative subject to the requirements of both FASB ASC 440-10 and FASB ASC 815-10, has the NFP complied with the disclosure requirements, in question 12 and those in FASB ASC 815-10-50? (See section II.D., "Derivative Instruments and Hedging Activities.")

    [FASB ASC 440-10-50-7; FASB ASC 815-10-50-6]

J. Risks and Uncertainties

1. Is a description of the principal services or activities performed by the NFP, including a description of each of its major classes of programs and the relative importance of each, and the revenue sources for the NFP's services included in the financial statements? *Note:* If the NFP has not commenced principal operations, it would describe the risks and uncertainties related to the activities in which the NFP is currently engaged and an understanding of what those activities are being directed toward.

    [FASB ASC 275-10-50 par. 2–2A]

2. Is an explanation that the preparation of financial statements in conformity with GAAP requires the use of management's estimates included in the financial statements?

    [FASB ASC 275-10-50-4]

3. Is disclosure regarding an estimate made when known information available before the financial statements are issued or are available to be issued indicates that it is at least reasonably possible that an estimate will change in the near term and the effect of the change will have a material effect on the financial statements?

    [FASB ASC 275-10-50 par. 6–9]

4. Does the disclosure in the preceding question 3 indicate the nature of the uncertainty including an indication that it is at least reasonably possible that a change in estimate will occur in the near term?

    [FASB ASC 275-10-50-9]

5. Has the optional disclosure been considered about the factors that cause the estimate in the preceding question 3 to be sensitive to change?

    [FASB ASC 275-10-50-9]

	Yes	No	N/A

6. If the NFP decides that the criteria in FASB ASC 275-10-50-8 are not met because the NFP uses risk-reduction techniques to mitigate losses or the uncertainty that may result from future events, have the disclosures in questions 3–5 and the disclosure of the risk-reduction techniques been considered?

[FASB ASC 275-10-50-10]

7. Is disclosure made of the concentrations described in FASB ASC 275-10-50-18 (including concentrations of contributions from a particular donor or fund raising event; concentrations of sources of labor, material, or services; or geographic concentrations), if, based on information known to management before the financial statements are issued or are available to be issued, a concentration that exists at the date of the statement of financial position makes the NFP vulnerable to the risk of a near-term severe impact, and it is at least reasonably possible that the events that could cause the impact will occur in the near term?

[FASB ASC 275-10-50 par. 16–22]

K. Related Parties

1. For related-party transactions, do disclosures include

   a. the nature of the relationship involved (for example, affiliate companies and officers)?

   b. a description of the transactions to which no amounts or nominal amounts were ascribed, for each of the periods for which a statement of activity is presented, and such other information deemed necessary to an understanding of the effects of the transactions on the financial statements?

   c. the dollar amount of transactions for each of the periods for which a statement of activities is presented and the effects of any change in the method of establishing the terms from that used in the preceding period?

   d. amounts due from or to related parties as of the date of each statement of financial position presented and, if not otherwise apparent, the terms and manner of settlement?

   [FASB ASC 850-10-50-1]

2. If management represents that related-party transactions were consummated on terms equivalent to those in an arms-length transaction, can that representation be substantiated?

[FASB ASC 850-10-50-5]

3. If the NFP and one or more other entities are under common control and the existence of that control could result in changes in net assets or financial position of the NFP being significantly different from that if the NFP were autonomous, is the nature of the control relationships disclosed (even if no transactions between the entities exist)?

[FASB ASC 850-10-50-6]

4. Are the disclosures in questions 1–3 provided for services received by the NFP from personnel of an affiliate?

[FASB ASC 958-720-50-3]

	Yes	No	N/A

5. In circumstances in which an NFP has little or no fundraising expense because of its relationship to other entities or individuals who raise funds for the NFP's use, has consideration been given to disclosing the relationships and their effect on fundraising expense?

[Q&A 6140.20]

L.   Subsequent Events

1. Are the financial statements adjusted for any changes in estimates resulting from subsequent events that provided additional evidence about conditions that existed at the statement of financial position date, including the estimates inherent in the process of preparing financial statements?

[FASB ASC 855-10-25-1]

2. Are subsequent events that provide evidence about conditions that did not exist at the statement of financial position date, but arose subsequent to that date adequately disclosed to keep the financial statements from being misleading?

[FASB ASC 450-20-50-9; FASB ASC 855-10-50-2]

3. Do the disclosures in question 2 include the following:

   a.   The nature of the event?

   b.   An estimate of the event's financial effect, or a statement that such an estimate cannot be made?

   [FASB ASC 855-10-50-2]

4. If a nonrecognized subsequent event is so significant, has consideration been given to presenting pro forma financial data, including the presentation of pro forma statements (usually a balance sheet only, in columnar form on the face of the historical statements)?

[FASB ASC 855-10-45-1; FASB ASC 855-10-50-3]

5. If the criteria in FASB ASC 360-10-45-9 for a long-lived asset (disposal group) classified as held for sale are met after the date of the statement of financial position but before the financial statements are issued or available to be issued

   a.   is the asset (group) classified as held and used?

   b.   is the carrying amount(s) of the major classes of assets and liabilities included as part of the disposal group disclosed in the notes?

   c.   is a description of the facts and circumstances leading to the expected disposal and the expected manner and timing of the disposal included in the notes?

   [FASB ASC 360-10-45-13; FASB ASC 205-10-50-1]

6. Do the financial statements disclose the date through which subsequent events have been evaluated, as well as whether that date is the date the financial statements were issued or the date the financial statements were available to be issued?

[FASB ASC 855-10-50-1]

	Yes	*No*	*N/A*

7. If the NFP revises financial statements for the correction of an error or the retrospective application of U.S. GAAP, has the NFP disclosed the dates through which subsequent events have been evaluated in both the issued (or available to be issued) financial statements and in the revised financial statements?

   [FASB ASC 855-10-50-4]

8. If the date of an acquisition is after the reporting date but before the financial statements are issued or available for issue, are the following disclosures included in the financial statements:

   a. The information required by questions 21–30 in section I.F., "Mergers and Acquisitions"?

   b. *For public entities:* The information required by question 33 in section I.F. if the acquirer is a public entity as defined in FASB ASC 958-805-20?

   c. If one or more of the disclosures in question 8a or 8b is not possible because the initial accounting for the acquisition is incomplete at the time the financial statements are issued (or are available to be issued), are the disclosures that could not be made described and the reason that they could not be made provided?

   [FASB ASC 805-10-50-4]

M. Pension and Other Postretirement Benefit Plans

Note

The requirements listed in the following questions are for a *nonpublic entity,* as defined in FASB ASC 715-20-20, because most NFPs are expected to meet that definition. If the NFP is a public entity — for example, because it is a conduit bond obligor for conduit debt securities that trade in a public market — or if it prefers to make an expanded set of disclosures, see paragraphs 1–4 of FASB ASC 715-20-50 and FASB ASC 958-715-50-1. (For defined benefit pension plans, accounting and reporting by the plans themselves should be in conformity with FASB ASC 960, *Plan Accounting—Defined Benefit Pension Plans.*)

Defined Benefit Plans

Note

FASB ASU No. 2018-14, *Compensation—Retirement Benefits—Defined Benefit Plans—General (Subtopic 715-20): Disclosure Framework—Changes to the Disclosure Requirements for Defined Benefit Plans,* issued in August 2018, is effective for all entities for fiscal years, and interim periods within those fiscal years, beginning after December 15, 2021. Early adoption is permitted.

FASB ASU No. 2018-14 removes disclosures about defined benefit pension plans that no longer are considered cost beneficial, modifies the disclosures for entities with two or more plans, and adds two new disclosures.

NFPs that have adopted ASU No. 2018-14 should mark questions 1i, 1m, 1n and 2d(ii) "N/A" and complete 1u, 1v, and 2d(iii). Other NFPs should mark questions 1u, 1v, and 2d(iii) "N/A" and complete questions 1i, 1m, 1n and 2d(ii).

	Yes	No	N/A

1. If there is a defined benefit plan, do disclosures include

   a. the benefit obligation, fair value of plan assets, and funded status of the plan?

      [FASB ASC 715-20-50-5]

   b. employer contributions, participant contributions, and benefits paid?

      [FASB ASC 715-20-50-5]

   c. the net periodic benefit cost recognized for each annual period for which an annual statement of activities is presented?

      [FASB ASC 715-20-50-5]

   d. the amounts and line item(s) used in the statement of activities to present the components of net benefit cost (other than the service cost component), if separate line item(s) are not used in the statement of activities?

      ["Pending Content" in FASB ASC 715-20-50-5]

   e. the amounts recognized in the statement of financial position, showing separately the postretirement benefit assets and current and noncurrent postretirement benefit liabilities?

      [FASB ASC 715-20-50-5; FASB ASC 958-715-50-1]

   f. the amounts recognized for the period as changes in net assets without donor restrictions arising from a defined benefit plan but not yet included in net periodic benefit cost, pursuant to paragraphs 11 and 21 of FASB ASC 715-30-35 and paragraphs 16 and 25 of FASB ASC 715-60-35 showing separately the net gain or loss and net prior service cost or credit?

      [FASB ASC 715-20-50-5; "Pending Content" in FASB ASC 958-715-50-1]

   g. the reclassification adjustments of the net gain or loss, the net prior service cost or credit, and the amortization of the net transition asset or obligation as those amounts are recognized as components of net periodic benefit cost?

      [FASB ASC 715-20-50-5; FASB ASC 958-715-50-1]

   h. the amounts that have been recognized as changes in net assets without donor restrictions arising from a defined benefit plan but not yet reclassified as components of net periodic benefit cost, showing separately the net gain or loss, net prior service cost or credit, and net transition asset or obligation?

      [FASB ASC 715-20-50-5; "Pending Content" in FASB ASC 958-715-50-1]

© 2020, Association of International Certified Professional Accountants

	Yes	No	N/A

i.   ***Prior to adoption of ASU No. 2018-14:*** on a weighted-average basis, the following assumptions used in the accounting for the plans: assumed discount rate, rate of compensation increase (for pay-related plans), and the expected long term rate of return on plan assets specifying, in a tabular format, the assumptions used to determine the benefit obligation and the net benefit cost?

[FASB ASC 715-20-50-5]

j.   the assumed health care cost trend rate(s) for the next year used to measure the expected costs of benefits covered by the plan (gross eligible charges) and a general description of the direction and pattern of change in the assumed trend rates thereafter, together with the ultimate trend rate(s) and when that rate is expected to be achieved?

[FASB ASC 715-20-50-5]

k.   if applicable, the amounts and types of securities of the employer and related parties included in plan assets, and the approximate amount of future annual benefits of plan participants covered by insurance contracts issued by the employer or related parties, and any significant transactions between the employer or related parties and the plan during the period?

[FASB ASC 715-20-50-5]

l.   the nature and effect of significant nonroutine events, such as amendments, combinations, divestitures, curtailments, and settlements?

[FASB ASC 715-20-50-5]

m.   ***Prior to adoption of ASU No. 2018-14:*** the amounts that have been recognized as changes in net assets without donor restrictions arising from a defined benefit plan but not yet reclassified as components of net periodic benefit cost that are expected to be recognized as components of net periodic benefit costs over the fiscal year that follows the most recent annual statement of financial position presented, showing separately the net gain or loss, net prior service cost or credit, and net transition asset or obligation?

[FASB ASC 715-20-50-5; "Pending Content" in FASB ASC 958-715-50-1]

n.   ***Prior to adoption of ASU No. 2018-14:*** the amount and timing of any plan assets expected to be returned to the employer during the 12-month period, or operating cycle if longer, that follows the most recent annual statement of financial position presented?

[FASB ASC 715-20-50-5]

© 2020, Association of International Certified Professional Accountants

	Yes	No	N/A

o.   the following information about the plan's investment policies and strategies:

    i.   Target allocation percentages or range of percentages considering the classes of plan assets, presented on a weighted-average basis as of the measurement date(s) of the latest statement of financial position presented, if applicable?

    ii.   Factors that are pertinent to an understanding of the policies or strategies such as investment goals, risk management practices, permitted and prohibited investments including the use of derivatives, diversification, and the relationship between plan assets and benefit obligations?

    iii.   For investment funds disclosed as classes, a description of the significant investment strategies of those funds?

    [FASB ASC 715-20-50-5]

p.   a narrative description of the basis used to determine the overall expected long term rate-of-return-on-assets assumption (for example, the general approach used, the extent to which the overall rate-of-return-on-assets assumption was based on historical returns, the extent to which adjustments were made to those historical returns in order to reflect expectations of future returns, and how those adjustments were determined)?

    [FASB ASC 715-20-50-5]

q.   for defined benefit pension plans, the accumulated benefit obligation?

    [FASB ASC 715-20-50-5]

r.   the benefits (as of the date of the latest statement of financial position presented) expected to be paid in each of the next five fiscal years, and in the aggregate for the five fiscal years thereafter? (*Note:* The expected benefits should be estimated based on the same assumptions used to measure the NFP's benefit obligation at the end of the year and should include benefits attributable to estimated future employee service.)

    [FASB ASC 715-20-50-5]

s.   the best estimate, as soon as it can reasonably be determined, of contributions expected to be paid to the plan during the next fiscal year (that is, beginning after the date of the latest statement of financial position presented)? (*Note:* Estimated contributions may be presented in the aggregate combining (i) contributions required by funding regulations or laws, (ii) discretionary contributions, and (iii) noncash contributions.)

    [FASB ASC 715-20-50-5]

	Yes	No	N/A

t.   if more than one defined benefit plan exists

     i.   are the preceding required disclosures either (1) aggregated for all of the employer's single-employer defined benefit pension plans and all of the employer's defined benefit postretirement plans or (2) disaggregated in groups, so as to provide the most useful information?

         [FASB ASC 715-20-50-2]

     ii.   if plans with assets in excess of accumulated benefit obligations are aggregated with plans that have accumulated benefit obligations that exceed plan assets and the required disclosures are combined, are the following amounts disclosed:

         (1)   The aggregate benefit obligation and the aggregate fair value of plan assets disclosed for plans with benefit obligations in excess of plan assets?

             [FASB ASC 715-20-50-3]

         (2)   The aggregate pension accumulated benefit obligation and the aggregate fair value of plan assets for pension plans with accumulated benefit obligations in excess of plan assets?

             [FASB ASC 715-20-50-3]

u.   *After adoption of ASU No. 2018-14:* on a weighted-average basis, the following assumptions used to determine the benefit obligation and the net benefit costs: discount rate, rate of compensation increase (for pay-related plans), the expected long term rate of return on plan assets and the interest crediting rates (for cash balance plans and other plans with promised interest crediting rates), in a tabular format?

     ["Pending Content" in FASB ASC 715-20-50-5]

v.   *After adoption of ASU No. 2018-14:* an explanation of the reasons for significant gains and losses related to changes in the benefit obligation for the period?

     ["Pending Content" in FASB ASC 715-20-50-5]

2.   If there is a defined benefit plan, do disclosures include the following information about plan assets:

   a.   The fair value of each class of plan assets as of each date for which a statement of financial position is presented, and are the asset classes based on the nature and risks of assets in an employer's plan(s)?

   b.   Additional classes of plan assets and further disaggregation of classes if that information is necessary to meet the objectives of FASB ASC 715-20-50-5(c)?

   c.   Information about the valuation technique(s) and inputs used to measure fair value and a discussion of changes in valuation techniques and inputs, if any, during the period?

         © 2020, Association of International Certified Professional Accountants

	Yes	*No*	*N/A*

d.   The following information for each class of plan assets included in question 2*a*:

     i.   The level within the fair value hierarchy in which the fair value measurements in their entirety fall?

     ii.   ***Prior to adoption of ASU No. 2018-14:*** A reconciliation of the beginning and ending balances for any plan assets measured at fair value using level 3 measures, reporting separately each of the following:

         (1)   Actual return on plan assets (as a component of net periodic pension cost or net periodic postretirement benefit costs), separately identifying the amount related to assets still held at the reporting date and the amount related to assets sold during the period?

         (2)   Purchases, sales, and settlements, net?

         (3)   Transfers in or out of level 3 (for example, transfers due to changes in the observability of significant inputs)?

     iii.   ***After adoption of ASU No. 2018-14:*** The amount of plan assets classified in level 3 purchased during the period and any transfers into or out of level 3, disclosed separately, for fair value measurements of plan assets classified in level 3?

         [FASB ASC 715-20-50-5; "Pending Content" in FASB ASC 715-20-50-5]

3.   If an NFP determines the measurement date of plan assets in accordance with FASB ASC 715-30-35-63A or 715-60-35-123A, is the following information disclosed in the financial statements:

   a.   The accounting policy election to measure plan assets and benefit obligations using the month-end that is closest to the NFP's fiscal year-end and the month-end measurement date?

   b.   If the employer contributes assets to the plan between the measurement date and its fiscal year-end, is the amount of the contribution disclosed to permit reconciliation of the total fair value of all the classes of plan assets to the ending balance of the fair value of plan assets? ***Note:*** The employer should not adjust the fair value of each class of plan assets for the effects of the contribution.

     ["Pending Content" in FASB ASC 715-20-50-5]

Defined Contribution Plans

4.   If there are defined contribution pension or other defined contribution postretirement plans, do the disclosures include the following items:

   a.   The amount of costs recognized for those plans during the period, disclosed separately from the amount of costs for defined benefit plans?

     [FASB ASC 715-70-50-1]

	Yes	No	N/A

b. A description of the nature and effect of any significant changes during the period affecting comparability, such as a change in the rate of employer contributions, a merger or acquisition, or a divestiture?

[FASB ASC 715-70-50-1]

5. If the pension plan has characteristics of both a defined benefit plan and a defined contribution plan and the substance of the plan is to provide a defined benefit, are the disclosures required in questions 1–2 provided?

[FASB ASC 715-70-35-2]

Multiemployer Plans

6. If there is a multiemployer pension or other postretirement plan, do disclosures include

a. the amount of contributions to multiemployer plans during the period?

[FASB ASC 715-80-50-9]

b. a description of the nature and effect of any changes during the period affecting comparability, such as a change in the rate of employer contributions, a business combination, or a divestiture?

[FASB ASC 715-80-50-6]

c. are the provisions of FASB ASC 450 applied if the situation arises in which withdrawal from a multiemployer pension or postretirement benefit plan may result in an employer's having an obligation to the plan for a portion of the plan's unfunded benefit obligation and it is probable or reasonably possible that

    i. an employer would withdraw from the plan under circumstances that would give rise to an obligation?

    ii. an employer's contribution to the fund would be increased during the remainder of the shortfall in the funds necessary to maintain the negotiated level of benefit coverage?

[FASB ASC 715-80-50-2; FASB ASC 715-80-35-2]

7. If there is a multiemployer pension plan, do disclosures include

a. a narrative description, both of the general nature of the multiemployer plans that provide pension benefits and of the employer's participation in the plans that would indicate how the risks of participating in these plans are different from single-employer plans?

[FASB ASC 715-80-50-4]

b. the following information for each individually significant multiemployer plan that provides pension benefits, in tabular format if possible:

    i. Legal name of the plan?

    ii. The plan's Employer Identification Number and, if available, its plan number?

© 2020, Association of International Certified Professional Accountants

	Yes	No	N/A

iii. For the most recently available certified zone status provided by the plan, the date of the plan's year-end to which the zone status relates and whether the plan has utilized any extended amortization provisions that affect the calculation of the zone status? _____ _____ _____

iv. If the zone status is not available, the total plan assets, the accumulated benefit obligations, and whether the plan was (1) less than 65% funded, (2) between 65% and 80% funded, or (3) more than 80% funded? _____ _____ _____

v. The expiration date(s) of the collective-bargaining agreement(s) requiring contributions to the plan, if any? _____ _____ _____

vi. Whether the employer's contributions represent more than 5% of total contributions to the plan as indicated in the plan's most recently available annual report (Form 5500 for U.S. plans) and the year-end date of the plan to which the annual report relates, presented for each period for which a statement of activities is presented? _____ _____ _____

vii. Whether a funding improvement plan or rehabilitation plan (for example, as those terms are defined by the Employment Retirement Security Act of 1974) had been implemented or was pending? _____ _____ _____

viii. Whether the employer paid a surcharge to the plan? _____ _____ _____

ix. A description of any minimum contribution(s), required for future periods by the collective bargaining agreement(s), statutory obligations, or other contractual obligations, if applicable? _____ _____ _____

[FASB ASC 715-80-50-5]

c. the following information (in a separate section of the tabular disclosure) for plans for which plan level information is not available in the public domain:

i. A description of the nature of the plan benefits? _____ _____ _____

ii. A qualitative description of the extent to which the employer could be responsible for the obligations of the plan, including benefits earned by employees during employment with another employer? _____ _____ _____

iii. Quantitative information to help users understand the financial information about the plan (to the extent available) as of the most recent date available, such as total plan assets, actuarial present value of accumulated plan benefits, and total contributions received by the plan? _____ _____ _____

[FASB ASC 715-80-50 par. 7–8]

d. if quantitative information in questions 6b(iii), 6b(vi), or 6c(iii) is not available, a description of the information has been omitted and why, along with any qualitative information as of the most recent date available that would help users understand the financial information that otherwise is required to be disclosed about the plan? _____ _____ _____

[FASB ASC 715-80-50-7]

	Yes	No	N/A

e.   the following information for each period for which a statement of activities is presented:

     i.   Its contributions made to each plan that is individually significant?

       [FASB ASC 715-80-50-5]

     ii.   Its total contributions made to all plans that are not individually significant?

       [FASB ASC 715-80-50-9]

f.   whether information about multiemployer pension plans is presented separately from multiemployer postretirement benefit plans?

    [FASB ASC 715-80-50-5; FASB ASC 715-80-50-11]

Medicare Prescription Drug, Improvement and Modernization Act of 2003

8.   Until an employer is able to determine whether benefits provided by its prescription drug plan are actuarially equivalent to Medicare Part D, does it disclose the following in financial statements for interim or annual periods:

a.   The existence of the Medicare Prescription Drug, Improvement and Modernization Act of 2003?

b.   The fact that measures of the accumulated postretirement benefit obligation or net periodic postretirement benefit cost do not reflect any amount associated with the subsidy because the employer is unable to conclude whether the benefits provided by the plan are actuarially equivalent to Medicare Part D under the act?

    [FASB ASC 715-60-50-6]

9.   In interim and annual financial statements for the first period in which an employer includes the effects of the Medicare Prescription Drug, Improvement and Modernization Act of 2003 subsidy in measuring the accumulated postretirement benefit obligation and the first period in which an employer includes the effects of the subsidy in measuring net periodic postretirement benefit cost, does it disclose the following:

a.   The reduction in the accumulated postretirement benefit obligation for the subsidy related to benefits attributed to past service?

b.   The effect of the subsidy on the measurement of net periodic postretirement benefit cost for the current period? That effect includes (i) any amortization of the actuarial experience gain in question 7a as a component of the net amortization called for by paragraphs 29–30 of FASB ASC 715-60-35, (ii) the reduction in current period service cost due to the subsidy, and (iii) the resulting reduction in interest cost on the accumulated postretirement benefit obligation as a result of the subsidy?

c.   Any significant change in the benefit obligation or plan assets not otherwise apparent, as required by FASB ASC 715-20-50-1(r)?

    [FASB ASC 715-60-50-3]

         © 2020, Association of International Certified Professional Accountants

	Yes	No	N/A

10. For purposes of the disclosures required by items (a) and (f) of FASB ASC 715-20-50-1, does an employer disclose gross benefit payments (paid and expected, respectively), including prescription drug benefits, and separately the gross amount of the Medicare Prescription Drug, Improvement and Modernization Act of 2003 subsidy receipts (received and expected, respectively)?

    [FASB ASC 715-60-50-4]

Defined Benefit Plan Terminated and Contributed to Defined Contribution Plan

11. If the NFP terminates a defined benefit plan and (*a*) contributes the assets withdrawn to a defined contribution plan, (*b*) the amount contributed is in excess of the employer's required (or maximum) annual contribution to the plan, and (*c*) the risk and rewards of the ownership of the assets in excess are retained by the employer, were the following considered for the defined contribution plan:

    a. Is the excess contribution that is not allocated to individual participants accounted for as an asset regardless of the source of funds?

    b. Is the unallocated amount treated as if it were part of the employer's investment portfolio and recorded as an asset?

    c. Is the investment return attributed to such securities including dividends, interest, and gains and losses reported in a manner consistent with the employer's reporting of similar items?

    [FASB ASC 715-70-55 par. 4–9]

N. Liquidity

1. Does the NFP provide

    a. qualitative information that is useful in assessing liquidity?

    b. qualitative information that communicates how the NFP manages its liquid resources available to meet cash needs for general expenditures within one year of the date of the statement of financial position?

    c. quantitative information that communicates the availability of an NFP's financial assets at the date of the statement of financial position to meet cash needs for general expenditures within one year of the date of the statement of financial position? (Availability of a financial asset may be affected by its nature, external limits imposed by donors, laws, and contracts with others, and internal limitations imposed by governing board decisions.)

    [FASB ASC 958-210-50-1A]

	Yes	*No*	*N/A*

O. Advertising Costs

Note

Fundraising by NFPs is not considered advertising. [FASB ASC 958-720-25-5]

1. Do the disclosures for advertising costs include

   a. the accounting policy, including whether such costs are expensed as incurred or the first time the advertising takes place?

   b. a description of the direct-response-advertising reported as assets (if any), the related accounting policy, and the amortization method and period?

   c. the amount charged to advertising expense for each statement of activities presented, with separate disclosure of amounts, if any, representing a write-down of the capitalized advertising costs to net realizable value?

   d. the amount of advertising reported as assets in each statement of financial position presented?

   [FASB ASC 720-35-50-1; FASB ASC 340-20-50-1]

P. Website Development and Cloud Computing Costs

Note

FASB ASU No. 2018-15, *Intangibles—Goodwill and Other—Internal-Use Software (Subtopic 350-40): Customer's Accounting for Implementation Costs Incurred in a Cloud Computing Arrangement That Is a Service Contract (a consensus of the FASB Emerging Issues Task Force)*, is effective for annual reporting periods beginning after December 15, 2020. Early adoption is permitted.

NFPs that have adopted ASU No. 2018-15 should complete questions 5–8. Other NFPs should mark those questions "N/A."

1. Are website development costs incurred in the planning stage expensed as incurred?

   [FASB ASC 350-50-25-2]

2. Are costs of software used to operate the website accounted for consistent with FASB ASC 350-50-25, unless a plan exists to market the software externally?

   [FASB ASC 350-50-25]

3. Are costs incurred to develop graphics (broadly defined as the "look and feel" of the website) accounted for as intangible assets, unless a plan exists to market them externally?

   [FASB ASC 350-50-25-8]

4. Are costs of operating the website accounted for in the same manner as other operating costs?

   [FASB ASC 350-50-25-14]

5. Are implementation costs of hosting arrangements (for example, cloud computing arrangements) capitalized or expensed in the same manner as capitalizing implementation costs incurred to develop or obtain internal-use software?

   ["Pending Content" in FASB ASC 350-40-25-18]

© 2020, Association of International Certified Professional Accountants

	Yes	No	N/A

6. Is the amortization of capitalized implementation costs of a hosting contract presented in the same line item in the statement of activities as the expense for fees for the associated hosting arrangement?

["Pending Content" in FASB ASC 350-40-45-1]

7. Are capitalized implementation costs of a hosting arrangement that is a service contract presented in the same line item in the statement of financial position as a prepayment of the fees for the associated hosting arrangement would be presented?

["Pending Content" in FASB ASC 350-40-45-2]

8. Does the NFP disclose the nature of its hosting arrangements that are service contracts?

["Pending Content" in FASB ASC 350-40-50-1]

Q. **Costs to Exit or Dispose of an Activity**

1. Are costs associated with an exit or disposal activity that does not involve a discontinued operation included in income from operations (if presented)?

[FASB ASC 958-220-45-11]

2. Are costs associated with an exit or disposal activity that involves a discontinued operation included in the results of discontinued operations?

[FASB ASC 420-10-45-2]

3. If an event or circumstance occurs that discharges or removes the NFP's responsibility to settle a liability for a cost associated with an exit or disposal activity recognized in a prior period, are the related costs reversed through the same line item(s) in the statement of activities used when those costs were recognized initially?

[FASB ASC 420-10-40-1]

4. In the period in which an exit or disposal activity is initiated and any subsequent period until the activity is completed, do the notes to the financial statements describe the exit or disposal activity, including the facts and circumstances leading to the expected activity and the expected completion date?

[FASB ASC 420-10-50-1]

5. For each major type of cost associated with the exit or disposal activity (for example, one-time termination benefits, contract termination costs, and other associated costs), has the NFP made the following disclosures:

   a. The total amount expected to be incurred in connection with the activity?

   b. The amount incurred in the period?

   c. The cumulative amount incurred to date?

   d. A reconciliation of the beginning and ending liability balances showing separately the changes during the period attributable to costs incurred and charged to expense, costs paid or otherwise settled, and any adjustments to the liability with an explanation of the reason(s) therefore?

	Yes	No	N/A

e.   The line item(s) in the statement of activities in which the costs are aggregated?

[FASB ASC 420-10-50-1]

6.   If a liability for a cost associated with the exit or disposal activity is not recognized because its fair value cannot be reasonably estimated, is that fact and the reasons why disclosed?

[FASB ASC 420-10-50-1]

R.   Fair Value Measurements

Note

FASB ASU No. 2018-13, *Fair Value Measurement (Topic 820): Disclosure Framework—Changes to the Disclosure Requirements for Fair Value Measurement*, issued in August 2018, is effective for all entities for fiscal years, and interim periods within those fiscal years, beginning after December 15, 2019. Early adoption is permitted upon issuance. An entity is permitted to early adopt any removed or modified disclosures upon issuance and delay adoption of the additional disclosures until their effective date.

FASB ASU No. 2018-13 removes disclosures about fair value measurement that no longer are considered cost beneficial. As a result, these disclosures are now identified in this checklist as optional.

FASB ASU also clarifies the requirements of certain existing disclosures, and adds two new disclosure requirements. However, the new disclosures are not required for nonpublic entities.

An NFP that is a conduit bond obligor for conduit debt securities that trade in a public market should complete question 7*f* and mark question 7*b* "N/A" if it has adopted ASU 2018-13. Other NFPs should complete question 7*b* and mark question 7*f* "N/A."

As noted in FASB ASC 820-10-35-54B, the disclosures in FASB ASC 820-10-50-2 do not apply to investments that are measured using net asset value as a practical expedient. Investments are not measured using the practical expedient if the investments are measured using a net asset value that is published and is the basis for current transactions (that is, the investment has a readily determinable fair value). Disclosures for investments that have a readily determinable fair value are found this section. Question 12 in Section II.C applies to investments measured using net asset value as a practical expedient.

---

1.   Has the NFP made the following disclosures for assets and liabilities that are measured at fair value in periods subsequent to initial recognition in the statement of financial position (for example, investments) for each period separately for each class of assets and liabilities:

a.   The fair value measurements at the end of the reporting period? (*Note:* For derivatives, amounts should be presented on a gross basis.)

b.   The level of the fair value hierarchy within which the fair value measurements are categorized in their entirety (level 1, level 2, or level 3)? (*Note:* For derivatives, information should be presented on a gross basis.)

c.   For recurring fair value measurements categorized within level 3 of the fair value hierarchy, a reconciliation from the opening balances to the closing balances, disclosing separately presenting changes during the period attributable to the following (disclosures for derivative assets and liabilities may be presented net):

     i.   Total gains or losses for the period recognized in changes in net assets, and the line item(s) in the statement of activities in which those gains and losses are recognized?

	Yes	No	N/A

      ii.   Purchases, sales, issuances, and settlements (each of those types of changes disclosed separately)?

      iii.   The amounts of any transfers into or out of level 3 of the fair value hierarchy and the reason for those transfers (for example, transfers due to changes in the observability of significant inputs)?

      iv.   In lieu of the information in (i)–(iii), does the NFP disclose changes during the period for purchases and issues (each of those types of changes disclosed separately) and the amounts of any transfers into or out of Level 3 (separately for transfers into Level 3 and transfers out of Level 3) and the reasons for those transfers? *Note*: This alternative is not available to a public entity.

   d.   The amount of the total gains or losses for the period in item *c*(i) in this question included in changes in net assets that is attributable to the change in unrealized gains or losses relating to those assets and liabilities held at the end of the reporting period and the line item(s) in the statement of activities in which those unrealized gains or losses are recognized?

      [FASB ASC 820-10-50-2; "Pending Content" in FASB ASC 820-10-50-2G]

2.   Are the disclosures in question 1 provided in sufficient detail to permit reconciliation of the fair value measurement disclosures for the various classes of assets and liabilities to the line items in the statement of financial position?

    [FASB ASC 820-10-50-2B]

3.   If the NFP has assets or liabilities that are measured at fair value on a nonrecurring basis in periods subsequent to initial recognition (for example, impaired assets), has the NFP disclosed the fair value measurement at the relevant measurement date and the reasons for the measurements?

    [FASB ASC 820-10-50-2]

4.   Has the NFP made the following disclosures for assets and liabilities that are measured at fair value in periods subsequent to initial recognition for each period separately for each class of assets and liabilities:

   a.   For fair value measurements within level 2 and level 3, a description of the valuation technique(s) and the inputs used in the fair value measurement?

   b.   If there has been a change in either or both a valuation approach and a valuation technique (for example, changing from matrix pricing to the binomial model or the use of an additional valuation technique), that change and the reason for making it?

    [FASB ASC 820-10-50-2]

	Yes	No	N/A

5. For fair value measurements categorized within level 3 of the fair value hierarchy, has the NFP provided the following information:

   a. Quantitative information about the significant unobservable inputs used in the fair value measurement? (*Note:* An NFP is not required to create quantitative information to comply with this disclosure requirement if quantitative unobservable inputs are not developed by the NFP when measuring fair value [for example, when the NFP uses prices from prior transactions or third-party pricing information without adjustment]. However, when providing this disclosure, the NFP cannot ignore quantitative unobservable inputs that are significant to the fair value measurement and are reasonably available to it. The requirement to provide quantitative information does not apply to a nonpublic entity reporting an indefinite-lived intangible asset at fair value.)   ____ ____ ____

   b. A description of the valuation processes used by the NFP (including, for example, how it decides its valuation policies and procedures and analyzes changes in fair value measurements from period to period)? (optional)   ____ ____ ____

   [FASB ASC 820-10-50-2; "Pending Content" in FASB ASC 820-10-50-2; FASB ASC 350-30-50-3A]

6. If a nonfinancial asset is measured in the statement of financial position at fair value in periods subsequent to initial recognition and its current use differs from its highest and best use, has the NFP disclosed that fact and why the nonfinancial asset is being used in a manner that differs from its highest and best use?   ____ ____ ____

   [FASB ASC 820-10-50-2]

7. *For public entities:* If the NFP is a public entity, has it provided the following information:

   a. The information about transfers between level 1 and level 2 of the fair value hierarchy required by FASB ASC 820-10-50-2(bb)? (optional)   ____ ____ ____

   b. *Prior to adoption of ASU No. 2018-13:* The information about the sensitivity of the fair value measurement to changes in unobservable inputs required by FASB ASC 820-10-50-2(g)?   ____ ____ ____

   c. The information required by FASB ASC 820-10-50-2E for each class of assets and liabilities not measured at fair value in the statement of financial position but for which the fair value is disclosed?   ____ ____ ____

   d. The information required by FASB ASC 820-10-50-2E if the fair value of a nonfinancial asset is disclosed and its current use differs from its highest and best use?   ____ ____ ____

© 2020, Association of International Certified Professional Accountants

	Yes	No	N/A

e. *After adoption of ASU No. 2018-13:* In complying with question 5a in this section, did the NFP provide the range and weighted average of significant unobservable inputs used to develop Level 3 fair value measurements and how it calculated the weighted average? *Note:* For certain unobservable inputs, an NFP may disclose other quantitative information, such as the median or arithmetic average, in lieu of the weighted average, if such information would be a more reasonable and rational method to reflect the distribution of unobservable inputs used to develop the Level 3 fair value measurement. An NFP does not need to disclose its reason for omitting the weighted average in these cases.

f. *After adoption of ASU No. 2018-13:* For recurring fair value measurements categorized within Level 3 of the fair value hierarchy, a narrative description of the uncertainty of the fair value measurement from the use of significant unobservable inputs (including all of the unobservable inputs disclosed when complying with item *e* of this question if those inputs reasonably could have been different at the reporting date? *Note:* If there are interrelationships between those inputs and other unobservable inputs used in the fair value measurement, the NFP should also provide a description of those interrelationships and of how they might magnify or mitigate the effect of changes in the unobservable inputs on the fair value measurement.

[FASB ASC 820-10-50-2; "Pending Content" in FASB ASC 820-10-50-2; FASB ASC 820-10-50-2E]

8. Are the quantitative disclosures required by this section in a tabular format?

[FASB ASC 820-10-50-8]

9. If the NFP reports assets and liabilities at fair value pursuant to the "Fair Value Option" subsections of FASB ASC 825-10, has it either (*a*) presented the aggregate of fair value and non-fair-value amounts in the same line item in the statement of financial position and parenthetically disclosed the amount measured at fair value included in the aggregate amount or (*b*) presented two separate line items to display the fair value and non-fair-value carrying amounts of similar assets and liabilities?

[FASB ASC 825-10-45-2]

10. As of each date for which a statement of financial position is presented, has the NFP disclosed the following information about items measured at fair value under the option in the "Fair Value Option" subsections of FASB ASC 825-10 or FASB ASC 815-15-25-4:

a. Management's reasons for electing a fair value option for each eligible item or group of similar eligible items?

b. The following information if the fair value option is elected for some but not all eligible items within a group of similar eligible items:

	Yes	No	N/A

          i.   A description of those similar items and the reasons for partial election?

          ii.   Information to enable users to understand how the group of similar items relates to individual line items on the statement of financial position?

      c.   The following information for each line item in the statement of financial position that includes an item or items for which the fair value option has been elected:

          i.   Information to enable users to understand how each line item in the statement of financial position relates to major categories or classes of assets and liabilities presented in accordance with fair value disclosure requirements in FASB ASC 820?

          ii.   The aggregate carrying amount of items included in each line item in the statement of financial position that are not eligible for the fair value option, if any?

          [FASB ASC 825-10-50-28]

11.   As of each date for which a statement of activities is presented, has the NFP disclosed the following information about items measured at fair value under the "Fair Value Option" subsections in FASB ASC 825-10 or the option in FASB ASC 815-15-25-4:

      a.   For each line item in the statement of financial position, the amounts of gains and losses from fair value changes during the period included in change in each of the net asset classes, and in an intermediate measure of operations, if one is presented, and in which line in the statement of activities those gains and losses are reported? (An NFP may meet this requirement by disclosing amounts that include gains and losses for other items measured at fair value.)

      b.   A description of how interest and dividends are measured and where they are reported in the statement of activities?

          [FASB ASC 825-10-50-30]

12.   Has the NFP disclosed the methods and significant assumptions used to estimate the fair value of items for which the fair value option has been elected?

      [FASB ASC 825-10-50-31]

13.   If an NFP elects the fair value option at a remeasurement event as described in items (d)–(e) of FASB ASC 825-10-25-4, has it disclosed the following for the period of the election:

      a.   Qualitative information about the nature of the event?

      b.   Quantitative information by line item in the statement of financial position indicating which line items in the statement of activities include the effect of initially electing the fair value option for an item?

          [FASB ASC 825-10-50-32]

© 2020, Association of International Certified Professional Accountants

	Yes	No	N/A

S. **Doubt about the NFP's Ability to Continue as a Going Concern**

1. If, after considering management's plans, substantial doubt about an NFP's ability to continue as a going concern is alleviated as a result of consideration of management's plans, do the notes disclose information that enables users of the financial statements to understand all of the following:

   a. Principal conditions or events that raised substantial doubt about the NFP's ability to continue as a going concern (before consideration of management's plans)?   ____ ____ ____

   b. Management's evaluation of the significance of those conditions or events in relation to the NFP's ability to meet its obligations?   ____ ____ ____

   c. Management's plans that alleviated substantial doubt about the NFP's ability to continue as a going concern?   ____ ____ ____

   [FASB ASC 205-40-50-12]

2. If, after considering management's plans, substantial doubt about an NFP's ability to continue as a going concern is not alleviated, do the notes disclose information that enables users of the financial statements to understand all of the following:

   a. That there is substantial doubt about the NFP's ability to continue as a going concern within one year after the date that the financial statements are issued? *Note:* A statement indicating that fact is required.   ____ ____ ____

   b. Principal conditions or events that raise substantial doubt about the NFP's ability to continue as a going concern?   ____ ____ ____

   c. Management's evaluation of the significance of those conditions or events in relation to the NFP's ability to meet its obligations?   ____ ____ ____

   d. Management's plans that are intended to mitigate the conditions or events that raise substantial doubt about the NFP's ability to continue as a going concern?   ____ ____ ____

   [FASB ASC 205-40-50-13]

3. If conditions or events continue to raise substantial doubt about an NFP's ability to continue as a going concern in subsequent annual or interim reporting periods, do the notes include all of the following:

   a. The required disclosures (questions 1 or 2 as appropriate) in those subsequent periods?   ____ ____ ____

   b. An explanation of how conditions or events have changed between reporting periods?   ____ ____ ____

   c. More extensive information about the relevant conditions or events and about management's plans?   ____ ____ ____

   [FASB ASC 205-40-50-14]

4. For the period in which substantial doubt no longer exists (before or after consideration of management's plans), does the NFP disclose how the relevant conditions or events that raised substantial doubt were resolved?   ____ ____ ____

   [FASB ASC 205-40-50-14]

II. Statement of Financial Position

	Yes	No	N/A

A. General

1. Does the statement of financial position report total assets, liabilities, and net assets as well as separate amounts for each of two classes of net assets: net assets without donor restrictions and net assets with donor restrictions, and do the captions used to describe the classes correspond to their meanings?

   [FASB ASC 958-210-45-1; FASB ASC 958-210-55-4]

2. Does the NFP provide information about liquidity by one or more of the following presentations:

   a. Sequencing assets according to their nearness of conversion to cash and sequencing liabilities according to the nearness of their maturity and resulting use of cash?

   b. Classifying assets and liabilities as current and noncurrent?

   c. Disclosing in notes to financial statements relevant information about the liquidity or maturity of assets and liabilities, including restrictions on the use of particular assets?

   [FASB ASC 958-210-45-8]

3. For classified statements of financial position, are assets and liabilities segregated into current and noncurrent classifications, with totals presented for current assets and current liabilities?

   [FASB ASC 210-10-45]

4. For classified statements of financial position, are assets that are not expected to be realized during the current operating cycle classified as noncurrent?

   [FASB ASC 210-10-45-4]

5. Are cash and other assets that are received with restrictions that limit their use to long term purposes or that are designated by the governing board for long term purposes (a) reported separately from similar assets that are available for current use and (b) described in the notes if the nature of the assets (for example, treasury bonds) is not apparent from the face of the statement of financial position?

   [FASB ASC 210-10-45-4; FASB ASC 958-210-45-6]

6. Are contractual limitations on the use of particular assets disclosed on the face of the financial statements or in the notes?

   [FASB ASC 958-210-45-7]

7. Are valuation allowances for assets shown as deductions from their related assets with appropriate disclosure?

   [FASB ASC 210-10-45-13]

8. Are assets offset against a related liability and reported at the net amount only when the NFP intends to set off and a valid right of setoff exists, as defined in FASB ASC 210-20-45-1?

   [FASB ASC 210-20-45-1; FASB ASC 210-10-45-4]

       © 2020, Association of International Certified Professional Accountants

	Yes	No	N/A

9. If derivative instruments, repurchase agreements, and reverse repurchase agreements, or securities borrowing and securities lending transactions are offset in accordance with either FASB ASC 210-20-45 or FASB ASC 815-10-45, is the following information disclosed in a tabular format, separately for assets and liabilities:

    a. The gross amounts of the recognized assets and those recognized liabilities?

    b. The amounts offset to determine the net amounts presented in the statement of financial position?

    c. The net amounts presented in the statement of financial position?

    d. The amounts subject to an enforceable master netting arrangement (or similar agreement) that is not included in item *b* either because management makes an accounting policy election not to offset or the amounts do not meet some or all of the guidance in either FASB ASC 210-20-45 or FASB ASC 815-10-45?

    e. The amounts related to financial collateral (including cash collateral) for an enforceable master netting arrangement (or similar agreement) that is not included in item *b*?

    f. The net amount after deducting the amounts in items *d–e* from the amounts in item *c*?

    g. A description of the rights of setoff (including the nature of those rights) associated with the NFP's recognized assets and recognized liabilities subject to an enforceable master netting arrangement (or similar agreement) disclosed in accordance with item *d*?

    [FASB ASC 210-20-50 par. 3–5; FASB ASC 860-30-50-8]

10. Are the total amounts disclosed in accordance with questions *9d–e* for an instrument less than or equal to the amount disclosed in accordance with question *9c* for that instrument and computed in accordance with FASB ASC 210-20-55-13?

    [FASB ASC 210-20-50-4; FASB ASC 210-20-55-13]

11. If the information required by question 9 is disclosed in more than a single note to the financial statements, are cross-references between those notes provided?

    [FASB ASC 210-20-50-6]

12. Does the NFP provide information about the nature and amounts of different types of limitations placed on net assets without donor restrictions, such as information about the amounts and purposes of board designations, reporting their amounts on the face of the statement of financial position or by including relevant details in notes to financial statements?

    [FASB ASC 958-210-50-3; FASB ASC 958-210-45-11]

13. Does the NFP provide information about self-imposed limits on the use of particular assets?

    [FASB ASC 958-210-50-1]

© 2020, Association of International Certified Professional Accountants

	Yes	No	N/A

B.   Cash and Cash Equivalents

1.   Is *cash* or *cash and cash equivalents* included as a separate line item on the statement of financial position?

[FASB ASC 230-10-45-4]

2.   Are restricted amounts appropriately segregated from other cash balances?

[FASB ASC 210-10-45-4; FASB ASC 958-210-45 par. 6–7]

3.   If a concentration of credit risk arises from deposits in excess of federally insured limits, is it disclosed?

[FASB ASC 825-10-50-20]

4.   If the NFP has material bank overdrafts or a material balance of undelivered checks as of the statement of financial position date, are

   a.   bank overdrafts presented as a separate caption within current liabilities?

   b.   undelivered checks classified as accounts payable?

     [Common Practice]

5.   Are short term highly liquid investments excluded from cash equivalents if they are purchased with resources that have donor restrictions that limit their use to long term investment — for example, as a permanent endowment fund?

[FASB ASC 958-230-55-2]

6.   Are requirements to hold cash in separate accounts disclosed?

[FASB ASC 958-210-50-2]

7.   Are certificates of deposit with original maturities of greater than 90 days excluded from "cash and cash equivalents"?

[Q&A 2130.39]

8.   Is information provided about the nature of restrictions on cash, cash equivalents, and amounts generally described as restricted cash or restricted cash equivalents?

["Pending Content" in FASB ASC 230-10-50-7]

C.   Investments Other Than Derivative Instruments

Note

For investments that are required to be consolidated or reported using the equity method, refer to section I.E, "Related Entities."

Investments in equity securities, general partnerships, limited partnerships, unincorporated joint ventures, limited liability companies, and other equity ownership interests fall within the scope of FASB ASC 958-321 unless they are required to be consolidated or are reported using the equity method of accounting.

Investments in debt securities and certain redeemable preferred stocks fall within the scope of FASB ASC 958-320.

All investments that do not fall within the scopes of FASB ASC 958-320 or 958-321 fall within the scope of FASB ASC 958-325, such as real estate, certificates of deposit, mortgage notes that are not debt securities, oil and gas, mineral interests, and timber.

	Yes	No	N/A

1. Are investments in equity securities with readily determinable fair values and all investments in debt securities measured at fair value in the statement of financial position?

   [FASB ASC 958-320-35-1; "Pending Content" in FASB ASC 958-320-35-1; "Pending Content" in FASB ASC 321-10-35-1]

2. Are other types of investments (such as real estate and oil and gas interests) reported in accordance with FASB ASC 958-325?

   [FASB ASC 958-325-35]

3. For each period for which a statement of financial position is presented, are the following disclosures made on the face of the financial statements or in the notes thereto:

   a. The aggregate carrying amount of investments by major types (for example, equity securities and corporate debt securities)?

      [FASB ASC 958-320-50-2; "Pending Content" in FASB ASC 958-321-50-1]

   b. The basis for determining the carrying amount for investments other than equity securities with readily determinable fair values and all debt securities?

      [FASB ASC 958-325-50-2]

   c. The methods and significant assumptions used to estimate the fair values of investments other than financial instruments, if those other investments are reported at fair value?

      [FASB ASC 958-325-50-2]

4. For the most recent period for which a statement of financial position is presented, does the entity disclose the nature of and carrying amount for every individual investment or group of investments that represents a significant concentration of market risk (market risk may result from the nature of the investments, a lack of diversity of industry, currency, or geographic location)?

   [FASB ASC 958-320-50-3; "Pending Content" in FASB ASC 958-321-50-1]

5. Are significant concentrations of credit risk, including those that arise from concentrations of investments in U.S. government securities, disclosed?

   [FASB ASC 825-10-50-21]

6. Are the appropriate disclosures made for investments in common stock accounted for under the equity method?

   [FASB ASC 323-10-50-3]

7. If the NFP enters into securities lending transactions or repurchase agreements, has it disclosed the following information:

   a. Its policy for requiring collateral or other security?

   b. The carrying amount and classification of assets and associated liabilities at the end of each period presented, including qualitative information about the relationship(s) between those assets and associated liabilities. For example, if assets are restricted solely to satisfy a specific obligation, include a description of the nature of restrictions placed on the assets?

	Yes	No	N/A

c.   A disaggregation of the gross obligation, by the class of collateral pledged, providing an appropriate level of disaggregation and classes determined on the basis of the nature, characteristics, and risks of the collateral pledged?   ___   ___   ___

d.   A reconciliation of total borrowings under securities lending agreements and repurchase agreements to the amount of the gross liability for securities lending transactions disclosed in accordance with FASB ASC 210-20-50-3(a) before any adjustments for offsetting if those amounts are different?   ___   ___   ___

e.   The remaining contractual maturity of the securities lending transactions, using maturity intervals that convey an understanding of the overall maturity profile of the entity's financing agreements?   ___   ___   ___

f.   A discussion of the potential risks associated with securities lending agreements and related collateral pledged, including obligations arising from a decline in the fair value of the collateral pledged and how those risks are managed?   ___   ___   ___

[FASB ASC 860-30-50-1A; FASB ASC 860-30-50-7]

8.   If the NFP has investments that would have been accounted for under the equity method if the NFP had not chosen to apply the guidance in the "Fair Value Option" subsections of FASB ASC 825-10 or in FASB ASC 815-15-25-4, has it disclosed for each period for which a statement of financial position is presented the information required by FASB ASC 323-10-50-3, excluding the disclosures in (a)(3), (b), and (d) of that paragraph?   ___   ___   ___

[FASB ASC 825-10-50-28]

9.   If equity investments without readily determinable fair value are neither reported at fair value nor reported at net asset value (question 12), are they measured at cost minus impairment, if any, plus or minus changes resulting from observable price changes in orderly transactions for the identical or a similar investment of the same issuer? *Note:* For investments that are required to be consolidated or reported using the equity method, refer instead to section I.E, "Related Entities."   ___   ___   ___

["Pending Content" in FASB ASC 958-321-35-2]

10.   If equity securities without readily determinable fair values are measured at cost minus impairment, if any, plus or minus changes resulting from observable price changes in orderly transactions for the identical or a similar investment of the same issuer, does the NFP disclose

a.   the carrying amount of equity securities without readily determinable fair values?   ___   ___   ___

b.   the amount of impairments and downward adjustments, if any, both annual and cumulative?   ___   ___   ___

c.   the amount of upward adjustments, if any, both annual and cumulative?   ___   ___   ___

© 2020, Association of International Certified Professional Accountants

	Yes	No	N/A

    d.   as of the date of the most recent statement of financial position, additional information (in narrative form) that is sufficient to permit financial statement users to understand the quantitative disclosures and the information that the NFP considered in reaching the carrying amounts and upward or downward adjustments resulting from observable price changes?

        ["Pending Content" in FASB ASC 321-10-50-3; "Pending Content" in FASB ASC 958-321-50-2]

11.   Have the necessary disclosures about financial instruments been made? (Refer to section II.E., "Financial Instruments.")

Note

Question 12 applies only to investments for which fair value is measured using net asset value per share (or its equivalent) as a practical expedient. Investments are not measured using the practical expedient if the investments are measured using a net asset value that is published and is the basis for current transactions (that is, the investment has a readily determinable fair value). Disclosures for investments that have a readily determinable fair value are found in section I.R.

12.   Does the NFP disclose all of the following information about its alternative investments for which ownership is represented by units of investments, such as shares of stock or partnership interests, for each interim and annual period, separately for each class of investment:

    a.   The fair value (as determined by applying paragraphs 59–62 of FASB ASC 820-10-35) of the investments in the class?

    b.   A description of the significant investment strategies of the investee(s) in the class?

    c.   For each class of investment that includes investments that can never be redeemed with the investees, but the NFP receives distributions through the liquidation of the underlying assets of the investees, the period of time over which the underlying assets are expected to be liquidated by the investees if the investee has communicated the timing to the NFP or announced the timing publicly, or if the timing is unknown, that fact?

    d.   The amount of the NFP's unfunded commitments related to investments in the class?

    e.   A general description of the terms and conditions upon which the investor may redeem investments in the class (for example, quarterly redemption with 60 days notice)?

    f.   The circumstances in which an otherwise redeemable investment in the class (or a portion thereof) might not be redeemable (for example, investments subject to a lockup or gate)?

    g.   When a restriction from redemption might lapse for those otherwise redeemable investments that are restricted from redemption as of the measurement date if the investee has communicated that timing to the NFP or announced the timing publicly, or if the timing is unknown, that fact and how long the restriction has been in effect?

© 2020, Association of International Certified Professional Accountants

	Yes	No	N/A

h. Any other significant restriction on the ability to sell investments in the class at the measurement date? ___ ___ ___

i. The plans to sell and any remaining actions required to complete the sale of any group of investments that would otherwise meet the criteria for probable sale except that the individual investments to be sold have not been identified? (The disclosure is made so the investments continue to qualify for the practical expedient in FASB ASC 820-10-35-59.) ___ ___ ___

[FASB ASC 820-10-50-6A; "Pending Content" in FASB ASC 820-10-50-6A]

D. Derivative Instruments and Hedging Activities

Note

FASB ASU No 2017-12, *Derivatives and Hedging (Topic 815): Targeted Improvements to Accounting for Hedging Activities,* issued in August 2017, changes the guidance for (1) fair value hedges of interest rate risk by adding the Securities Industry and Financial Markets Association (SIFMA) Municipal Swap Rate as an eligible benchmark interest rate in the United States, thereby allowing an entity that issues or invests in fixed-rate tax-exempt financial instruments to designate as the hedged risk changes in fair value attributable to interest rate risk related to the SIFMA Municipal Swap Rate rather than overall changes in fair value, (2) designating fair value hedges of interest rate risk, (3) measuring the change in fair value of the hedged item in fair value hedges of interest rate risk, and (4) recognizing and presenting the effects of the hedging instrument and the hedged item in the financial statements, by requiring the entire change in the fair value of the hedging instrument to be included in the same line item in the statement of activities that is used to present the change in value of the hedged item. The "Pending Content" also makes certain changes to cash flow hedges, which do not affect NFPs because they are not permitted to use cash flow hedge accounting.

ASU No. 2017-12, as amended by FASB ASU No. 2019-10, *Financial Instruments—Credit Losses (Topic 326), Derivatives and Hedging (Topic 815), and Leases (Topic 842): Effective Dates,* is effective for NFPs for fiscal years beginning after December 15, 2020, and interim periods within fiscal years beginning after December 15, 2021. Early application is permitted.

NFPs that have adopted the requirements of ASU No. 2017-12 should complete questions 23-28 and 30 and mark questions 12-14 and 17 "N/A." Other NFPs should complete questions 12-14 and 17 and mark questions 23-28 and 30 "N/A."

1. Are derivative instruments that are within the scope of FASB ASC 815, including certain derivative instruments embedded in other contracts, accounted for as assets or liabilities in the statement of financial position and measured at their fair values? ___ ___ ___

   [FASB ASC 815-10-25-1; FASB ASC 815-10-35-1]

2. Are gains and losses included in the change in net assets for

   a. derivative instruments that are not designated as a hedging instrument and derivative instruments that are designated as cash flow hedges? ___ ___ ___

   [FASB ASC 815-10-35-3]

   b. derivative instruments designated and qualifying as a fair value hedge, along with the offsetting loss or gain on the hedged item and the effects of hedge ineffectiveness? ___ ___ ___

   [FASB ASC 815-25-35-19]

	Yes	No	N/A

3. Are gains and losses on derivative instruments or nonderivative financial instruments that are designated and qualifying as hedges of a foreign currency exposure of a net investment in a foreign operation accounted for in the same manner as a translation adjustment, that is, are they reported separately in the statement of activities (by class of net assets affected) in accordance with FASB ASC 830, *Foreign Currency Matters*?

   [FASB ASC 815-35-35 par. 1–2; FASB ASC 815-10-50-4G]

4. Does the NFP disclose the following information about derivative instruments it holds or issues (or nonderivative instruments it holds or issues that are designated and qualify as hedging instruments pursuant to FASB ASC 815-20-25-58 and FASB ASC 815-20-25-66):

   a. Its objectives for holding or issuing those instruments?

   b. The context necessary to understand those objectives?

   c. Its strategies for achieving those objectives?

   [FASB ASC 815-10-50-1A]

5. Are the disclosures described in question 4 in the context of each instrument's primary underlying risk exposure (for example, interest rate, credit, foreign exchange rate, interest rate and foreign exchange rate, or overall price?

   [FASB ASC 815-10-50-1B]

6. Do the disclosures described in question 4 distinguish between instruments used for risk management purposes and those used for other purposes?

   [FASB ASC 815-10-50-1B]

7. Do the disclosures described in question 4 distinguish between instruments designated as (*a*) fair value hedging instruments, (*b*) cash flow hedging instruments, (*c*) hedges of foreign currency exposure of net investments in foreign operations, and (*d*) economic hedges and for other purposes related to the NFP's risk exposures?

   [FASB ASC 815-10-50-2]

8. For derivative instruments not designated as hedging instruments, does the NFP describe the purpose the derivative activity?

   [FASB ASC 815-10-50-4]

9. Does the NFP disclose information that enables users of its financial statements to understand the volume of its derivative activity?

   [FASB ASC 815-10-50-1A]

10. Did the NFP consider providing additional qualitative disclosures about its overall risk exposures relating to interest rate risk, foreign currency exchange rate risk, commodity price risk, credit risk, and equity price risk, even if the NFP does not manage those risks by using derivative instruments?

    [FASB ASC 815-10-50-5]

	Yes	No	N/A

11. Does the NFP disclose the location and fair value amounts of derivative instruments it holds or issues (or nonderivative instruments it holds or issues that are designated and qualify as hedging instruments pursuant to FASB ASC 815-20-25-58 and FASB ASC 815-20-25-66) in a tabular format that provides

    a. the fair value on a gross basis (even if the derivative instruments qualify for net presentation in the statement of financial position) and without netting any cash collateral payables and receivables associated with those instruments? ____ ____ ____

    [FASB ASC 815-10-50 par. 4A–4B; FASB ASC 820-10-50-3]

    b. separate asset and liability values segregated between derivatives that are designated and qualifying as hedging instruments and those that are not, and within those two broad categories, by type of derivative contract (for example, interest rate contracts, foreign exchange contracts, equity contracts, commodity contracts, credit contracts, and so forth)? ____ ____ ____

    [FASB ASC 815-10-50-4B]

    c. the line item(s) in the statement of financial position in which the fair value amounts for the preceding categories are included? ____ ____ ____

    [FASB ASC 815-10-50-4B]

12. Does the NFP disclose the location and amounts of the gains and losses reported in the statement of activities (by class of net assets affected) for derivative instruments it holds or issues (or nonderivative instruments it holds or issues that are designated and qualify as hedging instruments pursuant to FASB ASC 815-20-25-58 and FASB ASC 815-20-25-66) in a tabular format that provides

    a. the gains and losses on derivative instruments designated and qualifying as hedging instruments in fair value hedges and related hedged items designated and qualifying in fair value hedges)? ____ ____ ____

    b. the portion of gains and losses on derivative instruments designated and qualifying net investment hedges representing the amount of the hedge's ineffectiveness? ____ ____ ____

    c. the portion of gains and losses on derivative instruments designated and qualifying in net investment hedges representing the amount, if any, excluded from the assessment of hedge effectiveness? ____ ____ ____

    d. the gains and losses for derivative instruments not designated or qualifying as hedging instruments? (See question 15.) ____ ____ ____

    [FASB ASC 815-10-50 par. 4A, 4C, 4E, and 4G]

13. Do the disclosures described in question 12 present information separately by type of derivative contract (for example, interest rate contracts, foreign exchange contracts, equity contracts, commodity contracts, credit contracts, and other contracts)? ____ ____ ____

[FASB ASC 815-10-50-4D]

       © 2020, Association of International Certified Professional Accountants

	Yes	No	N/A

14. Do the disclosures described in question 12 identify the line item(s) in the statement of activities in which the gains and losses for the categories of derivative instruments are included and which class or classes of net assets are affected?

[FASB ASC 815-10-50-4D; FASB ASC 815-10-50-4G]

15. If the NFP excludes derivative instruments not designated or qualifying as hedging instruments from the disclosures described in question 12, has it disclosed the following information for those excluded instruments:

   a. The gains and losses on derivative and nonderivative instruments recognized in the statement of activities, separately by major types of items (for example, fixed income/interest rates, foreign exchange, equity, commodity, and credit)?

   b. The line item(s) in the statement of activities in which the gains and losses are recognized, separately by class of net assets affected?

   c. A description of the nature of its activities and related risks, and how the NFP manages those risks?

   [FASB ASC 815-10-50-4]

16. Does the NFP disclose the following information about derivative instruments it holds or issues (or nonderivative instruments it holds or issues that are designated and qualify as hedging instruments pursuant to FASB ASC 815-20-25-58 and FASB ASC 815-20-25-66) that have credit-risk-related contingent features and that are in a net liability position at the end of the reporting period:

   a. The existence and nature of the credit-risk-related contingent features and the circumstances in which the features could be triggered?

   b. The aggregate fair value amounts that are in a net liability position at the end of the period?

   c. The aggregate fair value of assets that are already posted as collateral at the end of the reporting period?

   d. The aggregate fair value of additional assets that would be required to be posted as collateral or the aggregate fair value of assets needed to settle the instrument immediately, if the credit-risk-related contingent features were triggered at the end of the reporting period?

   [FASB ASC 815-10-50-4H]

17. Is the following information about fair value hedges disclosed:

   a. The net gain or loss recognized in the change in net assets for the sum of (i) the amount of the hedge's ineffectiveness and (ii) the component of the derivative instrument's gain or loss, if any, excluded from the assessment of hedge effectiveness?

   [FASB ASC 815-25-50-1]

   b. The amount of net gain or loss recognized in earnings when a hedged firm commitment no longer qualifies as a fair value hedge?

   [FASB ASC 815-25-50-1]

	Yes	No	N/A

18. If the NFP elects to offset fair values for derivative instruments and cash collateral under a master netting arrangement, as described in paragraphs 5–6 of FASB ASC 815-10-45, does it disclose that accounting policy and the information required by FASB ASC 815-10-50-7A and FASB ASC 815-10-50-8?

    [FASB ASC 815-10-50 par. 7–8]

19. If the NFP holds or issues derivatives that have credit-risk-related contingent features (that is, clauses that would require the NFP to post additional collateral or to settle the instrument upon occurrence of a credit event, such as a downgrade in the NFP's long-term credit rating), do the financial statements contain the disclosures required by FASB ASC 815-10-50-4H?

    [FASB ASC 815-10-50-4H]

20. If the NFP is a party to a master netting arrangement for derivatives (including bifurcated embedded derivatives), have the required disclosures been made, irrespective of whether the NFP has offset amounts under the agreement? (Refer to section II.A. questions 9–11.)

    [FASB ASC 210-20-50-1]

21. If the NFP measures hybrid instruments (financial instruments containing embedded derivatives) at fair value in accordance with the election in FASB ASC 815-15-25-4 or the practicability exception in FASB ASC 815-15-30-1, has the NFP disclosed the information required by paragraphs 28–32 of FASB ASC 825-10-50?

    [FASB ASC 815-15-50-1]

22. Has the NFP provided information that will allow users to understand the effect of changes in the fair value of hybrid financial instruments measured at fair value on change in net assets?

    [FASB ASC 815-15-50-2]

23. Does the NFP disclose the location and amounts of the gains and losses reported in the statement of activities (by class of net assets affected) for derivative instruments it holds or issues (or nonderivative instruments it holds or issues that are designated and qualify as hedging instruments pursuant to FASB ASC 815-20-25-58 and FASB ASC 815-20-25-66) in a tabular format that provides

    a. the gains and losses on derivative instruments (and nonderivative instruments) designated and qualifying as hedging instruments in fair value hedges and related hedged items designated and qualifying in fair value hedges)?

    b. the portion of gains and losses on derivative instruments designated and qualifying in fair value hedges representing the amount, if any, excluded from the assessment of hedge effectiveness, separately for amounts recognized by an amortization approach (FASB ASC 815-20-25-83A) and amounts recognized directly in change in net assets (FASB ASC 815-20-25-83B)?

    c. the amount of net gain or loss recognized when a hedged firm commitment no longer qualifies as a fair value hedge?

       ["Pending Content" in FASB ASC 815-10-50 par. 4A, 4C, 4E, and 4G]

 © 2020, Association of International Certified Professional Accountants

	Yes	No	N/A

24. Does the NFP disclose in a tabular format the location and amounts of the gains and losses reported in the statement of activities for derivative instruments not designated or qualifying as hedging instruments, including the class(es) of net assets affected?

["Pending Content" in FASB ASC 815-10-50-4CC; "Pending Content" in FASB ASC 815-10-50-4E, FASB ASC 815-10-50-4G]

25. Do the disclosures described in questions 23–24 present information separately by type of derivative contract (for example, interest rate contracts, foreign exchange contracts, equity contracts, commodity contracts, credit contracts, and other contracts)?

[FASB ASC 815-10-50-4D]

26. Do the disclosures described in questions 23–24 identify the line item(s) in the statement of activities in which the gains and losses for the categories of derivative instruments are included and the total amount of those line item(s) in which the results of fair value hedges are recorded, including which class(es) of net assets are affected?

["Pending Content" in FASB ASC 815-10-15-4A; FASB ASC 815-10-50-4D; FASB ASC 815-10-50-4G]

27. Does the NFP disclose in tabular format the following for items designated and qualifying as hedged items in fair value hedges:

   a. The carrying amount of hedged assets and liabilities recognized in the statement of financial position?

   b. The cumulative amount of fair value hedging adjustments to hedged assets and liabilities included in the carrying amount of the hedged assets and liabilities recognized in the statement of financial position?

   c. The line item(s) in the statement of financial position that includes the hedged assets and liabilities? *Note:* Additional disclosures are required if last-of-layer method is used.

   d. The cumulative amount of fair value hedging adjustments remaining for any hedged assets and liabilities for which hedge accounting has been discontinued?

   ["Pending Content" in FASB ASC 815-10-50-4EE]

28. If the NFP elects to record changes in the fair value of amounts excluded from the assessment of effectiveness in change in net assets in accordance with FASB ASC 815-20-25-83B, is this accounting policy disclosed?

["Pending Content" in FASB ASC 815-10-50-4EEEE]

29. If the information required by questions 4–28 is disclosed in more than a single note, does each derivative notes cross-reference the other notes in which derivative-related information is disclosed?

[FASB ASC 815-10-50-4I; FASB ASC 815-10-50-4G]

30. For qualifying fair value hedges and qualifying net investment hedges, does the NFP present both of the following in the same line item in the statement of activities that is used to present the revenue or expense effect of the hedged item:

   a. The change in the fair value of the hedging instrument that is included in the assessment of hedge effectiveness?

	Yes	No	N/A

b.   Amounts excluded from the assessment of hedge effectiveness in accordance with paragraphs 83A–83B of FASB ASC 815-20-25?

["Pending Content" in FASB ASC 815-20-45-1A]

E.   Financial Instruments

1.   Are financial assets and financial liabilities presented separately by measurement category (for example, fair value, amortized cost) and form of financial asset (that is, securities or loans and receivables) in the statement of financial position or the accompanying notes to the financial statements?

["Pending Content" in FASB ASC 825-10-45-1A]

2.   Do disclosures of all significant concentrations of credit risk arising from all financial instruments (including derivative instruments accounted for under FASB ASC 815), whether from an individual counterparty or groups of counterparties (except for certain insurance and investment contracts, purchase and pension obligations), include

a.   information about the (shared) activity, region, or economic characteristic that identifies the concentration? Possible shared characteristics on which significant concentrations may be determined include, but are not limited to

i.   borrowers subject to significant payment increases.

ii.   loans with terms that permit negative amortization.

iii.   loans with high loan-to-value ratios. Judgment is required to determine whether loan products have terms that give rise to a concentration of credit risk.

b.   the maximum amount of loss due to credit risk that, based on the gross fair value of the financial instrument, the NFP would incur if parties failed completely to perform according to the terms of the contracts and the collateral (or other security, if any) for the amount due proved to be of no value to the NFP?

c.   the NFP's policy of requiring collateral or other security to support financial instruments subject to credit risk, information about the NFP's access to that collateral or other security, and the nature and a brief description of the collateral or other security supporting those financial instruments?

d.   the NFP's policy of entering into master netting arrangements to mitigate the credit risk of financial instruments, information about the arrangements for which the entity is a party, and a brief description of the terms of those arrangements, including the extent to which they would reduce the NFP's maximum amount of loss due to credit risk?

[FASB ASC 825-10-50-21]

     © 2020, Association of International Certified Professional Accountants

	Yes	No	N/A

Note

FASB ASC 860, *Transfers and Servicing*, establishes standards for resolving whether transfers of financial assets should be considered as sales or as secured borrowings if the transferor has some continuing involvement either with the assets transferred or with the transferee. Examples of continuing involvement with the transferred financial assets include, but are not limited to, any of the following: servicing arrangements, recourse arrangements, guarantee arrangements, agreements to purchase or redeem transferred financial assets, options written or held, derivative financial instruments that are entered into contemporaneously with, or in contemplation of, the transfer, arrangements to provide financial support, pledges of collateral, and the transferor's beneficial interests in the transferred financial assets. This checklist includes only the disclosure requirements for the more common activities engaged in by NFPs relating to transactions within the scope of FASB ASC 860. If the NFP services loans it did not originate or engages in securitizations or asset-backed financing arrangements, the additional disclosure requirements of FASB ASC 310, *Receivables*, and FASB ASC 860, not included herein, also should be considered.

3. If the NFP has transferred financial assets in a transaction described in FASB ASC 860, do disclosures provide the financial statement users with an understanding of the following:

   a. The NFP's continuing involvement, if any, with transferred financial assets?

   b. The nature of any restrictions on assets reported by the NFP in its statement of financial position that relate to a transferred financial asset, and the carrying amounts of such assets?

   c. How transfers accounted for as sales, if a transferor has continuing involvement with the transferred financial assets, affects the NFP's financial position, financial performance, and cash flows?

   d. How transfers accounted for as secured borrowings affect the NFP's financial position, financial performance, and cash flows?

   [FASB ASC 860-10-50-3]

4. If disclosures required by FASB ASC 860 are reported in the aggregate for similar transfers (which is permitted if the characteristics in FASB ASC 860-10-50-5 are considered and separate reporting of each transfer would not provide more useful information), does the NFP both

   a. disclose how similar transfers are aggregated?

   b. distinguish between transfers that are accounted for as secured borrowings and transfers that are accounted for as sales?

   [FASB ASC 860-10-50-3]

5. If the NFP transferred financial asset(s) and accounts for the transfer as a sale in accordance with FASB ASC 860 but entered into an agreement in contemplation of the initial transfer with the transferee that results in the NFP retaining substantially all of the exposure to the economic return on the transferred financial asset(s) throughout the term of the transaction, is the following information disclosed:

   a. The carrying amount of assets derecognized, as of the date of derecognition?

	Yes	No	N/A

b.   If the amounts that have been derecognized have changed significantly from the amounts that have been derecognized in prior periods or are not representative of the activity throughout the period, a discussion of the reasons for the change? ____ ____ ____

c.   The amount of gross cash proceeds received by the NFP for the assets derecognized, as of the date of derecognition? ____ ____ ____

d.   As of the reporting date, the fair value of assets derecognized by the NFP? ____ ____ ____

e.   Amounts reported in the statement of financial position arising from the transaction (for example, the carrying value or fair value of forward repurchase agreements or swap contracts)? ____ ____ ____

f.   A cross-reference to the appropriate line item in the derivative disclosures presented in accordance with FASB ASC 815-10-50-4B, if that disclosure is required? ____ ____ ____

g.   A description of the arrangements that result in the NFP retaining substantially all of the exposure to the economic return on the transferred financial assets and the risks related to those arrangements? ____ ____ ____

[FASB ASC 860-20-50 par. 4A–4C]

6.   If the NFP is a party to a master netting arrangement for repurchase agreements and reverse repurchase agreements, and securities borrowing and securities lending transactions, have the required disclosures been made, irrespective of whether the NFP has offset amounts under the agreement? (Refer to section II.A. questions 9–11.) ____ ____ ____

[FASB ASC 210-20-50-1]

7.   If an NFP takes advantage of the exception in FASB ASC 820-10-35-18D that permits a reporting entity to measure the fair value of a group of financial assets and financial liabilities on the basis of the price of the net risk exposure at the measurement date, has that fact been disclosed? ____ ____ ____

[FASB ASC 820-10-50-2D]

F.   Accounts, Notes, Contributions, and Loans Receivable

Note

FASB ASU No. 2016-13, *Financial Instruments—Credit Losses (Topic 326): Measurement of Credit Losses on Financial Instruments*, was issued in June 2016 to provide financial statement users with more decision-useful information about the expected credit losses on financial instruments and other commitments to extend credit held by a reporting entity at each reporting date. To achieve this objective, the amendments in this Update replace the incurred loss impairment methodology in current GAAP with a methodology that reflects expected credit losses and requires consideration of a broader range of reasonable and supportable information to inform credit loss estimates.

FASB ASU No. 2016-13, as amended by FASB ASU No. 2019-10, is effective for NFPs for fiscal years beginning after December 15, 2022, and interim periods within those fiscal years. Early adoption is permitted for fiscal years beginning after December 15, 2018, including interim periods within those fiscal years.

An NFP that has early adopted ASU No. 2016-13 should mark questions 10, 14–22, and 25–28 "N/A" and should complete questions 1–9, 11–13, 23–24, and 29–42. All others should complete questions 1–29 and 42 and mark questions 30–41 "N/A."

	Yes	No	N/A

1. Are major categories of loans and receivables presented separately on the face of the statement of financial position or in the notes (for example, contributions receivable, trade receivables, notes receivable, amounts due from governing board members, employees, or affiliated entities) with appropriate disclosures?

   [FASB ASC 310-10-45-2; FASB ASC 310-10-50-3]

2. If a classified statement of financial position is presented, are amounts due from affiliated entities and subsidiaries classified as current only if they are collectible within one year?

   [FASB ASC 310-10-45-9]

3. If a note is noninterest bearing or has an inappropriate stated interest rate

   a. is the discount or premium presented as a deduction from or addition to the face amount of the note?

   b. does the disclosure include the effective interest rate and face amount of the note?

   c. is amortization of discount or premium reported as interest in the statement of activity?

   [FASB ASC 835-30-45 par. 1A–3]

4. Are unearned discounts, finance charges, and interest included in the face amount of receivables shown as a deduction from the related receivables?

   [FASB ASC 310-10-45-8]

5. Are valuation allowances for receivables (such as those for doubtful accounts, credit losses, unearned income, unamortized discounts and premiums, or unamortized deferred fees and costs) shown as a deduction from the related receivable and the amounts disclosed in the financial statements?

   [FASB ASC 310-10-50 par. 4 and 14; FASB ASC 210-10-45-13]

6. If the NFP received unconditional promises to give, does it disclose the following:

   a. The amounts of promises receivable in less than one year, in one to five years, and in more than five years?

   b. The face amount of contributions promised to the NFP?

   c. The amount of any allowance for uncollectible promises receivable?

   d. Unamortized discount?

   e. Amounts pledged as collateral or otherwise limited as to use?

   [FASB ASC 958-310-50-1; FASB ASC 860-30-50-1A]

7. If the NFP received conditional promises to give, does it disclose the following:

   a. The total of the amounts promised?

   b. A description and amount for each group of promises having similar characteristics (such as amount of promises conditioned on establishing new programs, completing a new building, and raising matching gifts by a specified date)?

   [FASB ASC 958-310-50-4]

	Yes	No	N/A

8. If receivables are sold with recourse, is the amount of the recourse obligation computed and reported as a liability?

   [FASB ASC 860-20-25-1]

9. If the NFP has sold receivables in a transaction accounted for as a sale under FASB ASC 860 is the aggregate amount of gains or losses on the sales (including adjustments to record loans held for sale at the lower of cost or fair value presented separately in the statement of activities or disclosed in the notes to financial statements?

   [FASB ASC 860-20-50-5]

10. If an impairment of a loan has been recognized, have the following disclosures been made: (*Note:* Large groups of smaller balance homogeneous loans that are collectively evaluated for impairment — for example, student loans of a college — are exempt from this requirement unless restructured in a troubled debt restructuring.)

    a. As of the date of each statement of financial position presented, the total recorded investment in the impaired loans, the amount of that recorded investment in impaired loans for which there is a related allowance for credit losses and the amount of that allowance, and the amount of that recorded investment in impaired loans for which there is no related allowance for credit losses?

    b. The policy for recognizing interest income on impaired loans, including how cash receipts are recorded?

    c. For each period for which a statement of activity is presented, the average recorded investment in impaired loans, the related amount of interest income recognized for the time that the loan was impaired within the period, and, unless not practicable, the amount of interest income recognized using a cash-basis method of accounting during the time that the loan was impaired within the period?

       [FASB ASC 310-10-50-15; FASB ASC 310-40-50-5]

11. If the NFP has accepted collateral that it is permitted by contract or custom to sell or repledge, has it disclosed the following information about that collateral:

    a. The fair value of that collateral as of the date of each statement of financial position presented?

    b. The fair value of the portion of that collateral that it has sold or repledged?

    c. Information about the sources and uses of that collateral?

       [FASB ASC 860-30-50-1A]

12. As of each date for which a statement of financial position is presented, has the NFP disclosed the following information for assets measured at fair value under the elections in the fair value option subsections of FASB ASC 825-10 or FASB ASC 815-15-25-4:

    a. The difference between the aggregate fair value and the aggregate unpaid principal balance of loans and long term receivables (other than securities described in FASB ASC 958-320-15) that have contractual principal amounts?

    b. The aggregate fair value of loans that are 90 days or more past due?

	Yes	No	N/A

    c.   The aggregate fair value of loans in nonaccrual status, if the NFP's policy is to recognize interest income separately from other changes in fair value? ____ ____ ____

    d.   The difference between the aggregate fair value and the aggregate unpaid principal balance for loans that are 90 days or more past due, in nonaccrual status, or both? ____ ____ ____

    [FASB ASC 825-10-50-28]

13.   As of each date for which a statement of activities is presented, has the NFP disclosed the following information for loans and long term receivables measured at fair value under the fair value option subsections of FASB ASC 825-10 or FASB ASC 815-15-25-4:

    a.   The estimated amount of gains or losses included in the change in each of the net asset classes during the period, and in an intermediate measure of operations if one is presented, that is attributable to changes in instrument-specific credit risk? ____ ____ ____

    b.   How the gains or losses attributable to changes in instrument-specific credit risk were determined? ____ ____ ____

    [FASB ASC 825-10-50-30]

Note

Questions 14–16 apply to NFPs that (1) extend credit to customers (constituents) to encourage them to purchase products and services (for example, trade receivables including tuition receivables and conference or seminar fees receivable), (2) make mortgage loans, or (3) make secured or unsecured loans to constituents (for example, student loans). This checklist includes only the disclosure requirements for the more common activities relating to lending activities. If the NFP purchases or sells loans or servicing rights, holds impaired loans that have not been written off, forecloses on a loan, restructures a receivable in a troubled debt restructuring, or engages in other more complex lending activities, the additional disclosure requirements of FASB ASC 310 and FASB ASC 860, not included herein, also should be considered.

14.   Does the accounting policy note include the following:

    a.   The basis of accounting for loans and trade receivables? ____ ____ ____

    b.   The method for recognizing interest income on loan and trade receivables, including the NFP's policy for treatment of related fees and costs and the method of amortizing net deferred fees or costs? ____ ____ ____

    c.   The classification and method of accounting for receivables that can be contractually prepaid or otherwise settled in a way that the NFP would not recover substantially all of its recorded investment? ____ ____ ____

    d.   The accounting policies and methodology the NFP used to estimate its allowance for loan losses, allowance for doubtful accounts, any liability for off-balance sheet credit losses, and any related charges for credit losses, including a description of the factors that influenced management's judgment? ____ ____ ____

    e.   The policy for discontinuing accrual of interest on past due interest-bearing receivables, for recording payments on those past-due receivables, and the policy for resuming accrual of interest? ____ ____ ____

	Yes	No	N/A

f.   The policy for charging off uncollectible loans and receivables?   ____ ____ ____

g.   The policy for determining past due or delinquency status?   ____ ____ ____

[FASB ASC 310-10-50 par. 2 and 9; FASB ASC 310-10-50-6; FASB ASC 310-10-50 par. 4A and 11B]

15. Is the recorded investment in past due financing receivables (loans and receivables due in more than one year) on which accrual of interest has been discontinued disclosed for each date for which a statement of financial position is presented?   ____ ____ ____

[FASB ASC 310-10-50-7]

16. Is the recorded investment in financing receivables (loans and receivables due in more than one year) past due ninety days or more and still accruing disclosed for each date for which a statement of financial position is presented?   ____ ____ ____

[FASB ASC 310-10-50-7]

Note

Questions 17–23 apply to financing receivables, which are defined in FASB ASC 310-10-20 as "A financing arrangement that has both of the following characteristics: (*a*) It represents a contractual right to receive money either on demand or on fixed or determinable dates and (*b*) it is recognized as an asset in the entity's statement of financial position." The questions apply to financing receivables except for the following:

- Those measured at fair value with changes in fair value reported in the statement of activities

- Those measured at the lower of cost or market

- Trade accounts receivable with a contractual maturity of one year or less that arose from the sale of goods and services

- Loans acquired with deteriorated credit quality

17. Has the NFP provided an analysis, by class of financing receivable, of the age of its recorded investment in past due financing receivables at the end of the reporting period? (Past due is determined by the NFP's policy.)   ____ ____ ____

[FASB ASC 310-10-50-7A]

18. Does the accounting policy note for question 14 include the following:

a.   A discussion of risk characteristics relevant to each portfolio segment?   ____ ____ ____

b.   Identification of any change(s) to the entity's accounting policies or methodology from the prior period, the entity's rationale for the change(s), and the quantitative effect of the change(s) on the current period's provision for credit losses?   ____ ____ ____

[FASB ASC 310-10-50-11B]

19. Has the NFP provided the activity in the allowance for credit losses by portfolio segment, including all of the following:

a.   The balance in the allowance at the beginning and end of each period?   ____ ____ ____

b.   Current period provision?   ____ ____ ____

© 2020, Association of International Certified Professional Accountants

	Yes	No	N/A

    c.   Direct write-downs charged against the allowance? ____ ____ ____

    d.   Recoveries of amounts previously charged off? ____ ____ ____

        [FASB ASC 310-10-50-11B]

20. Is the following information reported for each portfolio segment at the end of each period, disaggregated on the basis of the impairment method used (for example, individually evaluated for impairment, collectively evaluated for impairment, acquired with deteriorated credit quality), as shown in FASB ASC 310-10-55-7:

    a.   The balance in the allowance for credit losses? ____ ____ ____

    b.   The recorded investment in financing receivables? ____ ____ ____

        [FASB ASC 310-10-50 par. 11B–11C]

21. Does the NFP disclose the following information about impaired loans that have been charged off partially:

    a.   The amount of impaired loans for each class of financing receivable? ____ ____ ____

    b.   The accounting for impaired loans for each class of financing receivable? ____ ____ ____

        [FASB ASC 310-10-50-14A]

    c.   The total unpaid principal balance of the impaired loans? ____ ____ ____

        [FASB ASC 310-10-50-15]

    d.   The NFP's policy for determining which loans to assess for impairment? ____ ____ ____

    e.   The factors considered in determining that the loan is impaired? ____ ____ ____

        [FASB ASC 310-10-50-15]

    f.   The amount of interest income on impaired loans that represents the change in present value attributable to the passage of time (applies to creditors that measure impairment based on the present value of expected future cash flows and choose to report the interest income component separately from bad-debt expense)? ____ ____ ____

        [FASB ASC 310-10-50-19]

22. Does the NFP provide the following information that enables financial statement users to understand how and to what extent the NFP monitors credit quality of its financing receivables:

    a.   A description of the credit quality indicator? ____ ____ ____

    b.   The recorded investment in financing receivables by credit quality indicator? ____ ____ ____

    c.   The date (or range of dates) in which the information was updated for each credit quality indicator? ____ ____ ____

    d.   If the NFP discloses internal risk ratings, the qualitative information on how those internal risk ratings relate to the likelihood of loss? ____ ____ ____

        [FASB ASC 310-10-50 par. 29–30]

	Yes	No	N/A

23. If the NFP as creditor has modified the terms of a receivable in a troubled debt restructuring transaction, has the NFP disclosed the information described in paragraphs 31–34 of FASB ASC 310-10-50?

    [FASB ASC 310-10-50 par. 31–34]

24. If the NFP as creditor, has foreclosed and repossessed assets or loans in the process of foreclosure, has the NFP disclosed the information described in paragraph 11 or 35 of FASB ASC 310-10-50, as applicable?

    [FASB ASC 310-10-50 pars. 11 and 35]

Note

Questions 25–28 (FASB ASC 310-30) apply to receivables and debt securities with a term in excess of one year that are acquired by an NFP by a transfer (that is, the NFP was not the original creditor if the receivable is an account, note, or loan receivable, nor was it the original donee if the receivable is a contribution receivable). Loans that are measured at fair value are excluded from the scope of FASB ASC 310-30 if all changes in fair value are included in the statement of activities and included in the performance indicator if a performance indicator is presented.

25. For an account, note, loan, or contribution receivable that was acquired by transfer rather than by origination

    a. does the valuation allowance reflect only those losses incurred by the NFP *after* acquisition? (**Note:** In other words, it is not appropriate, at acquisition, to establish a loss allowance.)

        [FASB ASC 310-30-30-1]

    b. is the excess between the receivable's contractually required payments and the amount of its cash flows expected at acquisition (nonaccretable difference) NOT displayed in the statement of financial position and NOT recognized as an adjustment of yield, a loss accrual, or a valuation allowance for credit risk?

        [FASB ASC 310-30-45-1]

    c. is the excess of all cash flows expected at acquisition over the NFP's initial investment in the receivable (accretable yield) recognized as a discount to be accreted over the life of the receivable as interest income and NOT displayed in the statement of financial position?

        [FASB ASC 310-30-35-2; FASB ASC 310-30-45-1]

    d. if the receivable is not a debt security within the scope of FASB ASC 958-320, are changes in the estimated cash flows expected to be collected over the life of the receivable accounted for under FASB ASC 450, FASB ASC 310-10-35, or FASB ASC 310-40-35 (if a decrease) or as an adjustment of the valuation allowance and accretable yield (if an increase)?

        [FASB ASC 310-30-35-10]

26. Do the notes to financial statements describe how prepayments are considered in the determination of contractual cash flows and cash flows expected to be collected?

    [FASB ASC 310-30-50-1]

	Yes	No	N/A

27. Is information about loans acquired with deteriorated credit quality (that is, are within the scope of FASB ASC 310-30), included in the disclosures required by paragraphs 15(a)–15(b) of FASB ASC 310-10-50 if it is probable that the loan has been impaired at the balance sheet date?

    [FASB ASC 310-10-50-18]

28. In addition to disclosures required by other GAAP, for each balance sheet presented, does an investor disclose the following information about loans that were acquired with deteriorated credit quality; that is, loans within the scope of FASB ASC 310-30:

    a. Separately for both those loans that are accounted for as debt securities and those loans that are not accounted for as debt securities

        i. the outstanding balance and related carrying amount at the beginning and end of the period?

        ii. the amount of accretable yield at the beginning and end of the period, reconciled for additions, accretion, disposals of loans, and reclassifications to or from nonaccretable difference during the period?

        iii. for loans acquired during the period, the contractually required payments receivable, cash flows expected to be collected, and fair value at the acquisition date?

        iv. for those loans within the scope of FASB ASC 310-30-15 for which the income recognition model in FASB ASC 310-30 is not applied in accordance with FASB ASC 310-30-35-3, the carrying amount at the acquisition date for loans acquired during the period and the carrying amount of all loans at the end of the period?

    b. Further, for those loans that are not accounted for as debt securities, does an investor disclose

        i. the amount of (1) any expense recognized pursuant to FASB ASC 310-30-35-10(a) and (2) any reductions of the allowance recognized pursuant to FASB ASC 310-30-35-10(b)(1) for each period for which a statement of activities is presented?

        ii. the amount of the allowance for uncollectible accounts at the beginning and end of the period?

        [FASB ASC 310-30-50-2]

Note

Questions 29–41 (FASB ASC 326-20) apply to financial assets measured at amortized cost basis (that is, not reported at fair value), including the following:

- Financing receivables
- Receivables that result from transactions within the scope of FASB ASC 605 on revenue recognition
- Receivables that result from transactions within the scope of FASB ASC 606 on revenue from contracts with customers
- Receivables that result from revenue transactions within the scope of FASB ASC 610 on other income
- Receivables that relate to repurchase agreements and securities lending agreements within the scope of FASB ASC 860
- Net investments in leases recognized by a lessor in accordance FASB ASC 842 on leases
- Off-balance-sheet credit exposures not accounted for as insurance.

	Yes	No	N/A

29. For financial assets measured at amortized cost within the scope of FASB ASC 326-20, has the NFP separately presented on the statement of financial position, the allowance for credit losses as a deduction from the amortized cost basis?

   ["Pending Content" in FASB ASC 326-20-45-1]

30. Has the NFP made the following disclosures regarding its accounting policy elections for accrued interest receivable:

   a. If the accrued interest receivable balance is presented within another statement of financial position line item, the amount of accrued interest, net of the allowance for credit losses (if any), and the line item on the statement of financial position in which that amount is presented?

   b. If the accrued interest receivable balance that is included in the amortized cost basis of financing receivables and held-to-maturity securities is excluded for the purposes of the disclosure requirements in FASB ASC 326-20-50-4 through 50-22, the total amount of accrued interest excluded from the disclosed amortized cost basis?

   c. If the NFP elects not to measure an allowance for credit losses for accrued interest receivables because it writes off the uncollectible accrued interest receivable balance in a timely manner, information about what time period(s), at the class of financing receivable or major security-type level, are considered timely?

   d. The accounting policy for writing off accrued interest receivables (for example, by reversing interest income or recognizing credit loss expense or a combination of both) and the amount of accrued interest receivables written off by reversing interest income by portfolio segment or major security type.

      ["Pending Content" in paragraphs 3A–3D of FASB ASC 326-20-50]

31. For financing receivables and net investments in leases (including unguaranteed residual assets) within the scope of FASB ASC 326-20, does the NFP provide quantitative and qualitative information by class of financing receivable about the credit quality, including all of the following: *Note:* These requirements do not apply to receivables measured at the lower of amortized cost basis or fair value, or to trade receivables due in one year or less.

   a. A description of the credit quality indicator(s)?

   b. The amortized cost basis, by credit quality indicator?

   c. For each credit quality indicator, the date or range of dates in which the information was last updated for that credit quality indicator?

      ["Pending Content" in FASB ASC 326-20-50-5; "Pending Content" in FASB ASC 326-20-50-9]

32. Does the NFP disclose all of the following about the allowance for credit losses by portfolio segment and major security type:

   a. A description of how expected loss estimates are developed?

	Yes	No	N/A

b. A description of the accounting policies and methodology to estimate the allowance for credit losses, as well as a discussion of the factors that influenced management's current estimate of expected credit losses, including past events, current conditions, and reasonable and supportable forecasts about the future? _____ _____ _____

c. A discussion of risk characteristics relevant to each portfolio segment? _____ _____ _____

d. A discussion of the changes in the factors that influenced management's current estimate of expected credit losses and the reasons for those changes? _____ _____ _____

e. Identification of changes to the NFP's accounting policies for the allowance for credit loss, changes to the methodology from the prior period, its rationale for those changes, and the quantitative effect of those changes? _____ _____ _____

f. Reasons for significant changes in the amount of writeoffs, if applicable? _____ _____ _____

g. A discussion of the reversion method applied for periods beyond the reasonable and supportable forecast period? _____ _____ _____

h. The amount of any significant purchases and sales of financial assets or reclassifications of loans held for sale during each reporting period? _____ _____ _____

["Pending Content" in FASB ASC 326-20-50-11]

33. If the NFP measures expected credit losses based on a discounted cash flow and reports the change in present value attributable to the passage of time as interest income, does it disclose the amount included in interest income that represents that change? _____ _____ _____

["Pending Content" in FASB ASC 326-20-50-12]

34. Does the NFP disclose the activity in the allowance for credit losses for each period, separately by portfolio segment, in a roll-forward that includes all of the following:

a. The beginning balance in the allowance for credit losses? _____ _____ _____

b. The current-period provision for expected credit losses? _____ _____ _____

c. Writeoffs charged against the allowance? _____ _____ _____

d. Recoveries collected? _____ _____ _____

e. The ending balance in the allowance for credit losses? _____ _____ _____

["Pending Content" in FASB ASC 326-20-50-13]

35. For financial assets that are past due as of the reporting date, does the NFP provide: *Note:* These disclosures do not apply to receivables measured at the lower of amortized cost basis or fair value or to trade receivables due in one year or less.

a. An explanation of when it considers a financial asset to be past due? _____ _____ _____

b. An aging analysis of the amortized cost basis, disaggregated by class of financing receivable? _____ _____ _____

["Pending Content" in FASB ASC 326-20-50-14; "Pending Content" in FASB ASC 326-20-50-15]

	Yes	No	N/A

36. For financial assets on nonaccrual status, does the NFP disclose all of the following, disaggregated by class of financing receivable: *Note:* These disclosures do not apply to receivables measured at the lower of amortized cost basis or fair value or to trade receivables due in one year or less.

   a. The amortized cost basis of financial assets on nonaccrual status as of the beginning of the reporting period? ____ ____ ____

   b. The amortized cost basis of financial assets on nonaccrual status as of the end of the reporting period? ____ ____ ____

   c. The amount of interest income recognized during the period on nonaccrual financial assets? ____ ____ ____

   d. The amortized cost basis of financial assets that are 90 days or more past due, but are not on nonaccrual status as of the reporting date? ____ ____ ____

   e. The amortized cost basis of financial assets on nonaccrual status for which there is no related allowance for credit losses as of the reporting date? ____ ____ ____

   ["Pending Content" in FASB ASC 326-20-50-16; "Pending Content" in FASB ASC 326-20-50-18]

37. Does the NFP include a summary of significant accounting policies for financial assets within the scope of FASB ASC 326-20, including all of the following: *Note:* These disclosures do not apply to receivables measured at the lower of amortized cost basis or fair value or to trade receivables due in one year or less.

   a. The policy for discontinuing accrual of interest? ____ ____ ____

   b. The policy for recording payments received on nonaccrual assets (such as the cost recovery method, cash basis method, or some combination of those methods)? ____ ____ ____

   c. The policy for resuming accrual of interest? ____ ____ ____

   d. The policy for determining past-due or delinquency status? ____ ____ ____

   e. The policy for recognizing writeoffs within the allowance for credit losses? ____ ____ ____

   ["Pending Content" in FASB ASC 326-20-50-17; "Pending Content" in FASB ASC 326-20-50-18]

38. For a financial asset for which the repayment (on the basis of an NFP's assessment as of the reporting date) is expected to be provided substantially through the operation or sale of the collateral and the borrower is experiencing financial difficulty, does the NFP describe, by class of financing receivable:

   a. The type of collateral? ____ ____ ____

   b. The extent to which collateral secures its collateral-dependent financial assets? ____ ____ ____

   c. Significant changes in the extent to which collateral secures its collateral-dependent financial assets, whether because of a general deterioration or some other reason? ____ ____ ____

   ["Pending Content" in FASB ASC 326-20-50-19]

© 2020, Association of International Certified Professional Accountants

	Yes	No	N/A

39. Are changes in the fair value of the collateral of a collateral-dependent financial asset reported as credit loss expense or a reversal of credit loss expense if the guidance in paragraphs 4–6 of FASB ASC326-20-35-4 is applied?

    ["Pending Content in FASB ASC 326-20-45-4]

40. For an NFP with off-balance-sheet credit exposures within the scope of FASB ASC 326 (including loan commitments, standby letters of credit, financial guarantees, and similar instruments), has the NFP presented the estimate of expected credit losses on the statement of financial position as a liability, separately from the allowance for credit losses related to the recognized financial instrument?

    ["Pending Content" in FASB ASC 326-20-45-2]

41. For an NFP with off-balance-sheet credit exposures, has the NFP disclosed

    a. a description of the accounting policies and methodology the entity used to estimate its liability for off-balance-sheet credit exposures and related charges for those credit exposures, including the factors that influenced management's judgment (for example, historical losses, existing economic conditions, and reasonable and supportable forecasts)?

    b. a discussion of risk elements relevant to particular categories of financial instruments?

       ["Pending Content" in FASB ASC 326-20-50-21]

42. Have the necessary disclosures about financial instruments been made for receivables, including unconditional promises to give cash? (Refer to section II.E.)

G. Beneficial Interests in Assets Held by Others

1. If the NFP is named by a donor as a beneficiary of a perpetual trust held by a third party

    a. is that beneficial interest measured at the fair value?

    b. is the contribution classified as donor-restricted support?

    c. are the annual distributions from the trust reported as investment income?

    d. is the amount of the beneficial interest remeasured annually and the adjustment reported as a gain or loss in net assets with donor restrictions?

       [FASB ASC 958-605-30-14; AAG 6.63–.64]

2. If the fair value of a beneficial interest in a perpetual trust is measured using the fair value of the trust assets, does the NFP disclose

    a. the terms of the trust and the practice of the trustee pertaining to distributions?

    b. that the NFP has used the fair value of the trust assets to determine the fair value of the beneficial interest?

       [FinREC recommendation in AAG 6.52]

© 2020, Association of International Certified Professional Accountants

	Yes	No	N/A

3. If the NFP transferred assets to another entity and specified itself or its affiliate as the beneficiary, has it

   a.   reported the transfer as an equity transaction if the criteria in FASB ASC 958-20-25-4 are met? _____ _____ _____

   b.   reported the transfer as an exchange of an asset for another asset if the criteria in FASB ASC 958-20-25-4 are not met? _____ _____ _____

   [FASB ASC 958-20-25 par. 5–6; FASB ASC 958-605-25-33]

4. If the NFP transferred assets to another entity and specified itself or its affiliate as the beneficiary, has it disclosed the following for each period in which a statement of financial position is presented:

   a.   The identity of the recipient entity to which the transfer was made? _____ _____ _____

   b.   Whether variance power was granted to the recipient entity and, if so, a description of the terms of the variance power? _____ _____ _____

   c.   The terms under which amounts will be distributed to the NFP or its affiliate? _____ _____ _____

   d.   The aggregate amount recognized in the statement of financial position for those transfers and whether that amount is recorded as an interest in the net assets of the recipient entity or as another asset (such as a beneficial interest in assets held by others or as a refundable advance)? _____ _____ _____

   [FASB ASC 958-605-50-6]

5. If the NFP is the beneficiary of transfers to a recipient entity and the NFP and that recipient entity are financially interrelated, has the NFP recognized the change in its interest in the net assets of the recipient NFP and classified that change

   a.   as if the contributions were received directly from the donor, because the NFP (beneficiary) can influence the operating and financial decisions of the recipient entity to such an extent that the NFP (beneficiary) can determine the timing and amount of distributions to it from the recipient entity? _____ _____ _____

   [FASB ASC 958-20-35-1; Q&A 6140.14 and .16–.17]

   b.   as changes in net assets with donor restrictions, because the NFP (beneficiary) cannot influence the operating and financial decisions of recipient entity to such an extent that the NFP (beneficiary) can determine the timing and amount of distributions to it from the recipient entity? _____ _____ _____

   [FASB ASC 958-20-35-1; Q&A 6140.15]

6. If the NFP is unable to obtain sufficient information to make a reasonable estimate of the fair value of a beneficial interest in a trust, has the NFP disclosed

   a.   The characteristics of the agreement, to the extent known? _____ _____ _____

   b.   The factor(s) that are limiting the ability to measure the beneficial interest(s)? _____ _____ _____

   c.   The amount received from the beneficial interest(s) in each of the periods for which a statement of activities is presented? _____ _____ _____

	Yes	No	N/A

d. The information in items *a–c* individually or each potentially material beneficial interest and in the aggregate for individually immaterial beneficial interests that are material collectively?

[FinREC recommendation in AAG 6.53]

H. Inventories

1. Are the major classes of inventory disclosed (for example, finished goods, work in process, raw materials)?

[Common Practice]

2. Is the method of determining inventory cost (for example, last in, first out and first in, first out) disclosed?

[FASB ASC 210-10-50-1]

3. Is the basis for stating inventory disclosed and, if necessary, the nature of a change in basis for stating inventory and the effect on change in net assets of such a change?

[FASB ASC 330-10-50-1]

4. If goods are stated above cost or at sales prices, has that fact been disclosed?

[FASB ASC 330-10-50-3; FASB ASC 330-10-50-4]

5. Are valuation allowances for inventory losses shown as a deduction from the related inventory?

[FASB ASC 210-10-45-13]

6. Are contributions of inventory reported in the period received at fair value?

[FASB ASC 958-605-25-2; FASB ASC 958-605-30-2; AAG 7.03]

7. Are substantial and unusual losses that result from the subsequent measurement of inventory disclosed in the financial statements?

[FASB ASC 330-10-50-2]

I. Property and Equipment

1. Are the following disclosed:

   a. Capitalization policy?

   b. Balances of major classes of depreciable assets by nature or function at the statement-of-financial-position date?

   c. Amounts recorded under capital leases, if applicable, are separately disclosed?

   d. Depreciation expense for each period?

   e. Accumulated depreciation, either by major classes of assets or in total?

   f. The method(s) used in computing depreciation with respect to major classes of depreciable assets?

   [FASB ASC 360-10-50-1; FASB ASC 840-30-50-1; FASB ASC 958-360-50-1]

2. Is the amount of capitalized interest disclosed?

[FASB ASC 835-20-50-1]

© 2020, Association of International Certified Professional Accountants

	Yes	No	N/A

3. Is donated property or equipment (including unconditional promises to give property and equipment) recognized at the date of the contribution at its fair value?

[FASB ASC 958-605-25-2; FASB ASC 958-605-30-2; AAG 9.04]

4. If tangible property is accepted solely to be saved for its potential future use in scientific or educational research and has no alternative use, and has an uncertain value (or no value) is the contributed property not recognized in the financial statements?

[FASB ASC 958-605-25-5]

5. Are material commitments for property expenditures disclosed?

[FASB ASC 440-10-50-1]

6. Is the basis of valuation of property and equipment disclosed (for example, cost for purchased items, fair value for contributed items)?

[FASB ASC 958-360-50-1]

7. Is separate disclosure of nondepreciable assets made?

[FASB ASC 958-360-50-2]

8. Is separate disclosure made of property and equipment not held for use in operations (for example, items held for sale, items held for investment purposes, and items held for construction in process)?

[FASB ASC 958-360-50-2]

9. Is separate disclosure made of assets restricted by donors for investment in property and equipment?

[FASB ASC 958-210-50-2]

10. If the NFP uses property and equipment to which another entity retains legal title during the term of the arrangement (other than a lease agreement), are the terms of the arrangement disclosed?

[FASB ASC 958-360-50-4]

11. If the NFP uses property and equipment in an exchange transaction (other than a lease transaction) and another entity retains legal title during the term of the arrangement, is the property or equipment reported as a contribution at fair value at the date received only if it is probable that the NFP will be permitted to keep the assets when the arrangement terminates?

[FASB ASC 958-605-55-25]

12. Are disclosures made concerning the liquidity of the NFP's property and equipment, including information about limitations on their use

    a. is information provided about property and equipment pledged as collateral or otherwise subject to lien?

    b. is information provided about property and equipment acquired with restricted assets where title may revert to another party, such as a resource provider?

    c. is information provided about donor or legal limitations on the use of or proceeds from the disposal of property and equipment?

[FASB ASC 958-360-50-4]

© 2020, Association of International Certified Professional Accountants

	Yes	No	N/A

13. If an impairment loss is recognized for a long-lived asset (asset group) to be held and used, are the following disclosures made in financial statements that include the period of the impairment write-down:

 a. A description of the impaired long-lived asset (asset group) and the facts and circumstances leading to the impairment?   ____ ____ ____

 b. The method or methods for determining fair value?   ____ ____ ____

 c. The amount of the impairment loss and the caption in the statement of activities in which the impairment loss is aggregated if that loss has not been presented as a separate caption or reported parenthetically on the face of the statement?   ____ ____ ____

 [FASB ASC 360-10-50-2]

14. If an impairment loss is recognized for a long-lived asset (asset group) to be held and used, is it reported as a component of changes in net assets before the effects of discontinued operations or accounting changes in the statement of activities and is it reported within the measure of operations, if that measure is presented?   ____ ____ ____

 [FASB ASC 360-10-45-4; FASB ASC 958-220-45-11]

15. If an NFP reports a measure of operations within its statement of activities, is the impairment loss referred to in question 14 recognized within that measure of operations?   ____ ____ ____

 [FASB ASC 360-10-45-4]

Note

Questions 16–20 apply only to long-lived asset disposals or classifications as held for sale that are not strategic shifts. NFPs with disposals representing a strategic shift in operations should complete section II.T, "Discontinued Operations."

16. If a long-lived asset (disposal group) is classified as held for sale, does the NFP

 a. measure the asset (group) at the lower of its carrying amount or fair value less cost to sell?   ____ ____ ____

 b. present separately the asset (or assets and liabilities of the disposal group, which may not be offset) in the statement of financial position?   ____ ____ ____

 c. separately disclose the major classes of assets and liabilities on the face of the statement of financial position or in the notes?   ____ ____ ____

 [FASB ASC 360-10-35-43; FASB ASC 360-10-45-14; FASB ASC 360-10-45-14; FASB ASC 205-20-45-10]

17. If a long-lived asset (disposal group) has either been sold or been classified as held for sale, are all of the following disclosed in the financial statements that include the period in which that sale or classification occurs:

 a. The carrying amount(s) of the major classes of assets and liabilities included as part of a disposal group, either separately presented on the face of the statement of financial position or in the notes?   ____ ____ ____

	Yes	No	N/A

b.   A description of the facts and circumstances leading to the expected disposal?

c.   The expected manner and timing of that disposal?

d.   The gain or loss recognized in accordance with paragraphs 37–45 of FASB ASC 360-10-35 and FASB ASC 360-10-40-5, and, if not separately presented, the caption on the face of the statement of activities that includes that gain or loss?

e.   If applicable, amounts of revenue and pretax net revenue or net expense (profit or loss) reported in discontinued operations?

     [FASB ASC 205-20-50-1; FASB ASC 360-10-50-3]

18.   If a long-lived asset (disposal group) is not a discontinued operation, do the statements of activities for the current period and any prior periods presented report any resulting gain or loss within the statement of activities

a.   as a component of change in net assets before the effects of discontinued operations or accounting changes?

b.   within the measure of operations, if that measure is presented?

     [FASB ASC 360-10-45-5; "Pending Content" in FASB ASC 360-10-45-5; FASB ASC 958-220-45-11]

19.   If the NFP decided not to sell a long-lived asset (disposal group) previously classified as held for sale, are all of the following included in the financial statements that included the period in which that decision occurs:

a.   Has the asset be reclassified to held and used?

b.   Is a description of the facts and circumstances leading to the decision to change the plan to sell provided?

c.   Is the effect of the decision on the change in net assets (and on the operating measure, if one is displayed) for the period and any prior periods presented disclosed?

     [FASB ASC 360-10-35-44; FASB ASC 360-10-45-8; FASB ASC 205-20-50-3]

20.   If a long-lived asset (disposal group) includes an individually significant component that either has been disposed of or is classified as held for sale and does not qualify for presentation and disclosure as a discontinued operation, is the following information about that individually significant component disclosed:

a.   The pretax change in net assets of the individually significant component for the period in which it is disposed of or is classified as held for sale, calculated in accordance with paragraphs 6–9 of FASB ASC 205-20-45?

b.   If the individually significant component includes a noncontrolling interest, the pretax change in net assets attributable to the parent for the period in which the component is disposed of or is classified as held for sale?

© 2020, Association of International Certified Professional Accountants

	Yes	No	N/A

c.   If the NFP has issued, or is a conduit bond obligor for, securities that are traded, listed, or quoted on an exchange or an over-the-counter market, is the information in items *a–b* presented for all prior periods presented?

   [FASB ASC 360-10-50-3A]

J.   Collections of Works of Art and Similar Items

Note

FASB ASU No. 2019-03, *Not-for-Profit Entities (Topic 958): Updating the Definition of Collections*, is effective for annual periods beginning after December 15, 2019, and to interim periods within annual periods beginning after December 15, 2020. Earlier application is permitted for financial statements not yet issued or made available for issuance.

NFPs that have adopted ASU No. 2019-03 should complete question 11. Other NFPs should mark that question "N/A."

1.   Does the NFP disclose its policy for capitalization of works of art, historical treasures, and similar items that meet the definition of *collections* in FASB ASC 958-360-20?

   [FASB ASC 958-360-50-1]

2.   Does the NFP recognize contributed collection items as revenues only if collections are capitalized and not recognize collection items if collections are not capitalized?

   [FASB ASC 958-605-25-19]

3.   Are works of art, historical treasures, and similar items capitalized if they are not added to a collection (either because the NFP chooses not to add the item to the collection or because the NFP does not maintain collections as defined in FASB ASC 958-360-20), and is the amount that is capitalized disclosed separately on the face of the statement of financial position or in the notes?

   [FASB ASC 958-360-45-3; FASB ASC 958-605-25-18]

4.   If the NFP adopts a policy of capitalizing collections that meet the definition in FASB ASC 958-360-20, does the statement of financial position include the total amount capitalized on a separate line item, entitled "Collections" or "Collection Items"?

   [FASB ASC 958-360-45-3]

5.   If the NFP capitalizes collections prospectively, are proceeds from sales and insurance recoveries of items not previously capitalized reported separately from revenues, expenses, gains, and losses?

   [FASB ASC 958-360-45-5]

6.   If the NFP does not capitalize collections or it capitalizes prospectively, are the following items disclosed:

a.   Description of collections including their relative significance?

b.   Accounting and stewardship policies for collections?

   [FASB ASC 958-360-50-6]

	Yes	No	N/A

7. If the NFP does not capitalize collections or it capitalizes collections prospectively, does a line item on the face of the statement of financial position (for example, "Collections (Note X)") refer to the disclosures required in question 6 and, if the NFP's policy is to capitalize prospectively, is that line item dated (for example, "Collections acquired since January 1, 19X1 (Note X)")?

    [FASB ASC 958-360-45-3]

8. If the NFP maintains collections that are not capitalized, are the following items reported separately on the statement of activities, separately from revenues, expenses, gains, and losses:

    a. Costs of collection items purchased as a decrease in the appropriate class of net assets?

    b. Proceeds from the sale of collection items as an increase in the appropriate class of net assets?

    c. Proceeds from insurance recoveries of lost or destroyed collection items as an increase in the appropriate class of net assets?

    [FASB ASC 958-360-45-5]

9. If collection items that are not capitalized are disposed of during the period, does the NFP also

    a. describe the items given away, damaged, destroyed, lost, or otherwise deaccessed during the period or disclose their fair value?

    b. reference the disclosures in the preceding question 9a on the "Collections" line item on the face of the statement of financial position?

    c. not include amounts on the face of the statement of activities as expenses or other decreases in net assets for the items given away or otherwise deaccessed?

    [FASB ASC 958-360-50-6; FASB ASC 958-360-45-3; FASB 958-360-40-3]

10. Are contributions *made by* the NFP of previously recognized collection items reported at fair value as expenses and decreases in assets in the period in which the contributions are made?

    [FASB ASC 958-360-40-2]

11. Does the NFP disclose the following information about its organizational policy for the use of proceeds from deaccessioned collection items:

    a. Whether those proceeds can be used for acquisitions of new collection items, the direct care of existing collections, or both?

    b. The NFP's definition of direct care if the NFP allows proceeds from deaccessioned collection items to be used for direct care?

    ["Pending Content" in FASB ASC 958-360-50-7]

            © 2020, Association of International Certified Professional Accountants

	Yes	No	N/A

K. Goodwill and Other Intangible Assets

Goodwill

1. Is the aggregate amount of goodwill presented as a separate line item in the statement of financial position?

    [FASB ASC 350-20-45-1; FASB ASC 350-20-45-5]

2. Is the aggregate amount of goodwill impairment losses presented as a separate line item in the statement of activities unless a goodwill impairment loss is associated with a discontinued operation?

    [FASB ASC 350-20-45-2; FASB ASC 350-20-45-6]

3. Is a goodwill impairment loss associated with a discontinued operation included (on a net-of-tax basis) within the results of discontinued operations?

    [FASB ASC 350-20-45-3, FASB ASC 350-20-45-7]

4. Has the NFP disclosed any changes in the carrying amount of goodwill during the period, including the following:

    a. The gross amount and accumulated impairment losses at the beginning of the period?

    b. Additional goodwill recognized during the period, except goodwill included in a disposal group that, on acquisition, meets the criteria to be classified as held for sale in accordance with FASB ASC 360-10-45-9?

    c. Adjustments resulting from the subsequent recognition of deferred tax assets during the period in accordance with paragraphs 2–4 of FASB ASC 805-740-25 and 805-740-45-2?

    d. Goodwill included in a disposal group classified as held for sale in accordance with FASB ASC 360-10-45-9 and goodwill derecognized during the period without having previously been reported in a disposal group classified as held for sale?

    e. Impairment losses recognized during the period in accordance with FASB ASC 350-10?

    f. Net exchange differences arising during the period in accordance with FASB ASC 830?

    g. Any other changes in the carrying amounts during the period?

    h. The gross amount and accumulated impairment losses at the end of the period?

        [FASB ASC 350-20-50-1]

	Yes	No	N/A

Note

FASB ASU No. 2017-04, *Intangibles—Goodwill and Other (Topic 350): Simplifying the Test for Goodwill Impairment*, is effective for annual or any interim goodwill impairment tests in fiscal years beginning after December 15, 2021. Early adoption is permitted for interim or annual goodwill impairment tests performed on testing dates after January 1, 2017.

The amendments in this ASU modify the concept of impairment from the condition that exists when the carrying amount of goodwill exceeds its implied fair value to the condition that exists when the carrying amount of a reporting unit exceeds its fair value. An entity no longer will determine goodwill impairment by calculating the implied fair value of goodwill by assigning the fair value of a reporting unit to all of its assets and liabilities as if that reporting unit had been acquired in a business combination. The amendments eliminate Step 2 from the goodwill impairment test.

FASB ASU No. 2019-06, *Intangibles—Goodwill and Other (Topic 350), Business Combinations (Topic 805), and Not-for-Profit Entities (Topic 958): Extending the Private Company Accounting Alternatives on Goodwill and Certain Identifiable Intangible Assets to Not-for-Profit Entities*, is effective upon issuance.

The amendments in this ASU allow certain identifiable intangible assets to be subsumed into goodwill and amortized at the time of an acquisition by an NFP, provided that the NFP also elects to amortize goodwill on a straight-line basis over 10 years (or less if a shorter period is more appropriate). This is referred to as the accounting alternative for subsequent measurement of goodwill.

NFPs that have elected the accounting alternative should complete question 6. Other NFPs should mark question 6 "N/A."

NFPs that have adopted the requirements of ASU No. 2017-04 or ASU No. 2019-06 should mark question 5c "N/A."

5. For each goodwill impairment loss recognized, has the NFP disclosed the following information in the notes to the financial statements that include the period in which the impairment loss is recognized:

    a. A description of the facts and circumstances leading to the impairment?

    b. The amount of the impairment loss and the method of determining the fair value of the associated reporting unit (whether based on quoted market prices, prices of comparable businesses or nonprofit activities, a present value or other valuation technique, or a combination thereof)?

    c. If a recognized impairment loss is an estimate that has not yet been finalized (refer to paragraphs 18–19 of FASB ASC 350-20-35), that fact and the reasons therefore and, in subsequent periods, the nature and amount of any significant adjustments made to the initial estimate of the impairment loss?

    [FASB ASC 350-20-50-2, FASB ASC 350-20-50-6]

6. If the NFP has elected the accounting alternative for subsequent measurement of goodwill in FASB ASC 350-20, does the NFP disclose

    a. For additions to goodwill, both (1) the amount assigned to goodwill in total and by major acquisition by a not-for-profit entity, or by reorganization event resulting in fresh-start reporting, and (2) the weighted-average amortization period in total and the amortization period by major acquisition by a not-for-profit entity, or by reorganization event resulting in fresh-start reporting?

	Yes	No	N/A

> b. The gross carrying amounts of goodwill, accumulated amortization, and accumulated impairment loss for each period for which a statement of financial position is presented?

> c. The aggregate amortization expense for each period presented?

> d. Goodwill included in a disposal group classified as held for sale in accordance with FASB ASC 360-10-45-9?

> e. Goodwill derecognized during the period without having previously been reported in a disposal group classified as held for sale?

> f. For each impairment loss recognized, the caption in the statement of activities in which the impairment loss is included?

> g. For each impairment loss recognized, the method of allocating the impairment loss to the individual amortizable units of goodwill?

> [Paragraphs 4–6 of FASB ASC 350-20-50]

Other Intangible Assets

7. At a minimum, are all intangible assets aggregated and presented as a separate line item in the statement of financial position? (This requirement does not preclude presentation of individual intangible assets or classes of intangible assets as separate line items.)

 [FASB ASC 350-30-45-1]

8. Are amortization expense and impairment losses for intangible assets presented in line items on the statement of activities?

 [FASB ASC 350-30-45-2]

9. For each period for which a statement of financial position is presented, does the NFP include the following information about intangible assets:

> a. The gross carrying amount, in total and by major intangible asset class, separately for intangible assets that are being amortized and those that are not?

> b. The accumulated amortization, in total and by major intangible asset class for intangible assets that are being amortized?

> c. The aggregate amortization expense for the period?

> d. The estimated amortization expense for each of the five succeeding periods?

> [FASB ASC 350-30-50-2]

10. If during the reporting period the NFP has acquired intangible assets that will be amortized, do the notes to the financial statements include

> a. the total amount of intangible assets acquired?

> b. the amount acquired in any major intangible asset class?

> c. the amount of any significant residual value, in total, for intangible assets acquired?

	Yes	No	N/A

    d. the amount of any significant residual value, by major class, for intangible assets acquired? ___ ___ ___

    e. the weighted-average amortization period, in total, for intangible assets acquired? ___ ___ ___

    f. the weighted-average amortization period, by major class, for intangible assets acquired? ___ ___ ___

    [FASB ASC 350-30-50-1]

11. If during the reporting period the NFP has acquired intangible assets and those intangible assets will not be amortized, do the notes to the financial statements include

    a. the total amount of intangible assets acquired? ___ ___ ___

    b. the amount acquired in any major intangible asset class? ___ ___ ___

    [FASB ASC 350-30-50-1]

12. If during the reporting period the NFP acquired research and development assets in a transaction other than an acquisition by an NFP, and wrote off those assets, do the notes to the financial statements indicate the amount written off and the line item in the statement of activities in which the amounts written off are aggregated? ___ ___ ___

    [FASB ASC 350-30-50-1]

13. If rights under intangible assets are subject to renewal or extension, does the NFP disclose

    a. its accounting policy on the treatment of costs incurred to renew or extend the term of a recognized intangible asset? ___ ___ ___

    b. information that enables users of financial statements to assess the extent to which the expected future cash flows associated with the recognized intangible assets are affected by the intent or ability to renew or extend the arrangement? ___ ___ ___

    c. in the period of acquisition or renewal, the weighted-average period prior to the next renewal or extension (both explicit and implicit), by major intangible asset class? ___ ___ ___

    d. the total amount of costs incurred in the period to renew or extend the term of a recognized intangible asset by major intangible asset class, for each period for which a statement of financial position is presented? ___ ___ ___

    [FASB ASC 350-30-50 par. 1–2 and 4]

14. If it is at least reasonably possible that either (*a*) the useful life or (*b*) the expected likelihood of renewal or extension of an intangible asset will change in the near future and the effect of the change would be material either individually or in aggregate by major intangible asset class, is the information about an estimate required by FASB ASC 275-10-50-8 (see section I.J., "Risks and Uncertainties")? ___ ___ ___

[FASB ASC 275-10-50-15A]

© 2020, Association of International Certified Professional Accountants

	Yes	No	N/A

15. For each impairment loss recognized related to an intangible asset, is the following information disclosed in the notes to the financial statements for the period in which the impairment loss is recognized:

    a.   A description of the impaired intangible asset and the facts and circumstances leading to the impairment? _____ _____ _____

    b.   The amount of the impairment loss and the method for determining fair value? _____ _____ _____

    c.   The caption in the statement of activities in which the impairment loss is aggregated? _____ _____ _____

    [FASB ASC 350-30-50-3]

L.   Other Assets and Deferred Charges

1. If the NFP has defined benefit pension plans for which the fair value of plan assets exceeds the projected benefit obligation

    a.   is the aggregate amount of all overfunded projected benefit obligations reported as an asset, separately from the asset for overfunded defined benefit postretirement plans other than pensions (if any)? _____ _____ _____

    b.   is the asset classified as a noncurrent asset if the NFP presents a classified statement of financial position? _____ _____ _____

    [FASB ASC 715-30-25-1; FASB ASC 715-20-45-3]

2. If the NFP has defined benefit postretirement plans other than pensions for which the fair value of plan assets exceeds the accumulated postretirement benefit obligation

    a.   is the aggregate amount of all overfunded plans reported as an asset, separately from the asset for overfunded defined benefit pension plans (if any)? _____ _____ _____

    b.   is the asset classified as a noncurrent asset if the NFP presents a classified statement of financial position? _____ _____ _____

    [FASB ASC 715-60-25-1; FASB ASC 715-20-45-3]

3. Are donated materials and supplies recognized when received at their fair values? _____ _____ _____

    [FASB ASC 958-605-25-2; FASB ASC 958-605-30-2; FASB ASC 958-605-55-26]

4. If the NFP holds insurance policies to fund the cost of providing employee benefits or protect against the loss of key persons, does it disclose any contractual restrictions on the ability to surrender a policy? _____ _____ _____

    [FASB ASC 325-30-50-1]

Note

FASB ASC 325-30 provides guidance for investments in life insurance contracts. It has two subsections; one for situations in which an entity purchases insurance and is either the owner or the beneficiary of the contract, and the other for life settlement contracts (contracts purchased by investors from the policy owner at an amount in excess of cash surrender value). Although not specifically applicable to NFPs if life insurance contracts are acquired by gift, NFPs may choose to analogize to this guidance if they hold life insurance policies as investments rather than as protection against loss. (For example, life insurance contracts on key personnel protect against loss.)

	Yes	No	N/A

5. Are investments in life insurance reported using one of the following measurements:

    a. Amounts that can be realized as of the statement-of-financial-position date?

    [FASB ASC 325-30-35-1]

    b. Transaction price plus policy premiums and all direct external costs, which is then tested for impairment? (**Note:** Transaction price is fair value at date of gift if policy is gifted.)

    [FASB ASC 325-30-30-1C; FASB ASC 325-30-35-8]

    c. Fair value?

    [FASB ASC 325-30-35-12]

6. If the NFP chooses to report using measurement *b* or *c* in the preceding question 5, do the financial statements include the disclosures required by paragraphs 2–10 of FASB ASC 325-30-50?

    [FASB ASC 325-30-50 par. 2–10]

7. Does the NFP disclose any contractual restrictions on the ability to surrender its policies?

    [FASB ASC 325-30-50-1]

M. Current Liabilities

1. For classified statements of financial position, do current liabilities include

    a. payables incurred in the acquisition of materials and supplies?

    b. collections received in advance of the delivery of goods or performance of services?

    c. debts that arise from operations directly related to the operating cycle, such as accruals for wages, salaries, commissions, rentals, royalties, and income and other taxes?

    d. other liabilities whose regular and ordinary liquidation is expected to occur within a relatively short time period?

    [FASB ASC 210-10-45 par. 8–9]

    e. obligations that, by their terms, are due on demand or will be due within one year (or operating cycle, if longer) from the balance-sheet date, even though liquidation may not be expected within that period?

    [FASB ASC 470-10-45-10]

    f. long term obligations that are or will be callable by the creditor because of the NFP's default at the date of the statement of financial position?

    [FASB ASC 470-10-45-11]

    g. serial maturities of long term debt and amounts required to be expended within one year under sinking fund provisions?

    [FASB ASC 210-10-45-9]

© 2020, Association of International Certified Professional Accountants

	Yes	No	N/A

2. In classified statements of financial position, do current liabilities exclude short term obligations that the NFP intends to refinance on a long term basis, provided the NFP demonstrates the ability to consummate the long term financing?

[FASB ASC 470-10-45-14]

3. In classified statements of financial position, is the current liability for defined benefit postretirement plans, including pensions, determined on a plan-by-plan basis as the amount by which the actuarial present value of benefits included in the benefit obligation payable in the next 12 months (or operating cycle if longer) exceeds the fair value of plan assets?

[FASB ASC 715-20-45-3]

N.　Notes Payable and Other Debt, Including Interfund Borrowings

1. Is there adequate disclosure of interest rates, maturities, and other terms and conditions, such as assets pledged as collateral, of loan agreements, bond indentures, and any special borrowing agreements?

[FASB ASC 440-10-50-1; FASB ASC 958-210-45-7; FASB ASC 958-210-50-2; Common Practice]

2. Are the combined aggregate amount of maturities and sinking fund requirements for all long-term borrowings disclosed for each of the five years following the date of the latest balance sheet presented?

[FASB ASC 470-10-50-1]

3. Has the NFP reclassified any assets pledged as collateral and reported them in its statement of financial position separately from other assets not so encumbered (for example, as security pledged to creditors) if the secured party has the right by contract or custom to sell or repledge the collateral?

[FASB ASC 860-30-45-1]

4. As of the date of the latest statement of financial position presented, does the NFP disclose

　　a. the carrying amount and classifications of any assets pledged as collateral, if the collateral is not reclassified and separately reported in the statement of financial position in accordance with FASB ASC 860-30-45-1?

　　b. the carrying amount and classifications of the associated liabilities?

　　c. qualitative information about the relationship(s) between those assets and associated liabilities (for example, if assets are restricted solely to satisfy a specific obligation, a description of the nature of restrictions placed on those assets)?

[FASB ASC 860-30-50-1A]

5. Is the following information about interest costs disclosed:

　　a. For an accounting period in which no interest is capitalized, the amount of interest cost incurred and charged to expense for the period?

	Yes	No	N/A

b.   For an accounting period in which interest is capitalized, the amount of interest cost incurred and the amount thereof that has been capitalized?

[FASB ASC 835-20-50-1]

6.   For unconditional purchase obligations that have been recorded in accordance with the unconditional purchase obligation subsections of FASB ASC 440, *Commitments*, are the amount of payments due in the aggregate and for each of the five years following the date of the latest statement of financial position presented disclosed?

[FASB ASC 440-10-50-6]

7.   If a note is noninterest bearing or has an inappropriate stated interest rate

     a.   is the discount or premium presented as a deduction from or addition to the face amount of the note?

     b.   does the disclosure include the effective interest rate and face amount of the note?

     c.   is amortization of the discount or premium reported as interest in the statement of activity?

     d.   are issue costs reported in the statement of financial position as deferred charges?

[FASB ASC 835-30-45-2]

8.   If a short-term obligation (including a long-term obligation that is callable because of default) is to be classified as a long-term borrowing, do disclosures include

     a.   general description of the financing agreement?

     b.   terms of any new obligation incurred or expected to be incurred, as a result of the refinancing?

[FASB ASC 470-10-50-4]

9.   If the NFP finances its activities from the proceeds of tax-exempt bonds and other obligations issued through state and local financing authorities, is such financing reported as liabilities in the statement of financial position?

[FASB ASC 958-470-25-1]

10.   If debt was considered to be extinguished by in-substance defeasance under the provisions of FASB Statement No. 76, *Extinguishment of Debt—an amendment of APB Opinion No. 26*, prior to December 31, 1996, is a general description of the transaction and the amount of debt that is considered extinguished at the end of the period disclosed so long if the debt remains outstanding?

[FASB ASC 470-50-50-1]

11.   If a troubled debt restructuring occurred during a period for which financial statements are presented, have the following disclosures been made:

     a.   A description of the principal changes in terms, the major features of settlement, or both?

     b.   The aggregate gain on restructuring of payables and the tax effect, if any?

     c.   The aggregate gain or loss on assets transferred to a creditor to settle a debt?

[FASB ASC 470-60-50-1]

© 2020, Association of International Certified Professional Accountants

	Yes	No	N/A

12. For periods after a troubled debt restructuring, have the following disclosures been made:

    a. The extent to which amounts contingently payable are included in the liability for the restructured payables? _____ _____ _____

    b. Total amounts contingently payable and the conditions under which those amounts would become payable or be forgiven? (This disclosure is required if it is reasonably possible that a liability for contingent payments will be incurred.) _____ _____ _____

    [FASB ASC 470-60-50-2]

13. If the NFP measures certain long term debt instruments at fair value under the fair value option subsections of FASB ASC 825-10 or FASB ASC 815-15-25-4, did it disclose the difference between the aggregate fair value and the aggregate unpaid principal balance of long term debt instruments that have contractual principal amounts? _____ _____ _____

    [FASB ASC 825-10-50-28]

14. If the NFP measures long term debt at fair value on a recurring basis and the obligation was issued with an inseparable third-party credit enhancement (for example, debt that is issued with a contractual third-party guarantee), does the NFP disclose the existence of a third-party credit enhancement? _____ _____ _____

    [FASB ASC 820-10-35-18A; FASB ASC 820-10-50-4A]

15. Are interfund receivables and payables clearly identified and arranged in the statement of financial position to eliminate their amounts when displaying total assets or liabilities? _____ _____ _____

    [FASB ASC 958-210-45-2]

16. Have the necessary disclosures about financial instruments been made? (Refer to section II.E.) _____ _____ _____

17. Are debt issuance costs related to a note reported in the statement of financial position as a direct deduction from the face amount of that note and is amortization of the debt issuance costs reported as interest expense? _____ _____ _____

    [FASB ASC 835-30-45 par. 1A and 3]

18. As of each date for which a statement of activities is presented, has the NFP disclosed the following information about liabilities that are measured at fair value under the "Fair Value Option" subsections of FASB ASC 825-10 or FASB ASC 815-15-25-4:

    a. The amount of change, during the period and cumulatively, of the fair value of the liability that is attributable to changes in the instrument-specific credit risk? _____ _____ _____

    b. How the gains and losses attributable to changes in instrument-specific credit risk were determined? _____ _____ _____

    ["Pending Content" in FASB ASC 825-10-50-30, "Pending Content" in FASB ASC 825-10-45-5]

© 2020, Association of International Certified Professional Accountants

	Yes	No	N/A

O.   Leases as Lessee

Note

FASB ASU No. 2016-02, *Leases (Topic 842)*, issued in February 2016, requires the recognition of lease assets and lease liabilities on the statement of financial position and the disclosure of key information about leasing arrangements.

For an NFP that has issued, or is a conduit bond obligor for, securities that are traded, listed, or quoted on an exchange or an over-the-counter market, ASU No. 2016-02 was effective for fiscal years beginning after December 15, 2018, including interim periods within those fiscal years. For all other NFPs, ASU No. 2016-02, as amended by FASB ASU No. 2019-10 is effective for fiscal years beginning after December 15, 2020, and interim periods within fiscal years beginning after December 15, 2021. Earlier application is permitted.

NFPs that have adopted ASU No. 2016-02 should complete questions 11–26; other NFPs complete questions 1–10.

---

1.   For capital leases, do disclosures include

    a.   gross amounts of assets recorded by major classes as of the date of each statement of financial position presented?

        [FASB ASC 840-30-50-1]

    b.   future minimum lease payments as of the date of the latest statement of financial position presented, in the aggregate and for each of the five succeeding fiscal years, with separate deductions therefrom for executory costs and imputed interest to reduce net minimum lease payments to present value?

        [FASB ASC 840-30-50-1]

    c.   total of future minimum sublease rentals under noncancelable subleases as of the date of the latest statement of financial position presented?

        [FASB ASC 840-30-50-1]

    d.   total contingent rentals actually incurred for each period for which a statement of activity is presented?

        [FASB ASC 840-30-50-1]

    e.   separate identification of

        i.   assets recorded under capital leases?

        ii.   accumulated amortization of capital leases?

        iii.   obligations under capital leases?

        iv.   amount of amortization of capital lease assets or the fact that the amortization of capital lease assets is included in depreciation expense?

        [FASB ASC 840-30-45 par. 1–3]

2.   For operating leases that have initial or remaining noncancelable lease terms in excess of one year, do disclosures include

    a.   future minimum rental payments required as of the date of the latest statement of financial position presented in the aggregate and for each of the five succeeding fiscal years?

    b.   total of future minimum rentals to be received under noncancelable subleases as of the date of the latest statement of financial position presented?

        [FASB ASC 840-20-50-2]

          © 2020, Association of International Certified Professional Accountants

	Yes	No	N/A

3. For all operating leases, do disclosures include rental expense for each period for which a statement of activities (or revenue and expenses) is presented, with separate amounts for minimum rentals, contingent rentals, and sublease rentals?

   [FASB ASC 840-20-50-1]

4. For operating leases, are contingent rentals recognized prior to the achievement of the specified target that triggers the contingent rental expense if the achievement of that target is considered probable?

   [FASB ASC 840-10-25-35]

5. Do disclosures include a general description of the lessee's leasing arrangements, including but not limited to

   a. bases for determining contingent rentals?

   b. existence and terms of any renewal or purchase options or escalation clauses?

   c. restrictions imposed by lease agreements (for example, those concerning dividends, additional debt, and further leasing?)

   [FASB ASC 840-10-50-2]

6. Is the nature and extent of leasing transactions with related parties disclosed?

   [FASB ASC 840-10-50-1]

7. If material, is the accounting policy used in recognizing amounts related to a modification of an operating lease (that does not change the lease classification) disclosed?

   [FASB ASC 840-20-55-6]

8. Is separate disclosure made of improvements to leased facilities and equipment?

   [FASB ASC 958-360-50-2]

9. If the NFP leases property or equipment under a sales-lease-back agreement, does the NFP disclose the terms of the sale-leaseback transaction, including future commitments, obligations, provisions, or circumstances that require or result in the seller-lessee's continuing involvement?

   [FASB ASC 840-40-50-1]

10. If the NFP indemnifies the lessor for preexisting environmental contamination and the likelihood of loss is reasonably possible, have the disclosures required by FASB ASC 840-40-50 been made?

   [FASB ASC 840-40-15-2]

11. Either on the face of the statement of financial position or in the notes, does the NFP disclose all of the following:

   a. Finance lease right-of-use assets and operating lease right-of-use as-sets, separately from each other and from other assets?

   b. Finance lease liabilities and operating lease liabilities, separately from each other and from other liabilities?

   ["Pending Content" in FASB ASC 842-20-45-1]

	Yes	No	N/A

12. If finance lease and operating lease right-of-use assets and lease liabilities are not reported as separate line items in the statement of financial position, does the NFP as lessee disclose the line items in the statement of financial position in which those right-of-use assets and lease liabilities are included?   _____ _____ _____

["Pending Content" in FASB ASC 842-20-45-2]

13. Are finance lease right-of-use assets reported on a different line item of the statement of financial position than operating lease right-of-use as-sets?   _____ _____ _____

["Pending Content" in FASB ASC 842-20-45-3]

14. Are finance lease liabilities reported on a different line item of the statement of financial position than operating lease liabilities?   _____ _____ _____

["Pending Content" in FASB ASC 842-20-45-3]

15. For finance leases, is interest expense on the lease liability presented in a manner consistent with how the NFP presents its other interest expense?   _____ _____ _____

["Pending Content" in FASB ASC 842-20-45-4]

16. For finance leases, is amortization of the right-of-use asset presented in a manner consistent with how the NFP presents depreciation or amortization of similar assets?   _____ _____ _____

["Pending Content" in FASB ASC 842-20-45-4]

17. Does the NFP as a lessee disclose information about the nature of its leases, including all of the following:

    a. A general description of those leases?   _____ _____ _____

    b. The basis and terms and conditions on which variable lease payments are determined?   _____ _____ _____

    c. The existence and terms and conditions of options to extend or terminate the lease, including a narrative disclosure about the options that are recognized as part of its right-of-use assets and lease liabilities and those that are not?   _____ _____ _____

    d. The existence and terms and conditions of residual value guarantees provided by the lessee?   _____ _____ _____

    e. The restrictions or covenants imposed by leases, for example, those relating to dividends or incurring additional financial obligations?   _____ _____ _____

["Pending Content" in FASB ASC 842-20-50-3]

18. Do the disclosures in question 17 identify the information included therein relating to subleases?   _____ _____ _____

["Pending Content" in FASB ASC 842-20-50-3]

19. Does the NFP as lessee disclose information about leases that have not yet commenced but that create for it significant rights and obligations, including the nature of any involvement with the construction or design of the underlying asset?   _____ _____ _____

["Pending Content" in FASB ASC 842-20-50-3]

	Yes	No	N/A

20. Does the NFP as lessee disclose information about significant assumptions and judgments made, which may include the following:

    a. The determination of whether a contract contains a lease (as described in paragraphs 2–27 of FASB ASC 842-10-15?

    b. The allocation of the consideration in a contract between lease and nonlease components (as described iny paragraphs 28–32 of FASB ASC 842-10-15?

    c. The determination of the discount rate for the lease (as described in paragraphs 2–4 of FASB ASC 842-20-30)?

["Pending Content" in FASB ASC 842-20-50-3]

21. For each period presented in the financial statements, does the NFP as lessee disclose the following amounts relating to total lease cost, which includes both amounts recognized in the statement of activities during the period and any amounts capitalized as part of the cost of another asset:

    a. Finance lease cost, segregated between the amortization of the right-of use assets and interest on the lease liabilities?

    b. Operating lease cost determined in accordance with paragraphs 6(a) and 7 of FASB ASC 842-20-25?

    c. Short-term lease cost, excluding expenses relating to leases with a lease term of one month or less, determined in accordance with FASB ASC 842-20-25-2?

    d. Variable lease cost determined in accordance with paragraphs 5(b) and 6(b) of FASB ASC 842-20-25?

    e. Sublease income, disclosed on a gross basis, separate from the finance or operating lease expense?

    f. Net gain or loss recognized from sale and leaseback transactions in accordance with FASB ASC 842-40-25-4?

["Pending Content" in FASB ASC 842-20-50-4]

22. Does the NFP as lessee disclose the following amounts, segregated between those for finance and operating leases:

    a. Cash paid for amounts included in the measurement of lease liabilities, segregated between operating and financing cash flows?

    b. Supplemental noncash information on lease liabilities arising from obtaining right-of-use assets?

    c. Weighted-average remaining lease term?

    d. Weighted-average discount rate?

["Pending Content" in FASB ASC 842-20-50-4]

23. Does the NFP as lessee disclose a maturity analysis of its lease liabilities, separately for its finance lease liabilities and its operating lease liabilities, and having the following characteristics:

    a. The undiscounted cash flows on an annual basis for a minimum of each of the first five years and a total of the amounts for the remaining years?

    b. A reconciliation of the undiscounted cash flows to the finance lease liabilities and the operating lease liabilities recognized in the statement of financial position?

["Pending Content" in FASB ASC 842-20-50-6]

	Yes	No	N/A

24. Do the disclosures required by FASB ASC 850, Related Party Disclosures, as described in section I.K., "Related Parties," include information about lease transactions between related parties?

    ["Pending Content" in FASB ASC 842-20-50-7]

25. For short term leases, does the NFP as lessee disclose both of the following:

    a.   The fact that the lessee accounts for short-term leases in accordance with FASB ASC 842-20-25-2 if the NFP does so?

    b.   The amount of the NFP's short-term commitments and the fact that lease expense for the period does not reasonably reflect NFP's short-term lease commitments, if that is the case?

    ["Pending Content" in FASB ASC 842-20-50-8]

26. If the NFP as lessee elects the practical expedient of not separating lease components from nonlease components (FASB ASC 842-10-15-37), does it disclose its accounting policy and for which class or classes of underlying assets it has elected to apply the practical expedient?

    ["Pending Content" in FASB ASC 842-20-50-9]

27. For sale and leaseback transactions, does the NFP as a seller-lessee dis-close both of the following:

    a.   The main terms and conditions of that transaction?

    b.   Any gains or losses arising from the transaction separately from gains or losses on disposal of other assets?

    ["Pending Content" in FASB ASC 842-40-50-2]

P.   **Other Liabilities and Deferred Credits**

1.   Are liabilities properly accrued and reported for employees' compensation for future absences, including sabbatical leaves?

    [FASB ASC 710-10-25]

2.   If an obligation for compensated absences or postemployment benefits is not accrued only because the amount cannot be reasonably estimated, is the fact that the benefits have not been accrued disclosed in the financial statements?

    [FASB ASC 710-10-50-1]

3.   Do the notes to the financial statements include information about an aging schedule of unconditional promises to give (showing the total amount separated into amounts payable in less than one year, in one to five years, and in more than five years) and the unamortized discount?

    [FASB ASC 958-405-50-1]

4.   If the NFP has incurred a legal obligation associated with the retirement of a tangible long-lived asset (including certain leases, such as coal or timber leases) that results from the acquisition, construction, or development and (or) normal operation of that long-lived asset (but not solely from a plan to sell or dispose of the asset), has it disclosed

    a.   the general description of the asset retirement obligation and the associated long-lived assets?

    b.   the fair value of assets that are legally restricted for purposes of settling the asset retirement obligation?

	Yes	No	N/A

    c. a reconciliation of the beginning and ending aggregated carrying amount of asset retirement obligations showing separately the changes attributable to (i) liabilities incurred in the current period, (ii) liabilities settled in the current period, (iii) accretion expense, and (iv) revisions in estimated cash flows, if there is a significant change in one or more of those four components during the reporting period?

    [FASB ASC 410-20-50-1]

5. If the NFP cannot reasonably estimate an asset retirement obligation, has it disclosed that fact and the reasons that it is unable to estimate the obligation?

    [FASB ASC 410-20-50-2]

6. If the NFP has defined benefit pension plans for which the projected benefit obligation exceeds the fair value of plan assets

    a. is the aggregate amount of all unfunded projected benefit obligations reported as a liability?

    b. if the NFP presents a classified statement of financial position, is the entire liability classified as a noncurrent unless there is a current portion? (Refer to question 3 in section II.M., "Current Liabilities.")

    [FASB ASC 715-30-25-1; FASB ASC 715-20-45-3]

7. If the NFP has defined benefit postretirement plans other than pensions for which accumulated postretirement benefit obligation exceeds the fair value of plan assets

    a. is the aggregate amount of all underfunded plans reported as a liability?

    b. if the NFP presents a classified statement of financial position, is the entire liability classified as a noncurrent unless there is a current portion? (Refer to section II.M. question 3.)

    [FASB ASC 715-60-25-1; FASB ASC 715-20-45-3]

8. If the NFP is obligated under a joint and several liability arrangement, has it disclosed

    a. the nature of the arrangement, including how the liability arose, the relationship with other co-obligors, and the terms and conditions of the arrangement?

    b. the total outstanding amount under the arrangement, which shall not be reduced by the effect of any amounts that may be recoverable from other entities?

    c. the carrying amount, if any, of an entity's liability and the carrying amount of a receivable recognized, if any?

    d. the nature of any recourse provisions that would enable recovery from other entities of the amounts paid, including any limitations on the amounts that might be recovered?

    e. in the period the liability is initially recognized and measured or in a period the measurement changes significantly, the corresponding entry and where the entry was recorded in the financial statements?

    [FASB ASC 405-40-50-1]

	Yes	No	N/A

9. Are deferred tax liabilities and assets, as well as any related valuation allowance,

   a.   classified as noncurrent amounts if a classified statement of financial position is presented? ____ ____ ____

   b.   offset and presented as a single noncurrent amount for a particular tax-paying component of the NFP and within a particular tax jurisdiction? *Note:* An NFP should not offset deferred tax liabilities and assets attributable to different tax-paying components of the entity or to different tax jurisdictions. ____ ____ ____

   [FASB ASC 740-10-45- 4 and FASB ASC 740-10-45-6]

Q.   Agency Transactions

1. If the NFP acts as an agent or intermediary, has it recorded a liability to the resource provider if the transfer is revocable or repayable? ____ ____ ____

   [FASB ASC 958-605-25-33]

2. If the NFP acts as an agent or intermediary in a transfer in which the resource provider specified itself or its affiliate as beneficiary, has it reported the transfer as

   a.   an equity transaction if the criteria in FASB ASC 958-20-25-4 are met? ____ ____ ____

   b.   a liability if the criteria in FASB ASC 958-20-25-4 are not met? ____ ____ ____

   [FASB ASC 958-605-25-33; FASB ASC 958-20-25 par. 4–7]

3. If the NFP acts as an agent or intermediary in a transfer in which the donor granted variance power and named an *unaffiliated* entity as the beneficiary, has it reported the transfer as a contribution? ____ ____ ____

   [FASB ASC 958-605-25-25]

4. If the NFP acts as an agent or intermediary in a transfer in which it is financially interrelated to the specified beneficiary (as defined in FASB ASC 958-20-20), has it reported the transfer as a contribution? ____ ____ ____

   [FASB ASC 958-20-25-1]

5. If the NFP acts as an agent or intermediary in a transfer that is not revocable or repayable, does not involve financially interrelated parties, and in which the donor did not grant variance power, has it reported the resources received as increases in assets and liabilities and has it reported the distribution of those resources to the beneficiaries as decreases in those accounts, except as noted in the following question 6? ____ ____ ____

   [FASB ASC 958-605-25-24]

6. If the NFP received nonfinancial assets in a transfer of the type described in question 5, did it report the receipt of those nonfinancial assets as assets and liabilities *only* if that is its accounting policy, it reports consistently from period to period, and it discloses that policy in the financial statements? ____ ____ ____

   [FASB ASC 958-605-25-24]

 © 2020, Association of International Certified Professional Accountants

	Yes	No	N/A

R. **Restricted Resources**

1. Are cash or other assets received with a donor-imposed restriction that limits their use to long term purposes reported separately from assets that are without donor restrictions and available for current use?

    [FASB ASC 958-210-45-6]

2. Does the NFP provide information about the nature and amounts of different types of donor-imposed restrictions by reporting their amounts on the face of the statement of financial position or by including relevant details in notes to financial statements?

    [FASB ASC 958-210-45-9]

3. Does the NFP provide the following information about its endowment:

    a. A description of the governing board's interpretation of the law(s) that underlies the NFP's net asset classification of donor-restricted endowment funds?

    b. A description of the NFP's policy(ies) for the appropriation of endowment assets for expenditure (its endowment spending policies)?

    c. A description of the NFP's endowment investment policies, including the following:

        i. The NFP's return objectives and risk parameters?

        ii. How those objectives relate to the NFP's endowment spending policies?

        iii. The strategies employed for achieving those objectives?

    d. The composition of the NFP's endowment by net asset class at the end of the period, in total and by type of endowment fund, showing donor-restricted endowment funds separately from board-designated endowment funds?

    [FASB ASC 958-205-50-1B]

    e. The aggregate amount of the deficiencies for all donor-restricted endowment funds, for which the fair value of the assets at the reporting date is less than the level required by donor stipulations or law?

    [FASB ASC 958-205-50-2]

4. Does the NFP provide a reconciliation of the beginning and ending balance of the NFP's endowment, in total and by net asset class, including, at a minimum, the following line items (as applicable):

    a. Investment return, net?

    b. Contributions?

    c. Amounts appropriated for expenditure?

    d. Other changes?

    [FASB ASC 958-205-50-1B]

5. Does the NFP provide the following information about its endowment:

    a. A description of the governing board's interpretation of the law(s) that underlies the NFP's ability to spend from underwater endowment funds?

© 2020, Association of International Certified Professional Accountants

	Yes	No	N/A

    b.   A description of any actions taken during the period to appropriate from underwater endowment funds?

        [FASB ASC 958-205-50-1B]

6.   For each period for which a statement of financial position is presented, does the NFP disclose each of the following, in the aggregate, for all underwater endowment funds:

    a.   The fair value of the underwater endowment funds?

    b.   The original endowment gift amount or level required to be maintained by donor stipulations or by law that extends donor restrictions?

    c.   The amount of the deficiencies of the underwater endowment funds ([a] less [b]).

        [FASB ASC 958-205-50-2]

S.   Mandatorily Redeemable Interests

1.   Are unconditional mandatorily redeemable financial instruments classified as liabilities if those instruments are mandatorily redeemable on fixed dates unless the redemption is required to occur only upon the liquidation or termination of the reporting entity? (**Note:** A mandatorily redeemable financial instrument is conditional if the obligation depends upon the occurrence of an event *not certain to occur.* Death is not uncertain of occurrence; thus, death is not a condition.)

    [FASB ASC 480-10-25-4]

2.   If all of the NFP's net assets are unconditional mandatorily redeemable financial instruments required to be classified as liabilities (that is, they are redeemable on fixed dates)

    a.   are those instruments described as *memberships subject to mandatory redemption* in statements of financial position to distinguish them from other liabilities?

    b.   are payments to holders of those instruments presented separately from payments to other creditors in statements of activities and cash flows?

    c.   are related accruals presented separately from amounts due to other creditors in statements of activities and cash flows?

        [FASB ASC 480-10-45-2; AAG 11.18–.22]

3.   If all of the NFP's net assets are unconditional mandatorily redeemable financial instruments required to be classified as liabilities (that is, they are redeemable on fixed dates) and the redemption price of those financial instruments exceeds the NFP's net assets, is the cumulative transition adjustment and any subsequent adjustments reported as an excess of liabilities over assets (a deficit net assets) and changes thereto even though the mandatorily redeemable shares are reported as a liability?

    [FASB ASC 480-10-45-2A]

4.   Does the NFP provide information about the nature and terms of mandatorily redeemable financial instruments and the rights and obligations embodied in those instruments, including information about settlement alternatives, if any, and who controls the settlement alternatives?

    [FASB ASC 480-10-50-1]

        © 2020, Association of International Certified Professional Accountants

		Yes	No	N/A

5. For all outstanding mandatorily redeemable financial instruments and for each settlement alternative, does the NFP provide information about

    a. the amount that would be paid determined under the conditions specified in the contract if the settlement were to occur at the reporting date?

    b. how changes in the fair value of the membership (dues or initiation fees) would affect those settlement amounts (for example, "the NFP is obligated to pay an additional y dollars in cash for each $100 increase in the fair value of the membership")?

    c. the maximum amount that the NFP could be required to pay to redeem the instruments or that the contract does not limit the amount that the issuer could be required to pay, as applicable?

    [FASB ASC 480-10-50-2]

T. Discontinued Operations

1. In the period(s) that a discontinued operation is classified as held for sale and for all prior periods presented, does the NFP

    a. measure the asset (group) at the lower of its carrying amount or fair value less cost to sell? *Note:* When an NFP presents the assets and liabilities of a discontinued operation in the statement of financial position of prior periods, the NFP should not measure those assets and liabilities in accordance with FASB ASC 360-10-35-43 as if they were held for sale in those prior periods.

    b. present separately the assets and liabilities of the discontinued operation in the asset and liability sections. respectively, of the statement of financial position, without offset as a single amount? *Note:* If the discontinued operation is part of a disposal group that includes other assets and liabilities (which are not part of the discontinued operation), an NFP may present the assets and liabilities of the disposal group.

    c. separately disclose the major classes of assets and liabilities of the discontinued operation on the face of the statement of financial position or in the notes? *Note:* Any loss recognized on a discontinued operation classified as held for sale should not be allocated to the major classes of assets and liabilities of the discontinued operation.

    [FASB ASC 360–10-35-43; FASB ASC 205-20-45 par. 10–11; FASB ASC 205-20-50-5B]

2. If the amounts in item *c* in question 1 are not reported on the face of the statement of financial position, are those amounts reconciled for all periods presented to the total assets and total liabilities of the disposal group, which is classified as held for sale and presented separately on the face of the statement of financial position? *Note:* If the disposal group includes assets and liabilities that are not part of the discontinued operation, those assets and liabilities should be presented as line items in the reconciliations, separately from the assets and liabilities of the discontinued operation.

    [FASB ASC 205-20-50-5C]

© 2020, Association of International Certified Professional Accountants

	Yes	No	N/A

3.   If a discontinued operation is disposed of before meeting the criteria in FASB ASC 205-20-45-1E to be classified as held for sale, are the assets and liabilities of the discontinued operation separately reported in the as-set and liability sections, respectively, of the statement of financial position for comparative periods (if any) before the period that includes the disposal? *Note:* When an NFP presents the assets and liabilities of a discontinued operation in the statement of financial position of prior periods, the NFP should not measure those assets and liabilities in accordance with FASB ASC 360-10-35-43 as if they were held for sale in those prior periods.

[FASB ASC 205-20-45-10]

4.   For an equity method investment that meets the criteria in FASB ASC 205-20-45-1B through 45-1C, is summarized information about the assets, liabilities, and results of operations of the investee disclosed if that information was disclosed in financial reporting periods before the disposal?

[FASB ASC 323-10-50-3(c); FASB ASC 205-20-50-7]

5.   For a discontinued operation in which an NFP retains an equity method investment after the disposal (the investee), do the financial statements include all of the following until the discontinued operation is no longer reported separately in discontinued operations:

    a.   Information that enables users of financial statements to compare the financial performance of the NFP from period to period assuming that the NFP held the same equity method investment in all periods presented in the statement of activities?

    b.   For each period after the period in which the discontinued operation was disposed of, the pretax income of the investee?

    c.   The NFP's ownership interest in the discontinued operation before the disposal transaction?

    d.   The NFP's ownership interest in the discontinued operation after the disposal transaction?

    e.   The NFP's share of the income or loss of the investee in the period(s) after the disposal transaction and the line item in the statement of activities that includes the income or loss?

    [FASB ASC 205-20-50-4B]

III. Statement of Activities

	Yes	No	N/A

A.   **General**

1.   Does the statement of activities report the amount of change in net assets for the period for the NFP as a whole (using a descriptive term such as "change in net assets" or "change in equity"), and does that amount articulate to the net assets reported in the statement of financial position?

[FASB ASC 958-220-45 par. 1–2]

© 2020, Association of International Certified Professional Accountants

	Yes	No	N/A

2. Does the statement of activities report the amount of change in net assets with donor restrictions and net assets without donor restrictions for the period?

   [FASB ASC 958-220-45-1]

3. Does the statement of activities report the following:

   a. Revenues as increases in net assets without donor restrictions unless the use of the assets received is limited by donor-imposed restrictions?

   b. Expenses as decreases in net assets without donor restrictions?

   c. Events that simultaneously increase one class of net assets and decrease another (reclassifications of net assets), including expiration of donor-imposed restrictions, separately from revenues, expenses, gains, and losses?

   d. Gains and losses as increases and decreases in net assets without donor restrictions unless a donor or law restricts their use?

   [FASB ASC 958-220-45 par. 3, 5, and 7–8]

4. If the NFP reports an intermediate measure of operations (for example, excess or deficit of operating revenues over expenses), is this intermediate measure reported only in a financial statement that, at a minimum, reports the change in net assets without donor restrictions for the period?

   [FASB ASC 958-220-45-10]

5. If the NFP reports an intermediate measure of operations and its use of the term *operations* is not apparent from the details provided on the face of the statement of activities, does a note to financial statements describe the nature of the reported measure of operations or the items excluded from operations?

   [FASB ASC 958-220-45-12; FASB ASC 958-220-50-1]

6. Does the statement of activities report gross amounts of revenues and expenses? (*Note:* Investment revenues may be reported net of related expenses.)

   [FASB ASC 958-220-45-14]

7. If the NFP reports net gains and losses on its statement of activities, do these net amounts result from peripheral or incidental transactions or from events largely beyond the control of the NFP and its management?

   [FASB ASC 958-220-45-17]

8. If special events and other fund raising activities are ongoing major or central activities of the NFP, are the revenues and expenses related to those events and activities reported as gross amounts?

   [FASB ASC 958-220-45-19]

9. Are costs that are netted against receipts from peripheral or incidental special events limited to direct costs?

   [FASB ASC 958-220-45-19]

10. Are sales revenues and cost of goods sold reported net of estimated returns?

    [FASB ASC 605-15-45-1]

© 2020, Association of International Certified Professional Accountants

	Yes	No	N/A

11. Are material events or transactions that an NFP considers to be of an unusual nature or of a type that indicates infrequency of occurrence, or both

    a.   reported as a separate component of change in net assets from continuing operations?

    b.   accompanied by disclosure of the nature and financial effects of each event?

       [FASB ASC 225-20-45-1]

12. If the NFP presents internal board designations, appropriations, and similar actions on the face of the financial statements, is an appropriate disaggregation and description by type of these actions presented in the notes to financial statements if that information is not provided on the face of the financial statement?

       [FASB ASC 958-220-50-1]

B.   Revenue Recognition (Other Than Contributions)

Note

FASB ASC 606 does not apply to contributions or to grants and awards that are conditional promises to give.

FASB ASC 606-10-50 has additional disclosure requirements for an NFP that has issued, or is a conduit bond obligor for, securities that are traded, listed, or quoted on an exchange or an over-the-counter market.

1. When one of the parties to a contract with a customer has performed, has the NFP presented the contract in the statement of financial position as a contract asset or a contract liability, depending on the relationship between the entity's performance and the customer's payment? (*Note:* Although FASB ASC 606 uses the terms contract asset and contract liability, an NFP may use an alternative description in the statement of financial position if the NFP provides sufficient information for a user of the financial statements to distinguish between receivables and contract assets.)

    ["Pending Content" in FASB ASC 606-10-45-1; "Pending Content" in FASB ASC 606-10-45-5]

2. Are any unconditional rights to consideration presented as a receivable, separately from contract assets?

    ["Pending Content" in FASB ASC 606-10-45-1]

3. Upon initial recognition of a receivable from a contract with a customer, is any difference between the measurement of the receivable in accordance with FASB ASC 326-20 and the corresponding amount of revenue recognized presented as a credit loss expense?

    ["Pending Content" in FASB ASC 606-10-45-4]

4. Is revenue recognized from contracts with customers presented separately from other sources of revenue?

    ["Pending Content" in FASB ASC 606-10-50-4]

5. Are any impairment losses recognized on any receivables or contract assets arising from an NFP's contracts with customers disclosed separately from impairment losses from other contracts?

    ["Pending Content" in FASB ASC 606-10-50-4]

      © 2020, Association of International Certified Professional Accountants

	Yes	No	N/A

6. Is revenue recognized from contracts with customers disaggregated into categories that depict how the nature, amount, timing, and uncertainty of revenue and cash flows are affected by economic factors, using the guidance in paragraphs 89–91 of FASB ASC 606-10-55 when selecting the categories used to disaggregate revenue? (See also question 7.)

["Pending Content" in FASB ASC 606-10-50-5]

7. If an NFP elects not to provide the disclosure described in question 6, (election is not available to an NFP that has issued, or is a conduit bond obligor for, securities that are traded, listed, or quoted on an exchange or an over-the-counter market) has the NFP instead disclosed the following information?

    a. Revenue disaggregated according to the timing of transfer of goods or services (for example, revenue from goods or services transferred to customers at a point in time and revenue from goods or services transferred to customers over time)

    b. Qualitative information about how economic factors (such as type of customer, geographical location of customers, and type of contract) affect the nature, amount, timing, and uncertainty of revenue and cash flows

    ["Pending Content" in FASB ASC 606-10-50-7]

8. Has the NFP disclosed the opening and closing balances of receivables, contract assets, and contract liabilities from contracts with customers, if not otherwise separately presented or disclosed?

["Pending Content" in FASB ASC 606-10-50-8(a)]

9. Has the NFP considered providing the optional disclosures about contract balances? *Note:* The disclosures are required if the NFP has issued, or is a conduit bond obligor for, securities that are traded, listed, or quoted on an exchange or an over-the-counter market.

["Pending Content" in FASB ASC 606-10-50-8(b); "Pending Content" in FASB ASC 606-10-50-9; "Pending Content" in FASB ASC 606-10-50-10]

10. Has the NFP disclosed the following information about its performance obligations in contracts with customers:

    a. When the NFP typically satisfies its performance obligations (for example, upon shipment, upon delivery, as services are rendered, or upon completion of service) including, if relevant, when performance obligations are satisfied in a bill-and-hold arrangement?

    b. The significant payment terms (for example, when payment typically is due, whether the contract has a significant financing component, whether the consideration amount is variable, and whether the estimate of variable consideration is typically constrained by the possibility of revenue reversal, per paragraphs 11–13 of FASB ASC 606-10-32)?

    c. The nature of the goods or services that the NFP has promised to transfer, highlighting any performance obligations to arrange for another party to transfer goods or services (that is, if the NFP is acting as an agent)?

	Yes	No	N/A

    d.   Obligations for returns, refunds, and other similar obligations? ____ ____ ____

    e.   Types of warranties and related obligations? ____ ____ ____

        ["Pending Content" in FASB ASC 606-10-50-12]

11.   Has the NFP considered providing the optional disclosure of revenue recognized in the reporting period from performance obligations satisfied (or partially satisfied) in previous periods — for example, changes in transaction price? *Note:* The disclosure is required if the NFP has issued, or is a conduit bond obligor for, securities that are traded, listed, or quoted on an exchange or an over-the-counter market. ____ ____ ____

    ["Pending Content" in FASB ASC 606-10-50-12A]

12.   Has the NFP considered providing the optional disclosures about its remaining performance obligations? *Note:* Certain of those disclosures are required if the NFP has issued, or is a conduit bond obligor for, securities that are traded, listed, or quoted on an exchange or an over-the-counter market. ____ ____ ____

    ["Pending Content" in paragraphs 13–15 of FASB ASC 606-10-50]

13.   Has the NFP disclosed the judgments, and changes in the judgments, used in determining the following?

    a.   The timing of satisfaction of performance obligations ____ ____ ____

    b.   The transaction price and the amounts allocated to performance obligations ____ ____ ____

    c.   Anything else that significantly affects the determination of the amount and timing of revenue from contracts with customers in accordance with FASB ASC 606 ____ ____ ____

        ["Pending Content" in FASB ASC 606-10-50-17]

14.   For performance obligations that are satisfied over time, has the NFP disclosed the methods used to recognize revenue (for example, a description of the output methods or input methods used and how those methods are applied)? ____ ____ ____

    ["Pending Content" in FASB ASC 606-10-50-18(a)]

15.   Has the NFP disclosed the methods, inputs, and assumptions used to assess whether an estimate of variable consideration is constrained? ____ ____ ____

    ["Pending Content" in FASB ASC 606-10-50-20(b); "Pending Content" in FASB ASC 606-10-50-21]

16.   Has the NFP considered providing the optional disclosures about significant judgments that affect the determination of the amount and timing of revenue from contracts with customers in accordance with FASB ASC 606? *Note:* The disclosures are required if the NFP has issued, or is a conduit bond obligor for, securities that are traded, listed, or quoted on an exchange or an over-the-counter market. ____ ____ ____

    ["Pending Content" in FASB ASC 606-10-50-18(b); "Pending Content" in FASB ASC 606-10-50-19; "Pending Content" in FASB ASC 606-10-50-20(a); "Pending Content" in FASB ASC 606-10-50-20(c); "Pending Content" in FASB ASC 606-10-50-20(d)]

        © 2020, Association of International Certified Professional Accountants

	Yes	No	N/A

17. Has the NFP considered providing the optional disclosure of the fact that it uses a practical expedient if it uses either the practical expedient for the existence of a significant financing component (FASB ASC 606-10-32-18) or the practical expedient for the incremental costs of obtaining a contract (FASB ASC 340-40-25-4)? *Note:* The disclosures are required if the NFP has issued, or is a conduit bond obligor for, securities that are traded, listed, or quoted on an exchange or an over-the-counter market.

    ["Pending Content" in FASB ASC 606-10-50-22; "Pending Content" in FASB ASC 606-10-50-23]

18. Does the NFP present the effects of financing (interest income or interest expense) separately from revenue from contracts with customers in the statement of activities?

    ["Pending Content" in FASB ASC 606-10-32-20]

19. In accounting for the effects of the time value of money, does the NFP present the discount and/or premium in the financial statements in accordance with paragraphs 1A–3 of FASB ASC 835-30-45? (See question 3 in section II.F, "Accounts, Notes, Contributions, and Loans Receivable" and question 18 in section II.N, "Notes Payable and Other Debt, Including Interfund Borrowing.")

    ["Pending Content" in FASB ASC 606-10-32-20]

20. Has the NFP disclosed its accounting policy if it makes any of the following elections:

    a. To account for shipping and handling as activities to fulfill the promise to transfer the goods, if shipping and handling activities are performed after a customer obtains control of the good?

    b. To exclude from the measurement of the transaction price all taxes assessed by a governmental authority that are both imposed on and concurrent with a specific revenue-producing transaction and collected by the entity from a customer (for example, sales, use, value added, and some excise taxes)?

    ["Pending Content" in FASB ASC 606-10-25-18B; "Pending Content in FASB ASC 606-10-32-2A]

21. If the NFP has the right to recover products from a customer upon settling a refund liability, is the asset to be recovered reported separately from the refund liability?

    ["Pending Content" in FASB ASC 606-10-55-27]

C. **Taxes**

1. Does the NFP disclose the following information about its tax status:

    a. Reference to the Internal Revenue Code section under which the NFP is exempt?

    b. Whether the NFP is classified as a private foundation?

    [Common Practice]

2. If the NFP's tax exempt status is in question by the IRS, is the potential impact disclosed?

    [FASB ASC 958-450-25-1]

	Yes	No	N/A

3. If the NFP incurs income tax expense, do the notes to the financial statements disclose the amount of the taxes and describe the nature of the activities that generated the taxes?

    [FASB ASC 958-720-50-1]

4. If the NFP incurs income tax expense, do the notes to the financial statements include the disclosures required by FASB ASC 740, *Income Taxes*?

    [FASB ASC 740-10-15-2; FASB ASC 740-10-50]

5. If the NFP has incurred any income tax penalties or interest, has it disclosed the total amounts of interest and penalties recognized in the statement of activities and the total amounts of interest and penalties recognized in the statement of financial position?

    [FASB ASC 740-10-50-15]

6. If the NFP has unrecognized tax benefits, has it displayed the benefits as required by paragraphs 10A–12 of FASB ASC 740-10-45 and disclosed the information about those benefits required by FASB ASC 740-10-50-15? (*Note:* NFPs that are public entities are subject to additional requirements of FASB ASC 740-10-50-15A.)

    [FASB ASC 740-10-50-15; FASB ASC 740-10-45; Q&A 5250.15]

D. Refunds Due To and Advances From Third Parties

1. Are advances from third parties for services not yet performed, as well as refunds due to third parties for amounts previously received, included as liabilities on the statement of financial position?

    [Common Practice; AAG 10.90]

E. Donated or Contributed Services

1. If the NFP receives contributed services, does it disclose the following:

    a. A description of the programs or activities for which those services were used?

    b. The nature and extent of contributed services received for the period?

    c. The amount recognized as revenues for the period?

    d. The fair value of contributed services received but not recognized, if practicable (optional)?

    e. Nonmonetary information such as the number and trends of donated hours received or service outputs provided by volunteer efforts (optional)?

    f. Dollar amount of contributions raised by volunteers (optional)?

    [FASB ASC 958-605-50-1]

F. Donated Materials and Facilities

1. If donated materials merely pass through the NFP to its charitable beneficiaries, and the NFP is only an agent or intermediary for the donors, has that donation been excluded from contribution revenues? (Refer to section II.Q., "Agency Transactions.")

    [FASB ASC 958-605-25 par. 23–24]

	Yes	No	N/A

2. If the NFP receives materials, supplies, utilities, or use of facilities without charge or at a price below fair value, is the contribution reported at the fair value in the period in which it is received and an expense reported in the period in which it is used?

[FASB ASC 958-605-55-23; FASB ASC 958-605-25-2]

3. If the NFP receives the unconditional use of facilities for a specified period of time at a price below fair value, is the fair value of that future use included in contributions in the period in which the donor promises the use, and is the amount recognized less than or equal to the fair value of the property at the time of the promise?

[FASB ASC 958-605-55-24; FASB ASC 958-605-25-2]

4. If the NFP has significant gift-in-kind activities, did the NFP disclose

   a. its accounting policies for gifts in kind?

   b. general sources of gifts in kind (such as governments, other NFPs, and private donors)?

   c. gifts in kind received in agency transactions?

   d. gifts in kind received from contributions?

   e. the amount utilized by the NFP in its own programs?

   f. the amount donated to other NFPs?

[FinREC recommendation in AAG 5.219, Examples 5–6 in AAG 5.220]

G. Fundraising

1. Do the financial statements disclose total fundraising expenses?

[FASB ASC 958-720-50-1]

2. If the NFP includes within its financial statements a ratio of fundraising expenses to amounts raised, has it disclosed how that ratio was computed?

[FASB ASC 958-205-50-3]

3. If the NFP performs a fund raising in conjunction with an activity that has program, management and general, membership development or other functional elements (joint activity), does the NFP

   a. report all costs of the activity as fundraising expenses if any of the criteria of purpose, audience, and content are not met?

   b. charge the costs of the activity that are identifiable with a particular function to that function and allocate the joint costs between fundraising and that other function if all three criteria of purpose, audience, and content are met?

   c. exclude costs of goods and services that are provided in exchange transactions that are part of the joint activity (for example, direct donor benefits of a special event) from fundraising expenses?

[FASB ASC 958-720-45-29]

4. If the NFP allocates joint costs of joint activities, are the following disclosures made:

   a. The types of activities for which joint costs have been incurred?

© 2020, Association of International Certified Professional Accountants

	Yes	No	N/A

b. A statement that joint costs have been allocated? ____ ____ ____

c. The total amount allocated during the period and the portion allocated to each functional expense category? ____ ____ ____

  [FASB ASC 958-720-50-2]

5. If the NFP allocates joint costs of joint activities, has it considered the optional disclosure of the amount of joint costs for each kind of joint activity? ____ ____ ____

  [FASB ASC 958-720-50-2]

6. If there are no significant benefits or duties connected with an NFP's membership, are the costs associated with membership-development activities reported as fundraising expense? ____ ____ ____

  [FASB ASC 958-720-55 par. 20–21]

H.   Contributions

Note

ASU No. 2018-08, *Clarifying the Scope and the Accounting Guidance for Contributions Received and Contributions Made*, was issued in June 2018 to improve the scope and the accounting guidance for contributions received and contributions made as it relates to revenue and expense recognition of grants and contracts by NFPs. It also clarifies requirements for the assessment of whether an agreement contains a donor-imposed condition. FASB ASU No. 2018-08 is effective as follows:

- For transactions in which an NFP has received a contribution, ASU No. 2018-08 is already effective.
- For transactions in which an NFP has made a contribution or is the resource provider, ASU No. 2018-08 is already effective for NFPs that has issued, or is a conduit bond obligor for, securities that are traded, listed, or quoted on an exchange or an over-the-counter market. All other NFPs should apply the amendments to transactions in which the NFP has made a contribution or serves as the resource provider in annual periods beginning after December 15, 2019, and interim periods within annual periods beginning after December 15, 2020.
- Early adoption is permitted.

1. Does the NFP distinguish between contributions received with donor-imposed restrictions and those received without donor-imposed restrictions, so that they are reported as donor-restricted support that increases net assets with donor restrictions or support that increases net assets without donor restrictions, respectively? ____ ____ ____

  [FASB ASC 958-605-45-3]

2. If donor-restricted contributions whose restrictions are met in the same reporting period are reported as support within net assets without donor restrictions, is such treatment consistent from period to period, is the policy disclosed, and does the NFP have a similar policy for the reporting of gains and investment income? ____ ____ ____

  [FASB ASC 958-220-45-6; "Pending Content" in FASB ASC 958-605-45-4A]

3. If donor-restricted contributions were initially conditional contributions and both the condition and the restriction have been met in the current period, has the NFP reported consistently from period to period and disclosed its accounting policy if it elects to report those contributions as support within net assets without donor restrictions? *Note:* An NFP may elect this policy without also having to elect it for other donor-restricted contributions or investment gains and income? ____ ____ ____

  ["Pending Content" in FASB ASC 958-605-45-4B]

	Yes	No	N/A

4. Does the NFP report receipt of unconditional promises to give with payments due in future periods as donor-restricted support, unless explicit donor stipulations or circumstances surrounding the receipt of the promise make clear that the donor intended the contribution to be used to support activities of the current period?

[FASB ASC 958-605-45-5]

5. Does an NFP that receives gifts of long-lived assets

    a. report such support as restricted if the donor stipulates how long the donated asset must be used?

    b. report such support as revenue without donor restrictions if the long-lived assets are received without donor stipulations about how long the donated asset must be used?

    [FASB ASC 958-605-45-6]

6. Does an NFP that receives unconditional promises to give in which cash promised will be received in future periods initially measure the fair value of the contribution and report subsequent accruals of the interest element as contribution revenue increasing net assets with donor restrictions if the underlying promise to give is donor-restricted or due in future periods? (**Note**: If the NFP elects to subsequently measure unconditional promises to give at fair value in accordance with the fair value option subsections of FASB ASC 825-10, it is not necessary to separately compute the interest element.)

[FASB ASC 958-605-30-4; FASB ASC 958-310-35-6]

I. Split-Interest Agreements

1. Are assets and liabilities recognized under split-interest agreements disclosed separately from other assets and liabilities in the statement of financial position or in the related notes?

[FASB ASC 958-30-45-6]

2. If a split-interest gift contains an embedded derivative (charitable remainder unitrusts with period-certain payments or period-certain-plus-life-dependent payments and certain lead interest trusts), is the embedded derivative reported at fair value?

[FASB ASC 958-30-30-9]

3. Is contribution revenue and changes in the value of split-interest agreements recognized under such agreements disclosed as separate line items in the statement of activities or in the related notes?

[FASB ASC 958-30-45-7]

4. Do the notes to the financial statements include the following disclosures related to split-interest agreements:

    a. A description of the general terms of existing split-interest agreements?

    b. The basis used for recognized assets?

    c. The discount rates and actuarial assumptions used in calculating present value?

    d. The existence of any legally mandated reserves?

    e. The existence of any limitations placed by state law, such as limitations on the instruments in which resources are invested?

	Yes	No	N/A

f. The disclosures required by the "Fair Value Option" subsection of FASB ASC 825-10-50, if an NFP elects the fair value option as described in FASB ASC 958-30-35-2? _____ _____ _____

g. The disclosures required by paragraphs 1–2 of FASB ASC 820-10-50 in the format described in FASB ASC 820-10-50-8, if the assets and liabilities of split-interest agreements are measured at fair value in periods after initial recognition? _____ _____ _____

[FASB ASC 958-30-50 par. 1–2]

5. Is contribution revenue recognized under split-interest agreements classified as

a. increases in net assets with donor restrictions if the donor has restricted the NFP's use of its interest? _____ _____ _____

b. increases in net assets without donor restrictions if the NFP has the immediate right to use its interest without restrictions? _____ _____ _____

[FASB ASC 958-30-45-1]

6. Are voluntary reserves that are set aside by the governing board for unexpected actuarial losses included as part of net assets without donor restrictions, and either presented as a separate component of board-designated net assets on the face of the statement of financial position or disclosed in the notes to financial statements? _____ _____ _____

[FASB ASC 958-30-50-3]

J.   Expenses

1. Do the notes to the financial statements describe the methods used to allocate costs among program and support functions? _____ _____ _____

[FASB ASC 958-220-50-1(d); FASB ASC 958-720-50-1(d)]

2. Are expenses that relate to more than one program or supporting activity allocated among the appropriate functions? _____ _____ _____

[AAG 13.77; FASB ASC 958-720-45-2A]

3. Are payments to affiliated NFPs reported by their functional classification to the extent that it is practicable and reasonable to do so? _____ _____ _____

[FASB ASC 958-720-45-26]

4. Are payments to affiliates that cannot be allocated to functions treated as a separate supporting service and reported in the statement of activities as a separate line item, and labeled "unallocated payments to affiliated NFPs"? _____ _____ _____

[FASB ASC 958-720-45-26]

5. If the components of the NFP's total program expenses are not evident from the details provided on the face of the statement of activities, do the notes to the financial statements disclose total program expenses and provide information about why total program expenses disclosed in the notes does not articulate with the statement of activities? _____ _____ _____

[FASB ASC 958-720-50-1]

	Yes	No	N/A

6. If in exchange for goods or services provided to the NFP, the NFP provides discounts or other reductions in amounts it charges for goods and services, are such reductions reported as expenses in the same functional classification in which the cost of the goods or services provided to the NFP are reported? (For example, if a college provided tuition remission to its employees as an employee benefit, it would report those reductions in the same functional class as the employees' salaries.)

[FASB ASC 958-720-25-7; FASB ASC 958-720-45-23]

7. If reductions in amounts the NFP charges for goods and services are given *other than* in exchange for goods or services provided to the NFP, are such amounts reported as follows:

   a. As expenses to the extent that the NFP incurs incremental expense in providing such goods or services?

   b. As discounts if the NFP incurs no incremental expense in providing such goods or services (discounts may be netted with related revenue or displayed immediately beneath the revenue amount)?

   [FASB ASC 958-720-25-8; FASB ASC 958-605-45-2]

8. Are accrued net losses on purchase commitments either (*a*) disclosed in the notes to the financial statements because expenses are reported by functional classification on the face of the statement of activities or (*b*) reported as a separate line item in a statement of activities that reports expenses by natural classification?

   [FASB ASC 330-10-50-5]

9. For deferred compensation agreements, are estimated amounts to be paid properly accrued?

   [FASB ASC 710-10-25 par. 9–11]

10. Does the NFP present the relationship between functional and natural classification for all expenses using an analysis that

    a. appears on the face of the statement of activities, as a separate statement, or as a note to the financial statements?

    b. disaggregates functional expense classifications by their natural expense classifications?

    c. excludes investment expenses that are netted against investment return?

    d. excludes items that are typically included in other comprehensive income (and are excluded from net income) of business entities, such as those items listed in FASB ASC 220-10-45-10A?

    e. reports by their natural classification in the analysis any expenses that are reported by other than their natural classification in the statement of activities (such as salaries included in cost of goods sold or facility rental costs of special events reported as direct benefits to donors)?

    [FASB ASC 958-720-50-1bb; FASB ASC 958-205-45-6; FASB ASC 958-220-50-1(c); FASB ASC 958-720-45-15]

© 2020, Association of International Certified Professional Accountants

	Yes	*No*	*N/A*

11. Does the NFP report the net gain or loss, the prior service costs or credits, and the transition asset or obligation as a separate line item or items, apart from expenses, outside an intermediate measure of operations, if one is presented, within changes in net assets without donor restrictions?

["Pending Content" in FASB ASC 958-715-45-1]

12. Does the NFP report the contra adjustment or adjustments to the net gain or loss, the prior service costs or credits, and the transition asset or obligation initially recognized pursuant to question 11 that result from the reclassification to net periodic pension cost and net period postretirement benefit cost in the same line item or items within changes in net assets without donor restrictions, apart from expenses, as the initially recognized amounts?

["Pending Content" in FASB ASC 958-715-45-2]

13. Is the service cost component of net periodic pension cost and net periodic postretirement benefit cost reported in the statement of activities in the same line item(s) as other compensation costs arising from services rendered by the pertinent employees during the period (except for the amount being capitalized, if appropriate, in connection with production or construction of an asset)?

["Pending Content" in FASB ASC 958-715-45-3]

14. Are the other components of net pension costs and net periodic postretirement benefit costs (other than service costs, as identified in FASB ASC 715-30-35-4 and 715- 60-35-9) reported separately from the service cost component and outside an intermediate measure of operations, if one is presented, within changes in net assets without donor restrictions?

["Pending Content" in FASB ASC 958-715-45-3]

15. Is the separate line item or items that are used to present the other components appropriately described and different from the separate line item or items used to present the net gain or loss, the prior service costs or credits, and the transition asset or obligation that would be recognized in other comprehensive income of a business entity in accordance with FASB ASC 715-30-35 and 715-60-35?

["Pending Content" in FASB ASC 958-715-45-3]

16. Are the service cost component and the other components of net periodic pension cost and net periodic postretirement benefit cost reported by functional expense classification?

["Pending Content" in FASB ASC 958-715-45-3]

17. If an NFP makes contributions to other NFPs, does it separately identify the contributions to other NFPs (both affiliated and other than affiliated NFPs) either in the statement of activities or notes to the financial statements?

[FinREC recommendation in AAG 13.33]

      © 2020, Association of International Certified Professional Accountants

	Yes	No	N/A

K.   Investments and Endowments

1.   If realized gains and losses arise from selling or otherwise disposing of investments for which unrealized gains and losses have been recognized in the statement of activities of prior reporting periods, does the amount reported in the statement of activities as gain or loss upon the sale or other disposition of the investments exclude the amount that has been previously recognized in the statement of activities? (The components of that gain or loss may be reported as the realized amount and the change in the unrealized amount, which was recognized in prior reporting periods.)

[AAG 4.53]

Note

All states but Pennsylvania have adopted the Uniform Prudent Management of Institutional Funds Act (UPMIFA)-based legislation. Endowments subject to Pennsylvania law should be reported in accordance with FASB ASC 958-205-45 par. 33–35 and FASB ASC 958-205-45 par. 16–21A.

---

2.   *For NFPs that have endowment funds subject to UPMIFA-based legislation*: Unless the NFP has made the election described in question 5 that follows, does the NFP report investment income and gains on donor-restricted endowment funds as increases in net assets with donor restrictions?

[FASB ASC 958-205-45-13D]

3.   *For NFPs that have endowment funds subject to UPMIFA-based legislation*: In the absence of donor stipulations or law to the contrary, does the NFP report losses on investments of donor-restricted endowment funds as decreases in net assets with donor restrictions?

[FASB ASC 958-205-45-13H]

4.   *This question is for investments that are not held in donor-restricted endowment funds*: Unless the NFP has made the election described in question 5 that follows, does the NFP report investment income and gains as increases in net assets without donor restrictions unless donors otherwise restrict those income and gains?

[FASB ASC 958-320-45 par. 1–3; "Pending Content" in FASB ASC 958-220-45-22]

5.   If the NFP has elected to report investment income and gains as increases in net assets without donor restrictions if the restrictions are met in the same period, are

a.   investment income and gains on which restriction have not been met reported as described in the preceding questions 2–4, as applicable?

b.   investment income and gains on which restrictions are met reported as increases in net assets without donor restrictions?

[FASB ASC 958-320-45-3; "Pending Content" in FASB ASC 958-220-45-24]

6.   If an NFP reports gains and investment income that are limited to specific uses by donor-imposed restrictions as increases in net assets without donor restrictions because the restrictions are met in the same reporting period as the gains and income are recognized, does the NFP

© 2020, Association of International Certified Professional Accountants

	Yes	No	N/A

a.   have a similar policy for reporting contributions received?   ____   ____   ____

b.   report consistently from period to period?   ____   ____   ____

c.   disclose its accounting policy?   ____   ____   ____

[FASB ASC 958-320-45-3; "Pending Content" in FASB ASC 958-220-45-24]

7.   Are significant net realized and net unrealized gains and losses that arose after the latest statement of financial position date, but before issuance of the financial statements, disclosed?   ____   ____   ____

[FASB ASC 855-10-25-3; FASB ASC 855-10-55-2]

L.   Discontinued Operations

1.   If a discontinued operation either has been disposed of or is classified as held for sale, are all of the following disclosed in the financial statements that cover the period in which that disposal or classification occurs:

    a.   A description of the facts and circumstances leading to the disposal or expected disposal?   ____   ____   ____

    b.   The expected manner and timing of that disposal?   ____   ____   ____

    c.   The gain or loss recognized, if not separately presented on the face of the statement of activities?   ____   ____   ____

    [FASB ASC 205-20-50-1]

2.   In a period in which a component (or a group of components) of an NFP either has been disposed of or is classified as held for sale, do the statements of activities for the current period and any prior periods report the disposal as a discontinued operation only if the disposal represents a strategic shift that has (or will have) a major effect on the NFP's operations and financial results?   ____   ____   ____

[FASB ASC 205-20-45-1B]

3.   In a period in which there is a discontinued operation, do the statements of activities for the current period and any prior periods presented

    a.   include the results of operations of the discontinued operation as a separate section of the statement that is identified discontinued operations?   ____   ____   ____

    b.   separately report the gain or loss recognized on the disposal (or loss recognized on classification as held for sale) on the face of the statement or in notes to the financial statements?   ____   ____   ____

    c.   include any subsequent increase in fair value less cost to sell (not in excess of cumulative losses recognized) in discontinued operations?   ____   ____   ____

    [FASB ASC 360-10-35-40; FASB ASC 205-20-45 par. 3–3C]

4.   In a period in which a component (or a group of components) of an NFP either has been disposed of or is classified as held for sale and that discontinued operation was not an equity method investment before the disposal, are all of the following disclosed for the periods in which the results of operations of the discontinued operation are presented in the statement of activities:

    a.   The pretax change in net assets of the discontinued operation?   ____   ____   ____

	Yes	No	N/A

b. The major classes of line items constituting the pretax change in net assets of the discontinued operation (for example, revenue, cost of sales, depreciation and amortization, and interest expense)? ____ ____ ____

c. Either (1) the total operating and investing cash flows of the discontinued operation or (2) the depreciation, amortization, capital expenditures, and significant operating and investing noncash items of the discontinued operation? ____ ____ ____

d. If the discontinued operation includes a noncontrolling interest, the pretax change in net assets attributable to the parent? ____ ____ ____

[FASB ASC 205-20-50-5B]

5. If the amounts for items *a–b* in question 4 do not appear on the face of the statement of activities, are those amounts reconciled to the after-tax amount for discontinued operations reported on the face of the statement of activities? *Note:* Amounts that are not major may be aggregated. ____ ____ ____

[FASB ASC 205-20-50 par. 5C–5D]

6. If the NFP has significant continuing involvement with a discontinued operation after the disposal date, does the NFP disclose the following information in the notes to the financial statements until the discontinued operation is no longer presented separately in the statement of activities:

a. The nature of the activities that give rise to the continuing involvement? ____ ____ ____

b. The period of time during which the involvement is expected to continue? ____ ____ ____

c. The amount of any cash inflows or outflows from or to the discontinued operation after the disposal transaction? ____ ____ ____

d. Revenues or expenses presented, if any, in continuing operations after the disposal transaction that before the disposal transaction were eliminated in consolidated financial statements as intraentity transactions? ____ ____ ____

[FASB ASC 205-20-50 par. 4A–4B]

7. In periods subsequent to that in which there is a discontinued operation, if there are adjustments to amounts reported in discontinued operations of a prior period

a. are the adjustments presented separately in the discontinued operations section of the current period's statement of activities? ____ ____ ____

b. are the nature and amount disclosed? ____ ____ ____

[FASB ASC 205-20-45-4; FASB ASC 205-20-50-3A]

8. If at any time the criteria for a component to be classified as held for sale in FASB ASC 205-20-45-1E are no longer met (except as permitted for by FASB ASC 205-20-45-1G for events or circumstances beyond an entity's control), are all of the following included in the financial statements that included the period in which that decision occurs:

a. Has the component (or group of components) been reclassified as held and used? ____ ____ ____

	Yes	No	N/A

    b.   Is a description of the facts and circumstances leading to the decision to change the plan for selling the discontinued operation provided?

    c.   Is the effect of the decision on the change in net assets (and on the operating measure, if one is displayed) for the period and any prior periods presented disclosed?

    [FASB ASC 205-20-45-1F; FASB ASC 205-20-50-3]

IV. Statement of Cash Flows

	Yes	No	N/A

1.   Is a statement of cash flows presented as a financial statement for each period for which both a statement of financial position and a statement of activities is presented?

    [FASB ASC 230-10-15-3]

2.   Does the statement of cash flows report net cash provided or used by operating, investing, and financing activities and the net effect of those flows on the total of cash, cash equivalents, and amounts generally described as restricted cash or restricted cash equivalents during the period in a manner that reconciles beginning and ending cash and cash equivalents?

    [FASB ASC 230-10-45-24]

3.   Are cash receipts and disbursements classified as cash flows from operating, investing, and financing activities in accordance with the classifications prescribed by FASB ASC 230, *Statement of Cash Flows*?

    [FASB ASC 230-10-45]

4.   Are amounts of cash receipts and cash disbursements reported gross unless the receipts and disbursements relate to (*a*) cash equivalents, (*b*) investments with an original maturity of three months or less, (*c*) loans receivable with an original maturity of three months or less, or (*d*) debt with an original maturity of three months or less?

    [FASB ASC 230-10-45-7]

5.   Are cash payments for debt issue costs classified as a financing activity?

    [FASB ASC 230-10-45-15]

6.   Are cash flows from purchases, sales, and insurance recoveries of unrecognized, noncapitalized collection items reported as investing activities?

    [FASB ASC 958-230-55-5A]

7.   Do the notes disclose the NFP's accounting policy for determining which items are treated as cash equivalents? (*Note:* Any change in policy for determining which items are treated as cash equivalents is a change in accounting principle.)

    [FASB ASC 230-10-50-1]

	Yes	No	N/A

8. If the direct method is used, does the statement of cash flows separately report (as applicable)

    a. cash received from contributors? ____ ____ ____

    b. cash received from service recipients? ____ ____ ____

    c. interest and dividends received? ____ ____ ____

    d. cash collected on contributions receivable? ____ ____ ____

    e. other operating cash receipts (if any)? ____ ____ ____

    f. cash paid to employees and suppliers? ____ ____ ____

    g. grants paid? ____ ____ ____

    h. interest paid? ____ ____ ____

    i. other operating cash payments (if any)? ____ ____ ____

    [FASB ASC 230-10-45-25; FASB ASC 958-205-55-19]

9. If the indirect method is used, is the change in net assets reconciled to net cash flow from operating activities within the statement of cash flows or in a separate schedule? ____ ____ ____

    [FASB ASC 230-10-45-28; FASB ASC 230-10-45-31]

10. If the indirect method is used, are amounts of interest paid (net of amounts capitalized) and income taxes paid, if any, disclosed? ____ ____ ____

    [FASB ASC 230-10-50-2]

11. Are investing and financing activities that affect recognized assets or liabilities but that do not result in cash receipts or cash payments, including gifts of property or investments, disclosed? ____ ____ ____

    [FASB ASC 230-10-50 par. 3–4]

12. In the statement of cash flows, are amounts received with donor-imposed stipulations that they must be used for long-term purposes reported simultaneously as cash flow from financing activities and cash outflow from investing activities? ____ ____ ____

    [FASB ASC 958-230-55-3]

13. If the NFP directed the sale of donated financial assets (for example, donated debt or equity instruments) upon receipt without imposing any limitations upon the sale (such as a limit order) and those financial assets were converted nearly immediately into cash, are the resulting cash receipts

    a. classified as cash flows from financing activities if the contributed resources were restricted by the donor for the purpose of (i) acquiring, constructing, or improving property, plant, equipment, or other long-lived assets or (ii) establishing or increasing a donor-restricted endowment fund? ____ ____ ____

    b. classified as cash flows from operating activities if the contributed resources were not restricted in the manner described in item *a* of this question? ____ ____ ____

    [FASB ASC 230-10-45-21A]

14. Is the reconciliation of the change in net assets to net cash used or provided by operating activities adjusted if noncash assets are contributed or if cash is received with donor imposed stipulations that require it to be used for long-term purposes (and thus is not included in "cash or cash equivalents" on the statement of financial position)? ____ ____ ____

    [FASB ASC 958-230-55-3]

© 2020, Association of International Certified Professional Accountants

	Yes	No	N/A

15. If contributions with donor-imposed restrictions limiting their use to the purchase of equipment are received and the equipment is purchased in a subsequent period, are both the proceeds of the sale of the assets restricted to equipment investment and the purchase of the equipment reported as cash flows from investing activities?

   [FASB ASC 958-230-55-3]

16. Are cash flows from agency transactions included in cash flows from operating activities?

   [FASB ASC 958-230-55-4]

17. If cash flows from derivative instruments that are accounted for as fair value hedges are classified in the same category as the cash flows of the item being hedged, is that accounting policy disclosed?

   [FASB ASC 230-10-45-27]

18. If an other-than-insignificant financing element is present at the inception of a derivative instrument (other than financing elements inherently included in at-the-market derivative instrument with no prepayments), are all cash inflows and outflows associated with that derivative instrument reported as financing activities?

   [FASB ASC 230-10-45-27]

19. If the indirect method is used and the NFP has issued zero-coupon debt instruments or other debt instruments with coupon interest rates that are insignificant in relation to the effective interest rate of the borrowing, such as an interest-free loan, does the amount of interest paid in question 10 include the portion of the debt payments that is attributable to accreted interest related to the debt discount?

   ["Pending Content" in FASB ASC 230-10-50-2]

20. Does the statement of cash flows report information in a manner that reconciles beginning and ending totals of cash, cash equivalents, and amounts generally described as restricted cash or restricted cash equivalents?

   ["Pending Content" in FASB ASC 230-10-45-24]

21. If cash, cash equivalents, and amounts generally described as restricted cash or restricted cash equivalents are presented in more than one line item within the statement of financial position, does the NFP, for each period that a statement of financial position is presented, present the following on the face of the statement of cash flows or in the notes to the financial statements:

   a. The amounts of cash, cash equivalents, and amounts generally described as restricted cash or restricted cash equivalents reported within the statement of financial position, disaggregated by the line item in which they appear within the statement of financial position?

   b. The sum of the amounts of cash, cash equivalents, and amounts generally described as restricted cash or restricted cash equivalents, which equals the amount shown in the statement of cash flows at the end of the corresponding period?

   ["Pending Content" in FASB ASC 230-10-50-8]

     © 2020, Association of International Certified Professional Accountants

	Yes	*No*	*N/A*

Note

ASU No. 2016-02 issued in February 2016, requires the recognition of lease assets and lease liabilities on the statement of financial position and the disclosure of key information about leasing arrangements.

For an NFP that has issued, or is a conduit bond obligor for, securities that are traded, listed, or quoted on an exchange or an over-the-counter market. ASU No. 2016-02 was effective for fiscal years beginning after December 15, 2018, including interim periods within those fiscal years. For all other NFPs, ASU No. 2016-02, as amended by FASB ASU No. 2019-10, is effective for fiscal years beginning after December 15, 2020, and interim periods within fiscal years beginning after December 15, 2021. Earlier application is permitted.

NFPs that have adopted ASU No. 2016-02 should complete question 22. Other NFPs should mark that question "N/A."

22. For leases, are

    a. repayments of the principal portion of the lease liability arising from finance leases presented within financing activities?

    b. interest on the lease liability arising from finance leases presented in accordance with the requirements for interest paid in FASB ASC 230, *Statement of Cash Flows*?

    c. payments arising from operating leases presented within operating activities, except to the extent that those payments represent costs to bring another asset to the condition and location necessary for its intended use, which should be classified within investing activities?

    d. variable lease payments and short-term lease payments not included in the lease liability presented within operating activities

    ["Pending Content" in FASB ASC 842-20-45-5]

Note

FASB ASU No. 2018-15, *Intangibles—Goodwill and Other—Internal-Use Software (Subtopic 350-40): Customer's Accounting for Implementation Costs Incurred in a Cloud Computing Arrangement That Is a Service Contract (a consensus of the FASB Emerging Issues Task Force)*, is effective for annual reporting periods beginning after December 15, 2020. Early adoption is permitted.

NFPs that have adopted ASU No. 2018-15 should complete question 23. Other NFPs should mark that question "N/A."

23. Are the cash flows from capitalized implementation costs of hosting arrangements presented in the same manner as the cash flows for the fees for the associated hosting arrangement?

    ["Pending Content" in FASB ASC 350-40-45-3]

© 2020, Association of International Certified Professional Accountants

Part 3
Auditors' Reports Checklist

.01 During the past year, the Auditing Standards Board (ASB) issued the following seven Statements on Auditing Standards (SASs), which are effective for audits of financial statements for periods ending on or after December 15, 2021:

- SAS No. 134, *Auditor Reporting and Amendments, Including Amendments Addressing Disclosures in the Audit of Financial Statements*, on May 8, 2019

- SAS No. 135, *Omnibus Statement on Auditing Standards — 2019*, on May 8, 2019

- SAS No. 137, *The Auditor's Responsibilities Relating to Other Information Included in Annual Reports*, on July 10, 2019

- SAS No. 138, *Amendments to the Description of the Concept of Materiality*, on December 5, 2019

- SAS No. 139, *Amendments to AU-C Sections 800, 805, and 810 to Incorporate Auditor Reporting Changes From SAS No. 134*, on March 10, 2020

- SAS No. 140, *Amendments to AU-C Sections 725, 730, 930, 935, and 940 to Incorporate Auditor Reporting Changes From SAS Nos. 134 and 137*, on April 8, 2020

- SAS No. 141, *Amendment to the Effective Dates of SAS Nos. 134–140*, on May 1, 2020

SAS Nos. 134 and 136–140 are designed to enhance the communicative value of the auditor's report while aligning generally accepted auditing standards (GAAS) with the standards of the International Auditing and Assurance Standards Board and the PCAOB The SASs are interrelated, because the ASB amended the auditor reporting model adopted in SAS No. 134 with the issuance of the SAS Nos. 136–140. The effective dates were aligned so that these SASs would be implemented as a suite, primarily to accommodate the amendments to the auditor reporting model. On May 1, 2020, the ASB issued SAS No. 141 to provide more time for firms to implement these SASs in light of the effects of the coronavirus pandemic. SAS No. 141 also lifts the prohibition in the earlier SASs against early implementation. Collectively, this checklist refers to the seven SASs as "The Suite of New Reporting Standards."

.02 This checklist has been developed by the staff of the Accounting and Auditing Publications Team of the AICPA as a nonauthoritative practice aid. It contains two sections. The first section (paragraph .09) is used for audits of financial statements for periods ending before December 15, 2021, provided the auditor did not chose to early adopt the suite of new reporting standards. The second section (paragraph .10) is used for audits of financial statements for periods ending on or after December 15, 2021, or if the auditor chooses to early adopt the suite of new reporting standards. Illustrations of auditor's reports that comply with this checklist are found in AU-C section 700B, *Forming an Opinion and Reporting on Financial Statements* (if the suite of new reporting standards has not yet been adopted), or in AU-C section 700, *Forming an Opinion and Reporting on Financial Statements* (if the suite of new reporting standards has been adopted).[1]

.03 This checklist contains the basic requirements for reporting on an audit of the financial statements in accordance with GAAS. It does not contain all requirements for reports required to be issued in audits in accordance with *Government Auditing Standards* (also referred to as the Yellow Book) or with the Office of Management and Budget *Uniform Administrative Requirements, Cost Principles, and Audit Requirements for Federal Awards* (Uniform Guidance) audit requirements. Illustrative auditor's reports are found in chapter 14, "Reports of Independent Auditors," of the AICPA Audit and Accounting Guide *Not-for-Profit Entities*. This checklist also does not contain requirements for an audit of internal control over financial reporting that is integrated with an audit of financial statements (integrated audit). If an auditor is engaged to perform an integrated audit,

---

[1] All AU-C sections can be found in AICPA *Professional Standards*.

the auditor should also refer to AU-C section 940, *An Audit of Internal Control Over Financial Reporting That Is Integrated With an Audit of Financial Statements.*

.04 This checklist is prepared for use in reporting on financial statements prepared in accordance with generally accepted accounting principles (GAAP). If an auditor is expressing an opinion on financial statements prepared in accordance with a cash, tax, regulatory, contractual, or another basis of accounting (referred to as a special-purpose framework), the auditor should comply with the requirements of AU-C section 800B, *Special Considerations — Audits of Financial Statements Prepared in Accordance With Special Purpose Frameworks* (if the suite of new reporting standards has not yet been adopted), and AU-C section 800, *Special Considerations — Audits of Financial Statements Prepared in Accordance With Special Purpose Frameworks* (if the suite of new reporting standards has been adopted). AU-C section 800B and AU-C section 800 address special considerations in the application of AU-C sections 200B–700B to an audit of financial statements prepared in accordance with a special purpose framework.

.05 This checklist is prepared for use in reporting on a complete set of financial statements. If an auditor is expressing an opinion on a single financial statement or a specific element, account, or item of a financial statement, the auditor should comply with the requirements of AU-C section 805B, *Special Considerations — Audits of Single Financial Statements and Specific Elements, Accounts, or Items of a Financial Statement* (if the suite of new reporting standards has not yet been adopted), and AU-C section 805, *Special Considerations — Audits of Single Financial Statements and Specific Elements, Accounts, or Items of a Financial Statement* (if the suite of new reporting standards has been adopted). AU-C section 805B and AU-C section 805 address special considerations in the application of AU-C sections 200B–700B to an audit of a single financial statement or of a specific element, account, or item of a financial statement.

.06 The PCAOB establishes standards for audits of *issuers*, as that term is defined by the Sarbanes-Oxley Act of 2002, or whose audit is prescribed by the rules of the SEC. Other entities are referred to as *nonissuers*. Because not-for-profit organizations (NFPs) are nonissuers, this checklist does not address PCAOB standards. Although uncommon, an auditor may be engaged to follow PCAOB auditing standards in the audit of an NFP. When the audit is not under the jurisdiction of the PCAOB but the entity desires, or is required by an agency, by a regulator, or by contractual agreement, to obtain an audit conducted under PCAOB standards, the AICPA Code of Professional Conduct requires the auditor to also conduct the audit in accordance with GAAS. SAS No. 131, *Amendment to Statement on Auditing Standards No. 122 Section 700*, Forming an Opinion and Reporting on Financial Statements (AU-C sec. 700B), clarifies the format of the auditor's report that should be issued when the auditor conducts an audit in accordance the standards of the PCAOB, but the audit is not under the jurisdiction of the PCAOB.

.07 If the auditor is engaged to audit both an NFPs's financial statements and management's assessment of the effectiveness of internal control over financial reporting in accordance with PCAOB auditing standards, refer to paragraphs .85–.98 of PCAOB Auditing Standard No. 2201, *An Audit of Internal Control Over Financial Reporting That Is Integrated with An Audit of Financial Statements*,[2] for the audit reports that should be used.

.08 Explanation of References:

AU-C = Reference to section number in AICPA *Professional Standards*

AAG = AICPA Audit and Accounting Guide *Not-for-Profit Entities* (as of March 1, 2020)

I. For Audits Conducted Prior to the Adoption of the Suite of New Reporting Standards

.09 Checklist Questionnaire for Financial Statements for Fiscal Years Ending Before December 15, 2021, If the Auditor Does Not Early Adopt the Suite of New Reporting Standards (see paragraph .01):

---

[2] All AS sections can be found in *PCAOB Standards and Related Rules.*

	Yes	No	N/A

Standard Auditor's Report

Title

1. Does the report have a title that includes the word "independent" to clearly indicate that it is the report of an independent auditor?

    [AU-C 700B.23–.24]

Addressee

2. Is the report addressed to those for whom the report is prepared, typically the entity whose financial statements are being audited or those charged with its governance as required by the circumstances of the engagement?

    [AU-C 700B.24 and .A19]

Introductory Paragraph

3. Does the introductory paragraph of the report

    a. identify the entity whose financial statements have been audited?

    b. state that the financial statements have been audited?

    c. identify the title of each statement that the financial statements comprise? (*Note:* the titles and dates of the financial statements that are referred to in the introductory paragraph of the auditor's report should match the titles and dates of the financial statements presented.)

    d. specify the date or period covered by each financial statement that the financial statements comprise?

    [AU-C 700B.25 and .A20–.A23]

Management's Responsibility for the Financial Statements

4. Does the report include a section with the heading "Management's Responsibility for the Financial Statements"?

    [AU-C 700B.26]

5. Does the report describe management's responsibility for the preparation and fair presentation of the financial statements including an explanation that management is responsible for

    a. the preparation and fair presentation of the financial statements in accordance with the applicable financial reporting framework?

    b. the design, implementation, and maintenance of internal control relevant to the preparation and fair presentation of financial statements that are free from material misstatement, whether due to fraud or error?

    [AU-C 700B.27 and .A24]

6. If management includes a separate statement about its responsibilities in a document containing the auditor's report, does the description of management's responsibility included in the auditor's report appropriately NOT refer to a management's statement?

    [AU-C 700B.28 and .A25]

© 2020, Association of International Certified Professional Accountants

	Yes	No	N/A

Auditor's Responsibility

7.   Does the report include a section with the heading "Auditor's Responsibility"?

[AU-C 700B.29]

8.   Does the report state that the responsibility of the auditor is to express an opinion on the financial statements based on the audit?

[AU-C 700B.30 and .A26]

9.   Does the report state that the audit was conducted in accordance with GAAS and identify the United States of America as the country of origin of those standards?

[AU-C 700B.31 and .A27–.A28]

10. Does the report state that GAAS requires the auditor to plan and perform the audit to obtain reasonable assurance about whether the financial statements are free from material misstatement?

AU-C 700B.31 and .A27–.A28]

11. If applicable, when the auditor's report refers to both GAAS and another set of auditing standards, does the auditor's report identify the other set of auditing standards as well as their origin?

[AU-C 700B.43]

12. Does the auditor's report describe an audit by stating that

a.   an audit involves performing procedures to obtain audit evidence about the amounts and disclosures in the financial statements?

b.   procedures selected depend on the auditor's judgment, including the assessment of the risks of material misstatement of the financial statements, whether due to fraud or error?

c.   in making those risk assessments, the auditor considers internal control relevant to the entity's preparation and fair presentation of the financial statements in order to design audit procedures that are appropriate in the circumstances but not for the purpose of expressing an opinion on the effectiveness of the entity's internal control, and accordingly, no such opinion is expressed — *unless the auditor has the responsibility to express and opinion on the effectiveness of internal control in conjunction with the audit of the financial statements?*

d.   an audit also includes evaluating the appropriateness of the accounting policies used and the reasonableness of significant accounting estimates made by management, as well as the overall presentation of the financial statements?

[AU-C 700B.32]

13. Does the auditor's report state whether the auditor believes that the audit evidence the auditor has obtained is sufficient and appropriate to provide a basis for the auditor's opinion?

[AU-C 700B.33]

          © 2020, Association of International Certified Professional Accountants

	Yes	No	N/A

Auditor's Opinion

14. Does the report include a section with the heading "Opinion"?

[AU-C 700B.34]

15. If an unmodified opinion is being expressed on the financial statements, does the auditor's opinion state that the financial statements present fairly, in all material respect, the financial position of the entity as of the balance sheet date, changes in its net assets, and its cash flows for the period then ended, in accordance with the applicable financial reporting framework?

[AU-C 700B.35 and .A29; AAG 14.02]

16. Does the auditor's opinion identify the applicable reporting framework and its origin?

[AU-C 700B.36 and .A31]

Other Reporting Responsibilities

17. If the auditor addresses other reporting responsibilities in addition to the auditor's responsibility under GAAS to report on the financial statements, are these other reporting responsibilities addressed in a separate section titled "Report on Other Legal and Regulatory Requirements" (or otherwise, as appropriate for its contents)?

[AU-C 700B.37 and .A32–.A33]

18. Does the section titled "Report on Other Legal and Regulatory Requirements" (or otherwise as appropriate) follow a section titled "Report on the Financial Statements," that contains the headings, statements, and explanations referred to in questions 4–15?

[AU-C 700B.38 and .A34]

Signature of the Auditor

19. Does the auditor's report include the manual or printer signature of the auditor's firm?

[AU-C 700B.39 and .A35–.A36]

Auditor's Address

20. Does the auditor's report name the city and state where the auditor practices? (*Note:* the city and state may be named in the firm's letterhead on which the report is presented. If the firm's letterhead includes multiple office locations, the auditor's report needs to indicate the city and state where the auditor practices.)

[AU-C 700B.40 and .A37]

Date of the Auditor's Report

21. Is the auditor's report dated no earlier than the date on which the auditor obtained sufficient appropriate audit evidence on which to base the auditor's opinion on the financial statements including evidence that

    a. the audit documentation has been reviewed?

    b. all statements that the financial statements comprise, including the related notes, have been prepared?

    c. management has asserted that they have taken responsibility for those financial statements?

    [AU-C 700B.41 and .A38–.A41]

© 2020, Association of International Certified Professional Accountants

	Yes	No	N/A

Comparative Financial Statements and Comparative Information

22. If comparative financial statements are presented, does the auditor's report refer to each period for which financial statements are presented and on which an audit opinion is expressed?

    [AU-C 700B.45 and .A48–.A49]

23. If a prior year(s) financial statements are summarized and therefore do not include the minimum information required for a complete set of financial statements, does the auditor's report make clear the degree of responsibility that the auditor is assuming in relation to the prior year(s) summarized information and is the introductory paragraph and the opinion paragraph silent as to the summarized information?

    [AU-C 700B.48 and .A54; AAG 14.05]

24. If comparative information is presented but not covered by the auditor's opinion, does the auditor's report clearly indicate the character of the auditor's work and degree of responsibility the auditor is taking for each period presented?

    [AU-C 700B.47 and .A52–.A53]

25. Does the report include appropriate language if different opinions are expressed on comparative financial statements?

    [AU-C 700B.A49]

Emphasis-of-Matter Paragraph or Other-Matter Paragraph

26. Has an emphasis-of-matter paragraph been added to the standard report when the auditor considers it necessary to draw users' attention to a matter appropriately presented or disclosed in the financial statements if, in the auditor's professional judgment, it is of such importance that it is fundamental to users' understanding of the financial statements? (*Note:* Such a paragraph should refer only to information presented or disclosed in the financial statements.)

    [AU-C 706B.06 and .A2–.A3]

27. If an emphasis-of-matter of paragraph has been included in the auditor's report,

    a. is it immediately after the opinion paragraph?

    b. does it have a heading "Emphasis of Matter" or other appropriate heading?

    c. does it include clear reference to the matter being emphasized and to where relevant disclosures that fully describe the matter can be found in the financial statements?

    d. does it indicate that the auditor's opinion is not modified with respect to the matter emphasized?

    [AU-C 706B.07 and .A4–.A5]

 © 2020, Association of International Certified Professional Accountants

	Yes	No	N/A

28. If any of the following events or circumstances has occurred, has an emphasis-of-matter paragraph been added to the auditor's report:

   a. An uncertainty relating to the future outcome of unusually important litigation or regulatory action?

   [AU-C 706B.A2]   ____ ____ ____

   b. A major catastrophe that has had, or continues to have, a significant effect on the entity's financial position?

   [AU-C 706B.A2]   ____ ____ ____

   c. Significant transactions with related parties?

   [AU-C 706B.A2]   ____ ____ ____

   d. Unusually important subsequent events?

   [AU-C 706B.A2]   ____ ____ ____

   e. If another set of financial statements has been prepared by the same entity in accordance with another general purpose framework and the auditor has issued a report on those financial statements and both frameworks are acceptable in the respective circumstances? (*Note:* For example, an entity might prepare one set of financial statements in accordance with accounting principles generally accepted in the United States of America and another set of financial statements in accordance with International Financial Reporting Standards promulgated by the International Accounting Standards Board and engage the auditor to report on both sets of financial statements.)

   [AU-C 706B.A9]   ____ ____ ____

   f. There has been a change in accounting principle or in the method of its application that has a material effect on the financial statements of any period presented? (*Note:* The auditor should evaluate and report on a change in accounting estimate that is inseparable from the effect of a related change in accounting principle like other changes in accounting principle.)

   [AU-C 706B.A14; AU-C 708B.07–.09 and .A4–.A9]   ____ ____ ____

   g. A change in the reporting entity that results in financial statements that, in effect, are those of a different reporting entity? (*Note:* A change in reporting entity that results from a transaction or event, such as the creation, cessation, or complete or partial purchase or disposition of a subsidiary or other business unit, does not require recognition in the auditor's report.)

   [AU-C 706B.A14; AU-C 708B.11 and .A11]   ____ ____ ____

   h. If an entity's financial statements contain an investment accounted for by the equity method and the investee makes a change in accounting principle that is material to the investing entity's financial statements?

   [AU-C 706B.A14; AU-C 708B.12]   ____ ____ ____

© 2020, Association of International Certified Professional Accountants

	Yes	No	N/A

i. When there are adjustments to correct a material misstatement in previously issued financial statements?

[AU-C 708B.13 and .A12–.A13]

j. If the auditor can demonstrate that due to unusual circumstances the financial statements or data would have been misleading if prepared in accordance with GAAP, a paragraph is necessary describing the departure, its approximate effects, if practicable, and the reasons why compliance with the principle would result in a misleading statement?

[AU-C 700B.A15]

29. Has an other-matter paragraph been included in the auditor's report when the auditor considers it necessary to communicate a matter other than those that are presented or disclosed in the financial statements if, in the auditor's professional judgment, it is relevant to users' understanding of the audit, the auditor's responsibilities, or the auditor's report?

[AU-C 706B.08 and .A6–.A11]

30. If an other-matter paragraph has been included in the auditor's report,

a. does it have the heading "Other Matter" or other appropriate heading?

[AU-C 706B.08]

b. if the other-matter paragraph draws users' attention to a matter relevant to their understanding of the audit of the financial statements, is the paragraph included immediately after the opinion paragraph and any emphasis-of-matter paragraph?

[AU-C 706B.08 and .A11]

c. if the other-matter paragraph draws users' attention to a matter relating to other reporting responsibilities addressed in the auditor's report, is the paragraph included in the section subtitled "Report on Other Legal and Regulatory Requirements"?

[AU-C 706B.A11]

d. if the other-matter paragraph is relevant to all the auditor's responsibilities or users' understanding of the auditor's report, the other-matter paragraph is included as a separate section following the "Report on the Financial Statements" and the "Report on Other Legal and Regulatory Requirements"?

[AU-C 706B.A11]

e. does the content reflect clearly that the other matter is not required to be presented and disclosed in the financial statements?

[AU-C 706B.A10]

© 2020, Association of International Certified Professional Accountants

	Yes	No	N/A

f. has the auditor not included information that he or she is prohibited from providing by law, regulation, or other professional standards (for example, ethical standards relating to the confidentiality of information) or information that is required to be provided by management?

[AU-C 706B.A10]

31. If any of the following events or circumstances has occurred, has an other-matter paragraph been added to the auditor's report:

a. The entity presents the supplementary information with the financial statements?

[AU-C 706B.A15; AU-C 725B.09; AU-C 730B.07]

b. A report on compliance is included in the auditor's report on the financial statements?

[AU-C 706B.A15; AU-C 806B.13]

c. The auditor's report contains an alert that restricts the use of the auditor's written communication?

[AU-C 706B.A15; AU-C 905B.07]

d. The auditor identifies a material inconsistency prior to the report release date that requires revision of the other information and management refuses to make the revision?

[AU-C 706B.A15; AU-C 720B.12]

e. In the rare circumstance in which the auditor wants to explain that he or she is unable to withdraw from an engagement even though the possible effect of an inability to obtain sufficient appropriate audit evidence due to a limitation on the scope of the audit imposed by management is pervasive?

[AU-C 706B.A6]

f. If the disclosures described in FASB *Accounting Standards Codification* (ASC) 958-205-50-4 concerning summarized comparative financial information are required but are not included in the financial statements? (**Note:** Such an explanatory paragraph should follow the opinion paragraph and should not be referred to in either the scope or opinion paragraphs.)

[AAG 14.06–.08]

Auditor's Opinion on the Comparative Statement Differs From Previously Expressed

32. If the auditor's opinion on the comparative financial statements for a prior period differs from the opinion the auditor previously expressed, does the report disclose the following matters in an emphasis-of-matter or other-matter paragraph, in accordance with AU-C section 706B, *Emphasis-of-Matter Paragraphs and Other-Matter Paragraphs in the Independent Auditor's Report*:

a. The date of the auditor's previous report?

b. The type of opinion previously expressed?

c. The substantive reason for the different opinion?

d. That the auditor's opinion on the amended financial statements is different from the auditor's previous opinion?

[AU-C 700B.54 and .A56]

© 2020, Association of International Certified Professional Accountants

	Yes	No	N/A

Prior Period Financial Statements Audited by a Predecessor Auditor

33. If the financial statements of the prior period were audited by a predecessor auditor and the predecessor auditor's report on the prior period's financial statements is not reissued, does the auditor's report include an other-matter paragraph with the following information:

    a. The financial statements of the prior period were audited by a predecessor auditor?

    b. The type of opinion expressed by the predecessor auditor and, if the opinion was modified, the reason(s) for the modification?

    c. The nature of an emphasis-of-matter paragraph or other-matter paragraph included in the predecessor auditor's report, if any?

    d. The date of the predecessor auditor's report?

    [AU-C 700B.55]

34. If a predecessor auditor is unable or unwilling to reissue the auditor's report on the prior period financial statements and those statements have been restated, does the auditor's report indicate in an other-matter paragraph that a predecessor auditor reported on the financial statements of the prior period before restatement, which is permitted if the auditor has audited the adjustments to the prior period financial statements?

    [AU-C 700B.A57]

Prior Period Financial Statements Not Audited

35. If the current period financial statements are audited and presented in comparative form with compiled or reviewed financial statements for a prior period and the report on the prior period is not reissued, does the auditor's report include an other-matter paragraph that includes the following information:

    a. The service performed in the prior period?

    b. The date of the report on that service?

    c. A description of any material modifications noted in that report?

    d. A statement that the service was less in scope than an audit and does not provide the basis for the expression of an opinion on the financial statements?

    [AU-C 700B.57 and .A58–.A59]

36. If the prior period financial statements were not audited, reviewed, or compiled, does the auditor's report include an other-matter paragraph that indicates that the auditor has not audited, reviewed, or compiled the prior period financial statements and that the auditor assumes no responsibility for them?

    [AU-C 700B.58 and .A60]

                    © 2020, Association of International Certified Professional Accountants

Considerations of Subsequent Events

37. If a subsequent event disclosed in the financial statements occurs after the original date of the auditor's report but before the issuance of the related financial statements, has the auditor followed one of the following two methods available for dating the report:

    a. Dual dating, in which the independent auditor's responsibility for events occurring subsequent to the original report date is limited to the specific event referred to in an explanatory note in the report (or otherwise disclosed)?   ____ ____ ____

    b. Dating the report as of the later date, in which the independent auditor's responsibility for subsequent events extends to the date of the report?   ____ ____ ____

    [AU-C 560B.13 and .A11–.A14]

38. If after the date of the auditor's report but before the report release date management revises the financial statements, does the auditor's report include an additional date to indicate that the auditor's procedures subsequent to the original date of the report are limited solely to the revision of the financial statements (that is, dual-date the auditor's report for that revision, for example, "February 16, 20CY, except as to Note X, which is as of [the date of completion of audit procedures limited to revision described in note X]")? (*Note:* The auditor may instead date the report as of the later date; however, the auditor's responsibility for subsequent events then extends to the date of the report and, accordingly, the procedures outlined in paragraph .13*a* of AU-C section 560B, *Subsequent Events and Subsequently Discovered Facts*, should be extended to that date.)   ____ ____ ____

    [AU-C 560B.13 and .A11–.A14]

39. If after the report release date management revises the financial statements because of a subsequently discovered fact, and the auditor's opinion on the revised financial statements differs from the opinion the auditor previously expressed, does an emphasis-of-matter or other-matter paragraph include

    a. the date of the auditor's previous report?   ____ ____ ____

    b. the type of opinion previously expressed?   ____ ____ ____

    c. the substantive reasons for the different opinion?   ____ ____ ____

    d. that the auditor's opinion on the revised financial statements is different from the auditor's previous opinion?   ____ ____ ____

    [AU-C 706B.A15; AU-C 560B.16*c*]

Considerations of Going Concern

40. If, after considering identified conditions or events and management's plans, the auditor concludes that there is substantial doubt about the entity's ability to continue as a going concern for a reasonable period of time (defined as the time required by FASB ASC 205-40-50-1, which is one year from the date that the financial statements are issued or, when applicable, from the date that the financial statements are available to be issued), does the auditor's report include an emphasis-of-matters paragraph? (*Note:* If the auditor disclaims an opinion on the financial statements because of uncertainties, the emphasis-of-matter paragraph is not included.)   ____ ____ ____

    [AU-C 706B.A14; AU-C 570B.24]

© 2020, Association of International Certified Professional Accountants

	Yes	No	N/A

41. Is the auditor's conclusion expressed through the use of terms consistent with those included in the applicable financial reporting framework? (*Note:* the auditor should not use conditional language in expressing a conclusion concerning the existence of substantial doubt about the entity's ability to continue as a going concern.)

    [AU-C 570B.25 and .A52–.A53]

Special Considerations of Group Audits

42. In a group audit, if the group engagement partner decides to assume responsibility for the work of a component auditor, is the auditor's report on the group financial statements silent about the component auditor?

    [AU-C 600B.31 and .A62]

43. In a group audit, if the group engagement partner decides not to assume responsibility for the work of a component auditor, does the auditor's report on the group financial statements make reference to the audit of a component auditor?

    [AU-C 600B.08]

44. If the auditor's report on the group financial statements makes reference to the audit of a component auditor,

    a. is the component auditor's report presented together with that of the auditor's report on the group financial statements?

        [AU-C 600B.29]

    b. has the component auditor issued an auditor's report that is not restricted as to use?

        [AU-C 600B.25]

    c. has the group engagement partner determined that the component auditor performed an audit of the financial statements of the component in accordance with the relevant requirements of GAAS?

        [AU-C 600B.25 and .A53]

    d. has the group engagement team read the component's financial statements and the component auditor's report thereon to identify significant findings and issues and, when considered necessary, communicated with the component auditor in this regard?

        [AU-C 600B.27]

    e. has the group engagement team performed the procedures required by AU-C section 600B, *Special Considerations — Audits of Group Financial Statements (Including the Work of Component Auditors),* except for those required by paragraphs .51–.65?

        [AU-C 600B.27]

45. If the auditor's report on the group financial statements makes reference to the audit of a component auditor, does the auditor's report on the group financial statements clearly indicate

    a. that the component was not audited by the auditor of the group financial statements but was audited by the component auditor?

    b. the magnitude of the portion of the financial statements audited by the component auditor?

	Yes	No	N/A

c. the set of auditing standards used by the component auditor and that additional audit procedures were performed by the component auditor to meet the relevant requirements of GAAS, if the component auditor's report on the component's financial statements does not state that the audit of the component's financial statements was performed in accordance with GAAS and the group engagement partner determined that the component auditor performed additional audit procedures in order to meet the relevant requirements of GAAS?

[AU-C 600B.28]

46. If the auditor's report on the group financial statements makes reference to the audit of a component auditor and the component's financial statements are prepared using a different financial reporting framework from that used for the group financial statements,

a. are the measurement, recognition, presentation, and disclosure criteria that are applicable to all material items in the component's financial statements under the financial reporting framework used by the component similar to the criteria that are applicable to all material items in the group's financial statements under the financial reporting framework used by the group?

[AU-C 600B.26]

b. has the group engagement team obtained sufficient appropriate audit evidence to evaluate the appropriateness of the adjustments to convert the component's financial statements to the financial reporting framework used by the group without the need to assume responsibility for, and, thus, be involved in, the work of the component auditor?

[AU-C 600B.26]

c. does the auditor's report on the group financial statements indicate the financial reporting framework used by the component?

[AU-C 600B.28]

d. does the auditor's report on the group financial statements indicate that auditor of the group financial statements is taking responsibility for evaluating the appropriateness of the adjustments to convert the component's financial statements to the financial reporting framework used by the group?

[AU-C 600B.28]

47. In a group audit, if the component auditor's report is modified or the component auditor's report includes an emphasis-of-matter or other-matter paragraph,

a. has the auditor of the group financial statements considered presenting the component auditor's report and making reference to those paragraphs and their disposition?

[AU-C 600B.A61]

b. is the report of the auditor of the group financial statements modified, or does it include an emphasis-of-matter paragraph or an other-matter paragraph, when deemed appropriate?

[AU-C 600B.30]

© 2020, Association of International Certified Professional Accountants

	Yes	No	N/A

Modifications to the Opinion in the Independent Auditor's Report

48. Has the auditor modified the opinion in the auditor's report if the auditor concludes that, either based on the audit evidence obtained, the financial statements as a whole are materially misstated or that the auditor is unable to obtain sufficient appropriate audit evidence to conclude that the financial statements as a whole are free from material misstatement?

    [AU-C 705B.07 and .A2–.A12]

49. Has the auditor expressed a qualified opinion if the auditor, having obtained sufficient appropriate audit evidence, concludes that misstatements, individually or in the aggregate, are material but not pervasive to the financial statements or the auditor is unable to obtain sufficient audit evidence on which to base the opinion, but the auditor concludes that the possible effects on the financial statements of undetected misstatements, if any, could be material but not pervasive?

    [AU-C 705B.08]

50. Has the auditor expressed an adverse opinion if the auditor, having obtained sufficient appropriate audit evidence, concludes that misstatements, individually or in the aggregate, are both material and pervasive to the financial statements?

    [AU-C 705B.09]

51. Has the auditor disclaimed an opinion if the auditor is unable to obtain sufficient appropriate audit evidence on which to base the opinion, and the auditor concludes that the possible effects on the financial statements of undetected misstatements, if any, could be both material and pervasive?

    [AU-C 705B.10 and .A13–.A14]

52. If the auditor is unable to obtain sufficient appropriate audit evidence due to a management-imposed limitation, and the auditor concludes that the possible effects on the financial statements of undetected misstatements, if any, could be both material and pervasive, has the auditor either disclaimed an opinion on the financial statements or, when practicable, withdrawn from the audit?

    [AU-C 705B.13]

53. If the auditor considers it necessary to express an adverse opinion or disclaim an opinion on the financial statements as a whole, has the auditor restrained from providing an unmodified opinion with respect to the same financial reporting framework on a single statement or one or more specific elements, accounts, or items of a financial statement? (*Note:* To include such an unmodified opinion in the same report would contradict the auditor's adverse opinion or disclaimer of opinion on the financial statements as a whole.)

    [AU-C 705B.15 and .A17–.A18]

54. If the auditor is not independent but is required by law or regulation to report on the financial statements, has the auditor disclaimed the opinion with respect to the financial statements and specifically stated that the auditor is not independent?

    [AU-C 705B.16 and .A19]

                    © 2020, Association of International Certified Professional Accountants

	Yes	*No*	*N/A*

55. If the auditor concludes that noncompliance with laws or regulations has a material effect on the financial statements and that the noncompliance has not been adequately reflected in the financial statements, has the auditor issued a qualified or adverse opinion (depending on the materiality effect on the financial statements as a whole)?

    [AU-C 250B.24 and .A27]

56. If the financial statements have been prepared using the going concern basis of accounting but, in the auditor's judgment, management's use of the going concern basis of accounting in the preparation of the financial statements is inappropriate, has the auditor expressed an adverse opinion?

    [AU-C 570B.23]

57. If adequate disclosure about an entity's ability to continue as a going concern for a reasonable period of time is not made in the financial statements, has the auditor expressed a qualified opinion or adverse opinion, as appropriate?

    [AU-C 570B.26]

Basis for Modification Paragraph

58. If the auditor has modified the opinion on the financial statements, has the auditor included a paragraph in the auditor's report

    a. that provides a description of the matter giving rise to the modification?

    b. that immediately precedes the opinion paragraph?

    c. that has a heading that includes "Basis for Qualified Opinion," "Basis for Adverse Opinion" or "Basis for Disclaimer of Opinion"?

    [AU-C 705B.17 and .A20]

59. If there is a material misstatement of the financial statements that relates to specific amounts in the financial statements (including quantitative disclosure), has the auditor included in the basis for modification paragraph a description and quantification of the financial effects of the misstatement, unless impracticable? If it is not practical to quantify the financial effects, has the auditor stated that in the basis for modification paragraph?

    [AU-C 705B.18 and .A21–.A23]

60. If there is a material misstatement of the financial statements that relates to narrative disclosures, has the auditor included an explanation of how the disclosures are misstated in the modification paragraph?

    [AU-C 705B.19]

61. If there is a material misstatement of the financial statements that relates to the omission of information required to be presented or disclosed, has the auditor described in the basis for modification paragraph the nature of the omitted information and include the omitted information (provided that it is practicable to do so and the auditor has obtained sufficient appropriate audit evidence about the omitted information)?

    [AU-C 705B.20 and .A24–.A25]

© 2020, Association of International Certified Professional Accountants

	Yes	No	N/A

62. If the modification results from the inability to obtain sufficient appropriate audit evidence, has the auditor included the reasons for that inability in the basis for modification paragraph?

   [AU-C 705B.21 and .A26]

63. If the auditor has expressed an adverse opinion or disclaimed an opinion on the financial statements, has the auditor described in the basis for modification paragraph any other matters of which the auditor is aware that would have required a modification to the opinion and the effects thereof?

   [AU-C 705B.22 and .A27]

64. If the auditor has expressed an adverse opinion or disclaimed an opinion on the financial statements, has the auditor considered the need to describe in an emphasis-of-matter or other-matter paragraph(s) any other matters of which the auditor is aware that would have resulted in additional communications in the auditor's report on the financial statements that are not modifications of the auditor's opinion?

   [AU-C 705B.22]

65. If the auditor makes reference to the work of an auditor's external specialist in the auditor's report because that reference is relevant to an understanding of a modification to the auditor's opinion, does the auditor's report state that the reference does not reduce the auditor's responsibility for that opinion?

   [AU-C 620B.15 and .A44]

Opinion Paragraph

66. If the auditor has modified the opinion, has the auditor used a heading that includes "Qualified Opinion," "Adverse Opinion," or "Disclaimer of Opinion"?

   [AU-C 705B.23 and .A28]

67. If the auditor has expressed a qualified opinion due to material misstatement in the financial statements, has the auditor stated in the opinion paragraph that, in the auditor's opinion, except for the effects of the matter(s) described in the basis for qualified opinion paragraph, the financial statements are presented fairly, in all material respects, in accordance with the applicable financial reporting framework?

   [AU-C 705B.24 and .A29–.A30]

68. If the auditor expressed a qualified opinion due to an inability to obtain sufficient appropriate audit evidence, has the auditor used the corresponding phrase "except for the possible effects of the matter(s) ..." for the modified opinion?

   [AU-C 705B.24]

69. If the auditor has expressed an adverse opinion, has the auditor stated in the opinion paragraph that, in the auditor's opinion, because of the significance of the matter(s) described in the basis for modification paragraph, the financial statements are not presented fairly in accordance with the applicable financial reporting framework?

   [AU-C 705B.25]

        © 2020, Association of International Certified Professional Accountants

	Yes	No	N/A

70. If the auditor has disclaimed an opinion due to an inability to obtain sufficient appropriate audit evidence, has the auditor stated in the opinion paragraph that

   a. because of the significance of the matter(s) described in the basis for disclaimer of opinion paragraph, the auditor has not been able to obtain sufficient appropriate audit evidence to provide a basis for an audit opinion?

   b. the auditor does not express an opinion on the financial statements?

   [AU-C 705B.26]

71. Is a qualified opinion or disclaimer of opinion expressed when the auditor's understanding of internal control raises doubts about the auditability of an entity's financial statements, such as

   a. concerns about the integrity of an entity's management cause the auditor to conclude that the risk of management misrepresentation in the financial statements is such that an audit cannot be conducted?

   b. concerns about the condition and reliability of an entity's records cause the auditor to conclude that it is unlikely that sufficient appropriate audit evidence will be available to support an unqualified opinion on the financial statements?

   [AU-C 315B.A110]

Description of the Auditor's Responsibility When the Auditor Expresses a Modified Opinion

72. If the auditor expressed a qualified or adverse opinion, has the auditor amended the description of the auditor's responsibility to state that the auditor believes that the audit evidence the auditor obtained is sufficient and appropriate to provide a basis for the auditor's modified opinion?

   [AU-C 705B.27]

73. If the auditor has disclaimed an opinion due to an inability to obtain sufficient appropriate audit evidence, has the auditor amended

   a. the introductory paragraph to state that the auditor was engaged to audit the financial statements?

   b. the description of the auditor's responsibility and scope of services of the audit to state only "Our responsibility is to express an opinion on the financial statements based on conducting the audit in accordance with auditing standards generally accepted in the United States of America. Because of the matter(s) described in the basis for disclaimer of opinion paragraph, however, we were not able to obtain sufficient appropriate audit evidence to provide a basis for an audit opinion"?

   [AU-C 705B.28]

Yes   *No*   *N/A*

Consideration of Other Information Presented In a Document Containing Audited Financial Statements

Other Information

Notes

"Other information" is financial and nonfinancial information (other than the financial statements and the auditor's report thereon) that is included in a document containing audited financial statements and the auditor's report thereon, excluding required supplementary information.
[AU-C 720B.05]

"Documents containing audited financial statements" refer to annual reports (or similar documents) issued to owners (or similar stakeholders) and annual reports of governments and organizations for charitable or philanthropic purposes made available to the public that contain audited financial statements and the auditor's report thereon.
[AU-C 720B.02]

If the auditor is engaged to report on whether supplementary information is fairly stated, in all material respects, in relation to the financial statements as a whole, then the provisions of AU-C section 725B, *Supplementary Information in Relation to the Financial Statements as a Whole*, apply, and auditors should refer to questions 75–81. Otherwise, the auditor is required to apply the provisions of AU-C section 720B, *Other Information in Documents Containing Audited Financial Statements*.

74. If other information is presented in a document containing audited financial statements, has the auditor considered including an other-matter paragraph disclaiming an opinion on the other information?

    [AU-C 720B.A2]

Supplementary Information

Notes

"Supplementary information" is information presented outside the financial statements that is not considered necessary for the financial statements to be fairly presented. Supplementary information includes additional details or explanations of items in or related to the financial statements, consolidating information, historical summaries of items extracted from the financial statements, statistical data, and other material, some of which may be from sources outside the accounting system or outside the entity.
[AU-C 725B.04 and .A7–.A8]

75. If supplementary information accompanies the financial statements and the auditor does not disclaim an opinion on the supplementary information, does the auditor include an emphasis-of-matter paragraph in the auditor's report that

    a. states that the audit is performed for the purpose of forming an opinion on the financial statements as a whole?

    b. specifically identifies the accompanying information?

    c. states that the accompanying information is presented for purposes of additional analysis and is not part of the financial statements?

    d. states that the supplementary information is the responsibility of management and was derived from, and relates directly to, the underlying accounting and other records used to prepare the financial statements?

    e. states that the supplementary information has been subjected to the auditing procedures applied in the audit of the financial statements?

        © 2020, Association of International Certified Professional Accountants

	Yes	*No*	*N/A*

f. states that, in addition to the auditing procedures applied in the audit, the supplementary information has been subjected to certain additional procedures, including comparing and reconciling such information directly to the underlying accounting and other records used to prepare the financial statements or to the financial statements themselves and other additional procedures, in accordance with auditing standards generally accepted in the United States of America?

[AU-C 725B.09]

76. If supplementary information is not presented with the financial statements and the auditor does not disclaim an opinion on the supplementary information, does the auditor include a separate report that includes all the items in question 66 as well as all of the following:

   a. A reference to the report on the financial statements?

   b. The date of that report?

   c. The nature of the opinion expressed on the financial statements?

   d. The report modifications, if any?

   [AU-C 725B.10 and .A3]

77. When reporting on supplementary information in a separate report, did the auditor consider whether to include an alert that restricts the use of the separate report solely to the appropriate specified parties, in accordance with AU-C section 905B, *Alert That Restricts the Use of the Auditor's Written Communication*, to avoid potential misinterpretation or misunderstanding of the supplementary information that is not presented with the financial statements?

[AU-C 725B.A16]

78. If the auditor issues an unmodified opinion on the financial statements and the auditor has concluded that the supplementary information is fairly stated, in all material respects, in relation to the financial statements as a whole, does the emphasis-of-matter paragraph or separate report state that, in the auditor's opinion, the supplementary information is fairly stated, in all material respects, in relation to the financial statements as a whole?

[AU-C 725B.09]

79. If the auditor issues a qualified opinion on the financial statements and the qualification has an effect on the supplementary information, does the emphasis-of-matter paragraph or separate report state that, in the auditor's opinion, except for the effects on the supplementary information of (refer to the paragraph in the auditor's report explaining the qualification), such information is fairly stated, in all material respects, in relation to the financial statements as a whole?

[AU-C 725B.09]

© 2020, Association of International Certified Professional Accountants

	Yes	No	N/A

80. If the auditor issues an adverse opinion or disclaims an opinion on the audited financial statements, and the auditor has been engaged to report on whether supplementary information, does the emphasis-of-matter paragraph or separate report state that because of the significance of the matter disclosed in the auditor's report, it is inappropriate to, and the auditor does not, express an opinion on the supplementary information? (*Note:* When permitted by law or regulation, the auditor may withdraw from the engagement to report on the supplementary information.)

    [AU-C 725B.11]

81. If the auditor concludes, on the basis of the procedures performed, that the supplementary information is materially misstated in relation to the financial statements as a whole and management does not revise that information, does the auditor either (*a*) modify the opinion on the supplementary information and describe the misstatement in the auditor's report or (*b*) if a separate report is being issued on the supplementary information, withhold the auditor's report on the supplementary information?

    [AU-C 725B.13]

II. For Audits Conducted After the Adoption of the Suite of New Reporting Standards

.10 Checklist Questionnaire for Financial Statements for Fiscal Years Ending on or after December 15, 2021, or if the Auditor Early Adopts the Suite of New Reporting Standards (see paragraph .01):

	Yes	No	N/A

Standard Auditor's Report

Title

1. Does the report have a title that clearly indicates that it is the report of an independent auditor?

    [AU-C 700.22 and .A25]

Addressee

2. Is the report addressed to those for whom the report is prepared, normally to those for whom the report is prepared, such as the entity whose financial statements are being audited or those charged with its governance as required by the circumstances of the engagement?

    [AU-C 700.23 and .A26]

Auditor's Opinion

3. Does the first section of the auditor's report include the auditor's opinion and have the heading "Opinion?"

    [AU-C 700.24]

4. Does the "Opinion" section of the report

    a. identify the entity whose financial statements have been audited?

    b. state that the financial statements have been audited?

		Yes	No	N/A

     c.   identify the title of each statement that the financial statements comprise? (*Note:* the titles and dates of the financial statements that are referred to in the "Opinion" paragraph of the auditor's report should match the titles and dates of the financial statements presented.) ____ ____ ____

     d.   refer to the notes? ____ ____ ____

     e.   specify the date or period covered by each financial statement that the financial statements comprise? ____ ____ ____

         [AU-C 700.25 and .A27–.A29]

5.   If an unmodified opinion is being expressed on the financial statements, does the auditor's opinion state that in the auditor's opinion, the accompanying financial statements present fairly, in all material respects, the financial position of the entity as of the date of the statement of financial position, and changes in its net assets, and its cash flows for the period then ended, in accordance with the applicable financial reporting framework? ____ ____ ____

     [AU-C 700.26 and .A17 and .A30–.A33; AAG 14.02]

6.   Does the auditor's opinion identify the applicable reporting framework and its origin? ____ ____ ____

     [AU-C 700.27 and .A34]

Basis for Opinion

7.   Does the auditor's report include a section, directly following the "Opinion" section, with the heading "Basis for Opinion?" ____ ____ ____

     [AU-C 700.28 and .A35]

8.   Does the "Basis for Opinion" section state that the audit was conducted in accordance with GAAS and identify the United States of America as the country of origin of those standards? ____ ____ ____

     [AU-C 700.28 and .A36–.A37]

9.   Does the "Basis for Opinion" section state refer to the section of the auditor's report that describes the auditor's responsibility under GAAS? ____ ____ ____

     [AU-C 700.28]

10. Does the "Basis for Opinion" section include a statement that the auditor is required to be independent of the entity and to meet the auditor's other ethical responsibilities, in accordance with the relevant ethical requirements relating to the audit? ____ ____ ____

     [AU-C 700.28 and .A38–.A39]

11. Does the "Basis for Opinion" section state whether the auditor believes that the audit evidence the auditor has obtained is sufficient and appropriate to provide a basis for the auditor's opinion? ____ ____ ____

     [AU-C 700.28]

Responsibility of Management for the Financial Statements

12. Does the auditor's report include a section with the heading "Responsibilities of Management for the Financial Statements?" ____ ____ ____

     [AU-C 700.31]

© 2020, Association of International Certified Professional Accountants

	Yes	No	N/A

13. Does the "Responsibilities of Management for the Financial Statements" section describe management's responsibility for the following:

    a.   The preparation and fair presentation of the financial statements in accordance with the applicable financial reporting framework?

    b.   The design, implementation, and maintenance of internal control relevant to the preparation and fair presentation of financial statements that are free from material misstatement, whether due to fraud or error?

    [AU-C 700.32 and .A41]

14. If management includes a separate statement about its responsibilities in a document containing the auditor's report, does the description of management's responsibility included in the auditor's report appropriately NOT refer to management's statement?

    [AU-C 700.33 and .A42]

Auditor's Responsibilities for the Audit of the Financial Statements

15. Does the auditor's report include a section with the heading "Auditor's Responsibilities for the Audit of the Financial Statements?"

    [AU-C 700.34]

16. Does the "Auditor's Responsibilities for the Audit of the Financial Statements" section state that the objectives of the auditor are to

    a.   obtain reasonable assurance about whether the financial statements as a whole are free from material misstatement, whether due to fraud or error?

    b.   issue an auditor's report that includes the auditor's opinion?

    [AU-C 700.35 and .A44]

17. Does the "Auditor's Responsibilities for the Audit of the Financial Statements" section state that

    a.   reasonable assurance is a high level of assurance but is not absolute assurance and therefore is not a guarantee that an audit conducted in accordance with GAAS will always detect a material misstatement when it exists?

    b.   the risk of not detecting a material misstatement resulting from fraud is higher than for one resulting from error, as fraud may involve collusion, forgery, intentional omissions, misrepresentations, or the override of internal control?

    c.   misstatements are considered material if there is a substantial likelihood that, individually or in the aggregate, they would influence the judgment made by a reasonable user based on the financial statements? *Note:* When the applicable financial reporting framework defines materiality differently from the definition in AU-C section 320, *Materiality in Planning and Performing an Audit*, the auditor's report may need to reflect the definition or description of materiality from the applicable financial reporting framework.

    [AU-C 700.35 and .A45–.A46]

 © **2020, Association of International Certified Professional Accountants**

	Yes	*No*	*N/A*

18. Does the "Auditor's Responsibilities for the Audit of the Financial Statements" section state that in performing an audit in accordance with GAAS, the auditor's responsibilities are to

   a. exercise professional judgment and maintain professional skepticism throughout the audit?

   b. identify and assess the risks of material misstatement of the financial statements, whether due to fraud or error, and design and perform audit procedures responsive to those risks and that such procedures include examining, on a test basis, evidence regarding the amounts and disclosures in the financial statements?

   c. obtain an understanding of internal control relevant to the audit in order to design audit procedures that are appropriate in the circumstances, but not for the purpose of expressing an opinion on the effectiveness of the entity's internal control, and that accordingly, no such opinion is expressed? *Note:* If the auditor has the responsibility to express an opinion on the effectiveness of internal control in conjunction with the audit of the financial statements, the auditor should omit the phrase "but not for the purpose of expressing an opinion on the effectiveness of the entity's internal control, and that accordingly, no such opinion is expressed."

   d. evaluate the appropriateness of accounting policies used and the reasonableness of significant accounting estimates made by management, as well as evaluate the overall presentation of the financial statements?

   e. conclude whether, in the auditor's judgment, there are conditions or events, considered in the aggregate, that raise substantial doubt about the entity's ability to continue as a going concern for a reasonable period of time?

   [AU-C 700.36]

19. Does the "Auditor's Responsibilities for the Audit of the Financial Statements" section state that the auditor is required to communicate with those charged with governance regarding, among other matters, the planned scope and timing of the audit, significant audit findings, and certain internal control–related matters that the auditor identified during the audit?

   [AU-C 700.37]

Other Information

20. If the entity includes in the basic financial statements information that is not required by the applicable financial reporting framework (whether required by law, regulation, or standards, or by voluntarily choice):

   a. Does the auditor's report cover that information if it cannot be clearly differentiated from the financial statements because of its nature and how it is presented?

   b. Do the financial statements identify the information as "unaudited" or "not covered by the auditor's report" if the auditor's opinion does not cover the information?

   [AU-C 700.61 and .A79–.A80]

© 2020, Association of International Certified Professional Accountants

	Yes	No	N/A

Annual Report

21. If the financial statements and the auditor's report thereon are included in an annual report that also includes other information, whether financial or nonfinancial information, does the auditor's report include a section with the heading "Other Information" [or another title, if appropriate, such as "Information Other Than the Financial Statements and Auditor's Report Thereon"] and completed question 98? *Note:* The auditor's report should not contain an "Other Information" section if the auditor disclaims an opinion on the financial statements.

 [AU-C 700.38; AU-C 705.30; AU-C 720.24]

Other Reporting Responsibilities

22. If the auditor addresses other reporting responsibilities that are in addition to the auditor's responsibility under GAAS, are those other reporting responsibilities addressed in a separate section of the auditor's report with the heading "Report on Other Legal and Regulatory Requirements" (or another heading, as appropriate for the contents of the section)? *Note:* When relevant, this section of the auditor's report may contain subheadings that describe the content of the other reporting responsibility paragraphs.

 [AU-C 700.39 and .A47–.A49]

23. If the auditor's report contains a section with the heading "Report on Other Legal and Regulatory Requirements" (or otherwise as appropriate), are the headings, statements, and explanations referred to in questions 1–19 presented under a heading "Report on the Audit of the Financial Statements?"

 [AU-C 700.40 and .A49]

24. Does the section titled "Report on Other Legal and Regulatory Requirements" (or otherwise as appropriate) follow the section titled "Report on the Audit of the Financial Statements?"

 [AU-C 700.40 and .A49]

Signature of the Auditor

25. Does the auditor's report include the manual or printer signature of the auditor's firm?

 [AU-C 700.41 and .A50–.A52]

26. If required by law or regulation, does the auditor's report also include the personal name and signature of the auditor, in addition to the auditor's firm?

 [AU-C 700.A52]

Auditor's Address

27. Does the auditor's report name the city and state where the audit report is issued? (*Note:* The city and state may be named in the firm's letterhead on which the report is presented. If the firm's letterhead includes multiple office locations, the auditor's report needs to indicate the city and state where the audit report is issued.)

 [AU-C 700.42 and .A53]

    © 2020, Association of International Certified Professional Accountants

	Yes	No	N/A

Date of the Auditor's Report

28. Is the auditor's report dated no earlier than the date on which the auditor obtained sufficient appropriate audit evidence on which to base the auditor's opinion on the financial statements, including evidence that

    a. all statements that the financial statements comprise, including the related notes, have been prepared? ___ ___ ___

    b. management has asserted that they have taken responsibility for those financial statements? ___ ___ ___

    c. The audit documentation has been reviewed, and if an engagement quality review is performed, that review has been completed? ___ ___ ___

    [AU-C 700.43 and .A54]

Audits Conducted in Accordance with Both GAAS and Another Set of Auditing Standards

29. If applicable, when the auditor's report refers to both GAAS and another set of auditing standards, does the auditor's report identify the other set of auditing standards as well as their origin? ___ ___ ___

    [AU-C 700.45]

30. When the auditor's report refers to both GAAS and another set of auditing standards, was the audit conducted in accordance with both sets of standards in their entirety? ___ ___ ___

    [AU-C 700.44 and .A58]

Audits Conducted in Accordance with Both Standards of the PCAOB and GAAS When the Audit is Not Within the Jurisdiction of the PCAOB

31. When the auditor's report refers to both GAAS and the standards of the PCAOB, does the report use the form required by the standards of the PCAOB, amended to state that the audit was also conducted in accordance with GAAS? ___ ___ ___

    [AU-C 700.46 and .A59–.A65]

Comparative Financial Statements and Comparative Information

32. If comparative financial statements are presented, does the auditor's report refer to each period for which financial statements are presented and on which an audit opinion is expressed? ___ ___ ___

    [AU-C 700.47 and .A66–.A67]

33. If comparative financial statements are presented, has the auditor updated the report on the financial statements of one or more prior periods presented on a comparative basis with those of the current period if the auditor is a continuing auditor? ___ ___ ___

    [AU-C 700.48 and .A68]

34. If comparative financial statements are presented, is the auditor's report dated on or after the date on which the auditor has obtained sufficient appropriate audit evidence on which to support the opinion for the most recent audit. ___ ___ ___

    [AU-C 700.48 and .A68–.A69]

© 2020, Association of International Certified Professional Accountants

	Yes	No	N/A

35. If comparative information is presented, such as the situation in which prior year(s) financial statements are summarized and therefore do not include the minimum information required for a complete set of financial statements, does the "Opinion" section of auditor's report exclude mention of the prior year(s) information?

[AU-C 700.50 and .A70–.A71; AAG 14.05]

36. If comparative information is presented but not covered by the auditor's opinion, does the auditor's report clearly indicate the character of the auditor's work, if any, and degree of responsibility the auditor is taking for each period presented? *Note:* Illustration No. 5, "An Auditor's Report on Financial Statements for a Single Year Prepared in Accordance With Accounting Principles Generally Accepted in the United States of America When Comparative Summarized Financial Information Derived From Audited Financial Statements for the Prior Year Is Presented," of AU-C section 700 provides an example of an auditor's report in these circumstances.

[AU-C 700.49 and .A70–.A71; AAG 14.05]

37. If comparative financial statements or comparative information are presented for the prior periods, has the auditor performed the procedures required by paragraphs .52–.55 of AU-C section 700?

[AU-C 700.51–.55 and .A73]

Auditor's Opinion on the Comparative Statement Differs From Previously Expressed

38. If the auditor's opinion on the comparative financial statements for a prior period differs from the opinion the auditor previously expressed, does the report disclose the following matters in an emphasis-of-matter or other-matter paragraph, in accordance with AU-C section 706, *Emphasis-of-Matter Paragraphs and Other-Matter Paragraphs in the Independent Auditor's Report:*

   a. The date of the auditor's previous report?

   b. The type of opinion previously expressed?

   c. The substantive reason for the different opinion?

   d. That the auditor's opinion on the amended financial statements is different from the auditor's previous opinion?

   [AU-C 700.56 and .A74, AU-C 706.A19; AU-C 703.92]

Prior Period Financial Statements Audited by a Predecessor Auditor

39. If the financial statements of the prior period were audited by a predecessor auditor and the predecessor auditor's report on the prior period's financial statements is not reissued, does the auditor's report include an other-matter paragraph with the following information:

   a. The financial statements of the prior period were audited by a predecessor auditor?

   b. The type of opinion expressed by the predecessor auditor and, if the opinion was modified, the reason(s) for the modification?

   c. The nature of an emphasis-of-matter paragraph or other-matter paragraph included in the predecessor auditor's report, if any?

	Yes	No	N/A

    d.   The date of the predecessor auditor's report? ____ ____ ____

           [AU-C 700.57; AU-C 703.93]

40.   If the prior period(s) financial statements are restated and the predecessor auditor agrees to issue a new auditor's report on the restated financial statements of the prior period, does the auditor express an opinion only on the current period? ____ ____ ____

           [AU-C 700.58]

41.   If prior period(s) financial statements are restated and a predecessor auditor is unable or unwilling to reissue the auditor's report on the restated financial statements, does the auditor's report include an other-matter paragraph indicating that the predecessor auditor reported on the financial statements of the prior period before restatement, if desired? ____ ____ ____

           [AU-C 700.A75]

42.   If the auditor is engaged to audit the adjustments to prior period financial statements that have been restated and the auditor obtains sufficient appropriate audit evidence to be satisfied about the appropriateness of the restatement, does the auditor's report include an other-matter paragraph that describes that the auditor

    a.   audited the adjustments described in Note X that were applied to restate the 20X1 financial statements? ____ ____ ____

    b.   expresses an opinion regarding whether the adjustments are appropriate and have been properly applied? ____ ____ ____

    c.   was not engaged to audit, review, or apply any procedures to the 20X1 financial statements of the entity other than with respect to the adjustments? ____ ____ ____

    d.   does not express an opinion or any other form of assurance on the 20X1 financial statements as a whole? ____ ____ ____

           [AU-C 700.A75]

Prior Period Financial Statements Not Audited

43.   If the current period financial statements are audited and presented in comparative form with financial statements for a prior period for which a compilation or review was performed, and the report on the prior period is not reissued, does the auditor's report of the current period include an other-matter paragraph that includes the following information with respect to the prior period:

    a.   The service performed in the prior period? ____ ____ ____

    b.   The date of the report on that service? ____ ____ ____

    c.   A description of any material modifications noted in that report? ____ ____ ____

    d.   If the service for the prior period was a review engagement, a statement that the service was substantially less in scope than an audit and does not provide the basis for the expression of an opinion on the financial statements as a whole? ____ ____ ____

    e.   If the service for the prior period was a compilation engagement, a statement that no opinion or other form of assurance is expressed on the financial statements? ____ ____ ____

           [AU-C 700.59 and .A76–.A77; AU-C 703.95]

© 2020, Association of International Certified Professional Accountants

	Yes	*No*	*N/A*

44. If the prior period financial statements were not audited, reviewed, or compiled, are the financial statements clearly marked to indicate their status, and does the auditor's report include an other-matter paragraph indicating that the auditor has not audited, reviewed, or compiled the prior period financial statements and that the auditor assumes no responsibility for them?

    [AU-C 700.60 and .A78; AU-C 703.96]

Key Audit Matters

45. If the auditor is engaged to communicate key audit matters in connection with an audit of a complete set of general purpose financial statements, does the auditor's report include a separate section under the heading "Key Audit Matters?" *Note:* The auditor is prohibited from communicating key audit matters when the auditor expresses an adverse opinion or disclaims an opinion on the financial statements, unless such reporting is required by law or regulation.

    [AU-C 701.04 and .10; AU-C 705.30]

46. Does the introductory language in the "Key Audit Matters" section of the auditor's report state the following:

    a. Key audit matters are those matters that were communicated with those charged with governance and, in the auditor's professional judgment, were of most significance in the audit of the financial statements of the current period.

    b. These matters were addressed in the context of the audit of the financial statements as a whole, and in forming the auditor's opinion thereon, and the auditor does not provide a separate opinion on these matters.

       [AU-C 701.10 and .A31–.A33]

47. Does the description of each key audit matter in the "Key Audit Matters" section of the auditor's report have an appropriate subheading and include a reference to the related disclosures, if any?

    [AU-C 701.10, .12, and .A34–.A41]

48. Does the description of each key audit matter address the following:

    a. Why the matter was considered to be one of most significance in the audit and therefore determined to be a key audit matter?

    b. How the matter was addressed in the audit?

       [AU-C 701.12 and .A42–.A50]

49. Does the "Key Audit Matters" section of the auditor's report include a reference to the following:

    a. The "Basis for Qualified Opinion" section of the auditor's report if matters give rise to a qualified opinion?

    b. The "Going Concern" section of the auditor's report if substantial doubt exists about an entity's ability to continue as a going concern for a reasonable period of time?

       [AU-C 701.14 and .A5]

          © 2020, Association of International Certified Professional Accountants

	Yes	*No*	*N/A*

50. If the auditor determines, depending on the facts and circumstances of the entity and the audit, that there are no key audit matters to communicate or that the only key audit matters communicated are those matters addressed by question 49, is a statement to this effect included in the "Key Audit Matters" section of the auditor's report?

    [AU-C 700.15 and .A56.–A57]

Emphasis-of-Matter Paragraph or Other-Matter Paragraph

51. Has an emphasis-of-matter paragraph been added to the standard report when the auditor considers it necessary to draw users' attention to a matter (or matters) presented or disclosed in the financial statements that are of such importance that it is (or they are) fundamental to users' understanding of the financial statements? (*Note:* Such a paragraph is not appropriate if the auditor would be required to modify the opinion in accordance with AU-C section 705, *Modifications to the Opinion in the Independent Auditor's Report*, as a result of the matter or if the matter has been determined to be a key audit matter to be communicated in the auditor's report in accordance with AU-C section 701, *Communicating Key Audit Matters in the Independent Auditor's Report*.)

    [AU-C 706.01, .06, and .08]

52. If an emphasis-of-matter of paragraph has been included in the auditor's report, does the auditor's report

    a. include a separate section with the heading "Emphasis of Matter" or another appropriate heading?

    b. include clear reference to the matter being emphasized and to where relevant disclosures that fully describe the matter can be found in the financial statements?

    c. indicate that the auditor's opinion is not modified with respect to the matter emphasized?

       [AU-C 706.09 and .A6–.A8]

53. If any of the following events or circumstances has occurred, has an emphasis-of-matter paragraph been added to the auditor's report:

    a. An uncertainty relating to the future outcome of unusually important litigation or regulatory action?

       [AU-C 706.A4]

    b. A significant subsequent event that occurs between the date of the financial statements and the date of the auditor's report?

       [AU-C 706.A4]

    c. A major catastrophe that has had, or continues to have, a significant effect on the entity's financial position or change in net assets?

       [AU-C 706.A4]

    d. Significant transactions with related parties?

       [AU-C 706.A4]

	Yes	No	N/A

e.   Another set of financial statements has been prepared by the reporting entity in accordance with another general purpose framework and the auditor has issued a report on those financial statements and both frameworks are acceptable in the respective circumstances? (*Note:* For example, an entity might prepare one set of financial statements in accordance with accounting principles generally accepted in the United States of America and another set of financial statements in accordance with International Financial Reporting Standards promulgated by the International Accounting Standards Board and engage the auditor to report on both sets of financial statements.)

[AU-C 706.A12]

f.   There has been a change in accounting principle or in the method of its application that has a material effect on the financial statements of any period presented? (*Note:* The auditor should evaluate and report on a change in accounting estimate that is inseparable from the effect of a related change in accounting principle like other changes in accounting principle.)

[AU-C 706.A18; AU-C 708.07–.10 and .A4–.A10]

g.   A change in the reporting entity that results in financial statements that, in effect, are those of a different reporting entity? (*Note:* A change in reporting entity that results from a transaction or event, such as the creation, cessation, or complete or partial purchase or disposition of a subsidiary or other business unit, does not require recognition in the auditor's report.)

[AU-C 706.A18; AU-C 708.11 and .A11]

h.   If an entity's financial statements contain an investment accounted for by the equity method and the investee makes a change in accounting principle that is material to the investing entity's financial statements?

[AU-C 706.A18; AU-C 708.12]

i.   When there are adjustments to correct a material misstatement in previously issued financial statements?

[AU-C 706.A18; AU-C 708.13 and .A12–.A13]

j.   When the financial statements are prepared using a special purpose framework? *Note:* If the special purpose financial statements are prepared in accordance with a regulatory basis of accounting, and the special purpose financial statements together with the auditor's report are intended for general use, the auditor should not include the emphasis-of-matter paragraph.]

[AU-C 706.A18; AU-C 800.22]

          © 2020, Association of International Certified Professional Accountants

	Yes	No	N/A

k. The entity presents supplementary information with the financial statements and the auditor does not prepare a separate report on the supplementary information? *Note:* The separate section should use the heading "Supplementary Information," or other appropriate heading. *Note:* If the auditor's report on the financial statements contains an adverse opinion or a disclaimer of opinion, the auditor is precluded from expressing an opinion on the supplementary information.

   [AU-C 725.09]

54. Has an other-matter paragraph been included in the auditor's report when the auditor considers it necessary to draw users' attention to any matters other than those that are presented or disclosed in the financial statements that are relevant to users' understanding of the audit, the auditor's responsibilities, or the auditor's report? (*Note:* Such a paragraph is not appropriate if the matter has been determined to be a key audit matter to be communicated in the auditor's report, in accordance with AU-C section 701.)

   [AU-C 706.01, .06, and .10]

55. If an other-matter paragraph has been included in the auditor's report

a. is the other matter included in a separate section with the heading "Other Matter" or other appropriate heading?

   [AU-C 706.11 and .A13–.A15]

b. does the content reflect clearly that the other matter is not required to be presented and disclosed in the financial statements?

   [AU-C 706.A13]

c. does the content not include information that the auditor is prohibited from providing by law, regulation, or other professional standards (for example, ethical standards relating to the confidentiality of information) or information that is required to be provided by management?

   [AU-C 706.A13]

56. If any of the following events or circumstances has occurred, has an other-matter paragraph been added to the auditor's report:

a. A subsequently discovered fact becomes known to the auditor after the report release date, management revises the financial statements, and the auditor's opinion on the revised financial statements differs from the opinion the auditor previously expressed?

   [AU-C 706.A19; AU-C 560.16]

b. A report on compliance is included in the auditor's report on the financial statements?

   [AU-C 706.A19; AU-C 806.13]

	Yes	No	N/A

c.   Financial statements are prepared in accordance with a contractual basis of accounting, a regulatory basis of accounting, or an other basis of accounting when required pursuant to paragraph .06 of AU-C section 905, *Alert That Restricts the Use of the Auditor's Written Communication*, and the auditor restricts the use of the auditor's report?

[AU-C 706.A19; AU-C 905.06]

d.   The auditor restricts the use of the auditor's report to certain users of the financial statements?

[AU-C 706.A19; AU-C 905.06]

e.   In the rare circumstance in which the auditor is unable to withdraw from an engagement and wants to explain that fact, such as when the auditor unable to obtain sufficient appropriate audit evidence due to a limitation on the scope of the audit imposed by management that is pervasive?

[AU-C 720.A50–.A51; AU-C 706.A9]

f.   If the disclosures described in FASB ASC 958-205-50-4 concerning summarized comparative financial information are required but are not included in the financial statements?

[AAG 14.06–.08]

Considerations of Subsequent Events

57.   If a subsequent event disclosed in the financial statements occurs after the original date of the auditor's report but before the issuance of the related financial statements, has the auditor followed one of the following two methods available for dating the report:

a.   Dual dating, in which the independent auditor's responsibility for events occurring subsequent to the original report date is limited to the specific event referred to in an explanatory note in the report (or otherwise disclosed)?

b.   Dating the report as of the later date, in which the independent auditor's responsibility for subsequent events extends to the date of the report?

[AU-C 560.13 and .A11–.A16]

58.   If after the date of the auditor's report but before the report release date management revises the financial statements, does the auditor's report include an additional date to indicate that the auditor's procedures subsequent to the original date of the report are limited solely to the revision of the financial statements (that is, dual-date the auditor's report for that revision, for example, "February 16, 20CY, except as to Note X, which is as of [the date of completion of audit procedures limited to revision described in note X]")? (*Note:* The auditor may instead date the report as of the later date; however, the auditor's responsibility for subsequent events then extends to the date of the report and, accordingly, the procedures outlined in paragraph .13a of AU-C section 560, *Subsequent Events and Subsequently Discovered Facts*, should be extended to that date.)

[AU-C 560.13 and .A11–.A16]

	Yes	No	N/A

59. If after the report release date management revises the financial statements because of a subsequently discovered fact, and the auditor's opinion on the revised financial statements differs from the opinion the auditor previously expressed, does an emphasis-of-matter or other-matter paragraph include

    a. the date of the auditor's previous report? ___ ___ ___

    b. the type of opinion previously expressed? ___ ___ ___

    c. the substantive reasons for the different opinion? ___ ___ ___

    d. that the auditor's opinion on the revised financial statements is different from the auditor's previous opinion? ___ ___ ___

    [AU-C 706.A18–.A19; AU-C 560.16*c*]

Considerations of Going Concern

60. If the financial statements have been prepared using the going concern basis of accounting but, in the auditor's judgment, management's use of the going concern basis of accounting in the preparation of the financial statements is inappropriate, does the auditor express an adverse opinion? ___ ___ ___

    [AU-C 570.23, .A48–.A50, and .A54]

61. If, after considering identified conditions or events and management's plans, the auditor concludes that there is substantial doubt about the entity's ability to continue as a going concern for a reasonable period of time (defined as the time required by FASB ASC 205-40-50-1, which is one year from the date that the financial statements are issued or, when applicable, from the date that the financial statements are available to be issued), does the auditor's report include a "Key Audit Matters" section that refers to the "Substantial Doubt About the Entity's Ability to Continue as a Going Concern" section of the auditor's report? *Note:* Those sections are not required if the auditor concludes that substantial doubt has been alleviated by management's plans. ___ ___ ___

    [AU-C 701.14 and .A5; AU-C 570.24]

62. Does the "Substantial Doubt About the Entity's Ability to Continue as a Going Concern" section

    a. draw attention to the note in the financial statements that discloses (1) the conditions or events identified and management's plans that deal with these conditions or events and (2) that these conditions or events indicate that substantial doubt exists about the entity's ability to continue as a going concern for a reasonable period of time? ___ ___ ___

    b. state that the auditor's opinion is not modified with respect to the matter? ___ ___ ___

    [AU-C 570.24 and .A53–.A58]

63. Is the auditor's conclusion expressed through the use of terms consistent with those included in the applicable financial reporting framework? (*Note:* the auditor should not use conditional language in expressing a conclusion concerning the existence of substantial doubt about the entity's ability to continue as a going concern.) ___ ___ ___

    [AU-C 570.25 and .A52–.A53]

© 2020, Association of International Certified Professional Accountants

	Yes	No	N/A

64. If adequate disclosure about an entity's ability to continue as a going concern for a reasonable period of time is not made in the financial statements:

    a. Did the auditor express a qualified opinion or adverse opinion, as appropriate? _____ _____ _____

    b. Does the "Basis for Qualified (Adverse) Opinion" section of the auditor's report, state that either (1) substantial doubt exists about the entity's ability to continue as a going concern and that the financial statements do not adequately disclose this matter or (2) substantial doubt about the entity's ability to continue as a going concern has been alleviated by management's plans but the financial statements do not adequately disclose this matter, as appropriate? _____ _____ _____

    [AU-C 570.26; AU-C 705]

Special Considerations of Group Audits

65. In a group audit, if the group engagement partner decides to assume responsibility for the work of a component auditor, is the auditor's report on the group financial statements silent about the component auditor? _____ _____ _____

    [AU-C 600.31 and .A62]

66. In a group audit, if the group engagement partner decides not to assume responsibility for the work of a component auditor, does the auditor's report on the group financial statements make reference to the audit of a component auditor? _____ _____ _____

    [AU-C 600.08]

67. If the auditor's report on the group financial statements makes reference to the audit of a component auditor,

    a. is the component auditor's report presented together with that of the auditor's report on the group financial statements? _____ _____ _____

    [AU-C 600.29]

    b. has the component auditor issued an auditor's report that is not restricted as to use? _____ _____ _____

    [AU-C 600.25]

    c. has the group engagement partner determined that the component auditor performed an audit of the financial statements of the component in accordance with the relevant requirements of GAAS? _____ _____ _____

    [AU-C 600.25 and .A53]

    d. has the group engagement team read the component's financial statements and the component auditor's report thereon to identify significant findings and issues and, when considered necessary, communicated with the component auditor in this regard? _____ _____ _____

    [AU-C 600.27]

    e. has the group engagement team performed the procedures required by AU-C section 600, *Special Considerations — Audits of Group Financial Statements (Including the Work of Component Auditors)*, except for those required by paragraphs .51–.65? _____ _____ _____

    [AU-C 600.27]

          © 2020, Association of International Certified Professional Accountants

	Yes	No	N/A

68. If the auditor's report on the group financial statements makes reference to the audit of a component auditor, does the auditor's report on the group financial statements clearly indicate

   a.   that the component was not audited by the auditor of the group financial statements but was audited by the component auditor?   ____   ____   ____

   b.   the magnitude of the portion of the financial statements audited by the component auditor?   ____   ____   ____

   [AU-C 600.28]

69. If the auditor's report on the group financial statements makes reference to the audit of a component auditor and the component auditor's report on the component's financial statements does not state that the audit of the component's financial statements was performed in accordance with GAAS or the standards of the PCAOB, did the group engagement partner determine that the component auditor performed additional audit procedures in order to meet the relevant requirements of GAAS and does the auditor's report on the group financial statements clearly indicate

   a.   the set of auditing standards used by the component auditor?   ____   ____   ____

   b.   that additional audit procedures were performed by the component auditor to meet the relevant requirements of GAAS?   ____   ____   ____

   [AU-C 600.28]

70. If the auditor's report on the group financial statements makes reference to the audit of a component auditor and the component's financial statements are prepared using a different financial reporting framework from that used for the group financial statements,

   a.   are the measurement, recognition, presentation, and disclosure criteria that are applicable to all material items in the component's financial statements under the financial reporting framework used by the component similar to the criteria that are applicable to all material items in the group's financial statements under the financial reporting framework used by the group?   ____   ____   ____

   [AU-C 600.26]

   b.   has the group engagement team obtained sufficient appropriate audit evidence to evaluate the appropriateness of the adjustments to convert the component's financial statements to the financial reporting framework used by the group without the need to assume responsibility for, and, thus, be involved in, the work of the component auditor?   ____   ____   ____

   [AU-C 600.26]

   c.   does the auditor's report on the group financial statements indicate the financial reporting framework used by the component?   ____   ____   ____

   [AU-C 600.28]

© 2020, Association of International Certified Professional Accountants

	Yes	*No*	*N/A*

    d.   does the auditor's report on the group financial statements indicate that auditor of the group financial statements is taking responsibility for evaluating the appropriateness of the adjustments to convert the component's financial statements to the financial reporting framework used by the group?

    [AU-C 600.28]

71.   In a group audit, if the component auditor's report is modified or the component auditor's report includes an emphasis-of-matter or other-matter paragraph,

    a.   has the auditor of the group financial statements considered presenting the component auditor's report and making reference to those paragraphs and their disposition?

    [AU-C 600.30 and .A61]

    b.   is the report of the auditor of the group financial statements modified, or does it include an emphasis-of-matter paragraph or an other-matter paragraph, when deemed appropriate?

    [AU-C 600.30]

Modifications to the Opinion in the Independent Auditor's Report

72.   Has the auditor modified the opinion in the auditor's report if the auditor concludes that, either based on the audit evidence obtained, the financial statements as a whole are materially misstated or that the auditor is unable to obtain sufficient appropriate audit evidence to conclude that the financial statements as a whole are free from material misstatement?

    [AU-C 705.07 and .A2–.A13]

73.   Has the auditor expressed a qualified opinion if either (1) the auditor, having obtained sufficient appropriate audit evidence, concludes that misstatements, individually or in the aggregate, are material but not pervasive to the financial statements or (2) the auditor is unable to obtain sufficient audit evidence on which to base the opinion, but the auditor concludes that the possible effects on the financial statements of undetected misstatements, if any, could be material but not pervasive?

    [AU-C 705.08; AU-C 705.13]

74.   Has the auditor expressed an adverse opinion if the auditor, having obtained sufficient appropriate audit evidence, concludes that misstatements, individually or in the aggregate, are both material and pervasive to the financial statements?

    [AU-C 705.09]

75.   Has the auditor disclaimed an opinion if the auditor is unable to obtain sufficient appropriate audit evidence on which to base the opinion, and the auditor concludes that the possible effects on the financial statements of undetected misstatements, if any, could be both material and pervasive?

    [AU-C 705.10 and .A14–.A15]

              © **2020, Association of International Certified Professional Accountants**

	Yes	*No*	*N/A*

76. If the auditor is unable to obtain sufficient appropriate audit evidence due to a management-imposed limitation, and the auditor concludes that the possible effects on the financial statements of undetected misstatements, if any, could be both material and pervasive, has the auditor either disclaimed an opinion on the financial statements or, when practicable, withdrawn from the audit?

    [AU-C 705.13 and .A16–.A17]

77. If the auditor considers it necessary to express an adverse opinion or disclaim an opinion on the financial statements as a whole, has the auditor restrained from providing an unmodified opinion with respect to the same financial reporting framework on a single statement or one or more specific elements, accounts, or items of a financial statement? (*Note:* To include such an unmodified opinion in the same report would contradict the auditor's adverse opinion or disclaimer of opinion on the financial statements as a whole.)

    [AU-C 705.15 and .A18–.A19]

78. If the auditor is not independent but is required by law or regulation to report on the financial statements, has the auditor disclaimed an opinion with respect to the financial statements and specifically stated that the auditor is not independent?

    [AU-C 705.16 and .A20]

79. If the auditor concludes that noncompliance with laws or regulations has a material effect on the financial statements and that the noncompliance has not been adequately reflected in the financial statements, has the auditor issued a qualified or adverse opinion (depending on the materiality effect on the financial statements as a whole)?

    [AU-C 250.24 and .A27]

80. Is a qualified opinion, an adverse opinion, or a disclaimer of opinion expressed when the auditor's understanding of internal control raises doubts about the auditability of an entity's financial statements, such as

    a. concerns about the integrity of an entity's management cause the auditor to conclude that the risk of management misrepresentation in the financial statements is such that an audit cannot be conducted?

    b. concerns about the condition and reliability of an entity's records cause the auditor to conclude that it is unlikely that sufficient appropriate audit evidence will be available to support an unqualified opinion on the financial statements?

    [AU-C 315.A128–.A129]

Opinion

81. If the auditor has modified the opinion on the financial statements, does the auditor's report use a heading that includes "Qualified Opinion," "Adverse Opinion" or "Disclaimer of Opinion" instead of using "Opinion?"

    [AU-C 705.17 and .A21–.A23]

© 2020, Association of International Certified Professional Accountants

		Yes	No	N/A

82. If the auditor expresses a qualified opinion due to a material misstatement in the financial statements, does the auditor's opinion state, "except for the effects of the matters described in the 'Basis for Qualified Opinion' section of the auditor's report, the accompanying financial statements present fairly, in all material respects, […] in accordance with [the applicable financial reporting framework]?

   [AU-C 705.18. and .A24–.A25]

83. If the auditor expresses a qualified opinion due to the inability to obtain sufficient appropriate audit evidence, does the auditor's opinion state, "except for the possible effects of the matters described in the 'Basis for Qualified Opinion' section of the auditor's report, the accompanying financial statements present fairly, in all material respects, […] in accordance with [the applicable financial reporting framework]?

   [AU-C 705.18 and .A24–.A25]

84. If the auditor expresses an adverse opinion, does the auditor's opinion state, "because of the significance of the matters described in the 'Basis for Adverse Opinion' section of the auditor's report, the accompanying financial statements do not present fairly […] in accordance with [the applicable financial reporting framework]?

   [AU-C 705.19]

85. If the auditor disclaims an opinion due to an inability to obtain sufficient appropriate audit evidence, does the auditor's report state that;

   a.   "the auditor does not express an opinion on the accompanying financial statements?"

   b.   "because of the significance of the matters described in the "Basis for Disclaimer of Opinion" section of the auditor's report, the auditor has not been able to obtain sufficient appropriate audit evidence to provide a basis for an audit opinion on the financial statements?"

   c.   "the auditor was engaged to audit the financial statements," rather than "the financial statements have been audited?"

   [AU-C 705.20]

Basis for Modification Paragraph

86. If the auditor has modified the opinion on the financial statements, does the auditor's report use a heading that includes "Basis for Qualified Opinion," "Basis for Adverse Opinion" or "Basis for Disclaimer of Opinion" instead of using "Basis for Opinion?"

   [AU-C 705.21]

87. Is a description of the matter giving rise to the modification included in the "Basis for … Opinion" section referred to in question 86?

   [AU-C 705.21]

88. If there is a material misstatement of the financial statements that relates to specific amounts in the financial statements (including quantitative disclosures):

   a.   Does the "Basis for … Opinion" section include a description and quantification of the financial effects of the misstatement, unless impracticable?

© 2020, Association of International Certified Professional Accountants

	Yes	No	N/A

b.   If it is not practicable to quantify the financial effects, does the auditor's report state that fact in the "Basis for . . . Opinion" section?

[AU-C 705.22 and .A27–.A28]

89.   If there is a material misstatement of the financial statements that relates to qualitative disclosures, does the auditor's report include an explanation of how the disclosures are misstated in the "Basis for . . . Opinion" section?

[AU-C 705.23]

90.   If there is a material misstatement of the financial statements that relates to the omission of information required to be presented or disclosed, does the auditor's report include in the "Basis for . . . .Opinion" section:

a.   A description of the nature of the omitted information?

b.   the omitted information (provided that it is practicable to do so and the auditor has obtained sufficient appropriate audit evidence about the omitted information)?

[AU-C 705.24 and .A29–.A30]

91.   If the modification results from the inability to obtain sufficient appropriate audit evidence, does the auditor's report include the reasons for that inability in the "Basis for. ... Opinion" section?

[AU-C 705.25 and .A31]

92.   When the auditor expresses a qualified or an adverse opinion, does the auditor's report state that "the audit evidence obtained is sufficient and appropriate to provide a basis for the auditor's qualified opinion" or that "the audit evidence obtained is sufficient and appropriate to provide a basis for the auditor's adverse opinion" rather than the similar language in the standard report?

[AU-C 705.26]

93.   If the auditor disclaims an opinion on the financial statements, does the auditor eliminate from the "Basis for ... Opinion" section of the auditor's report the following elements:

a.   a reference to the section of the auditor's report where the auditor's responsibilities are described?

b.   a statement about whether the audit evidence obtained is sufficient and appropriate to provide a basis for the auditor's opinion?

[AU-C 705.27]

94.   Even if the auditor has expressed an adverse opinion or disclaimed an opinion on the financial statements, has the auditor described in the "Basis for. ... Opinion" section the reasons for any other matters of which the auditor is aware that would have required a modification to the opinion and the effects thereof?

[AU-C 705.28 and .A32–.A33]

95.   If the auditor has expressed an adverse opinion or disclaimed an opinion on the financial statements, has the auditor considered the need to describe in an emphasis-of-matter or other-matter paragraph(s) any other matters of which the auditor is aware but that would not require a modification of the auditor's opinion?

[AU-C 705.A33]

© 2020, Association of International Certified Professional Accountants

	Yes	No	N/A

96.   If the auditor makes reference to the work of an auditor's external specialist in the auditor's report because that reference is relevant to an understanding of a modification to the auditor's opinion, does the auditor's report state that the reference does not reduce the auditor's responsibility for that opinion?

[AU-C 620.15 and .A44]

Description of the Auditor's Responsibility for the Audit of the Financial Statements When the Auditor Disclaims an Opinion

97.   If the auditor has disclaimed an opinion due to an inability to obtain sufficient appropriate audit evidence, has the auditor amended the "Auditor's Responsibilities for the Audit of the Financial Statements" to state only that:

    a.   the auditor's responsibility is to conduct an audit of the entity's financial statements in accordance with auditing standards generally accepted in the United States of America and to issue an auditor's report?"

    b.   however, because of the matters described in the "Basis for Disclaimer of Opinion" section of the auditor's report, the auditor was not able to obtain sufficient appropriate audit evidence to provide a basis for an audit opinion on the financial statements?"

    c.   the auditor is required to be independent and to meet other ethical responsibilities, in accordance with the relevant ethical requirements relating to the audit, required by paragraph .28*c* of section 700

    [AU-C 705.29]

Consideration of Other Information Presented In a Document Containing Audited Financial Statements

Notes

"Other information" is financial and nonfinancial information (other than the financial statements and the auditor's report thereon) that is included in an entity's annual report, excluding supplemental information addressed by AU-C section 725, *Supplementary Information in Relation to the Financial Statements as a Whole,* or required supplementary information addressed by AU-C section 730, *Required Supplementary Information.*

[AU-C 720.09 and 720.12]

"Annual report" is a document, or combination of documents, typically prepared on an annual basis by management or those charged with governance in accordance with law, regulation, or custom, the purpose of which is to provide owners (or similar stakeholders) with information on the entity's operations and the entity's financial results and financial position as set out in the financial statements. An annual report contains, accompanies, or incorporates by reference the financial statements and the auditor's report thereon and usually includes information about the entity's developments, its future outlook and risks and uncertainties, a statement by the entity's governing body, and reports covering governance matters. Annual reports include annual reports of governments and organizations for charitable or philanthropic purposes that are available to the public.

[AU-C 720.12]

	Yes	No	N/A

98. Does the "Other Information" section in the auditor's report on the financial statements should include:

    a.   a statement that management is responsible for the other information?

    b.   an identification of other information and a statement that the other information does not include the financial statements and the auditor's report thereon?

    c.   a statement that the auditor's opinion on the financial statements does not cover the other information and that the auditor does not express an opinion or any form of assurance thereon?

    d.   a statement that, in connection with the audit of the financial statements, the auditor is responsible to read the other information and consider whether a material inconsistency exists between the other information and the financial statements or the other information otherwise appears to be materially misstated?

    e.   a statement that, if, based on the work performed, the auditor concludes that an uncorrected material misstatement of the other information exists, the auditor is required to describe it in the auditor's report?

    f.   a statement that the auditor has concluded that an uncorrected material misstatement of the other information exists and a description of it, if the auditor has concluded that an uncorrected material misstatement of the other information exists?

    [AU-C 720.24 and .A56]

99. In rare circumstances, if the refusal to correct a material misstatement of the other information casts such doubt on the integrity of management and those charged with governance that it calls into question the reliability of audit evidence in general, has the auditor considered a disclaimer of opinion on the financial statements?

    [AU-C 720.A49]

Consideration of Supplementary Information Presented In a Document Containing Audited Financial Statements

---

Notes

"Supplementary information" is information presented outside the basic financial statements, excluding required supplementary information that is not considered necessary for the financial statements to be fairly presented in accordance with the applicable financial reporting framework. Such information may be presented in a document containing the audited financial statements or separate from the financial statements. Supplementary information does not include required supplementary information, which is information that a designated accounting standard setter requires to accompany an entity's basic financial statements. See AU-C section 730.

[AU-C 725.04, and .A1, .A7–.A8]

© 2020, Association of International Certified Professional Accountants

	Yes	No	N/A

100. If supplementary information accompanies the financial statements and the auditor does not disclaim an opinion on the supplementary information, does the auditor include an emphasis-of-matter paragraph in the auditor's report that

    a. states that the audit is performed for the purpose of forming an opinion on the financial statements as a whole? _____ _____ _____

    b. specifically identifies the accompanying information? _____ _____ _____

    c. states that the supplementary information is presented for purposes of additional analysis and is not a required part of the financial statements? _____ _____ _____

    d. states that the supplementary information is the responsibility of management and was derived from, and relates directly to, the underlying accounting and other records used to prepare the financial statements? _____ _____ _____

    e. states that the supplementary information has been subjected to the auditing procedures applied in the audit of the financial statements and certain additional procedures, including comparing and reconciling such information directly to the underlying accounting and other records used to prepare the financial statements or to the financial statements themselves and other additional procedures, in accordance with auditing standards generally accepted in the United States of America? _____ _____ _____

    [AU-C 725.09 and .A17]

101. If supplementary information is not presented with the financial statements and the auditor does not disclaim an opinion on the supplementary information, does the auditor include a separate report that includes all the items in question 100 as well as all of the following:

    a. A reference to the report on the financial statements? _____ _____ _____

    b. The date of that report? _____ _____ _____

    c. The nature of the opinion expressed on the financial statements? _____ _____ _____

    d. The report modifications, if any? _____ _____ _____

    [AU-C 725.10 and .A16]

102. When reporting on supplementary information in a separate report, did the auditor consider whether to include an alert that restricts the use of the separate report solely to the appropriate specified parties, in accordance with AU-C section 905, to avoid potential misinterpretation or misunderstanding of the supplementary information that is not presented with the financial statements? _____ _____ _____

    [AU-C 725.A16]

103. If the auditor issues an unmodified opinion on the financial statements and the auditor has concluded that the supplementary information is fairly stated, in all material respects, in relation to the financial statements as a whole, does the "Supplementary Information" section of the auditor's report or the separate report state that, in the auditor's opinion, the supplementary information is fairly stated, in all material respects, in relation to the financial statements as a whole? _____ _____ _____

    [AU-C 725.09]

 © 2020, Association of International Certified Professional Accountants

	Yes	No	N/A

104. If the auditor issues a qualified opinion on the financial statements and the qualification has an effect on the supplementary information, does the "Supplementary Information" section of the auditor's report or the separate report state that, in the auditor's opinion, except for the effects on the supplementary information of (refer to the paragraph in the auditor's report explaining the qualification), such information is fairly stated, in all material respects, in relation to the financial statements as a whole?

 [AU-C 725.09]

105. If the auditor issues an adverse opinion or disclaims an opinion on the audited financial statements, and the auditor has been engaged to report on supplementary information, does the "Supplementary Information" section of the auditor's report or the separate report state that because of the significance of the matter disclosed in the auditor's report, it is inappropriate to, and the auditor does not, express an opinion on the supplementary information? (*Note:* When permitted by law or regulation, the auditor may withdraw from the engagement to report on the supplementary information.)

 [AU-C 725.11]

106. If the auditor concludes, on the basis of the procedures performed, that the supplementary information is materially misstated in relation to the financial statements as a whole and management does not revise that information, does the auditor either (*a*) modify the opinion on the supplementary information and describe the misstatement in the auditor's report or (*b*) if a separate report is being issued on the supplementary information, withhold the auditor's report on the supplementary information?

 [AU-C 725.13]

© 2020, Association of International Certified Professional Accountants

Part 4

Auditors' Reports Checklist for Audits Performed in Accordance With *Government Auditing Standards* and the Uniform Guidance

---

This checklist is based on *Government Auditing Standards (2018 Revision)* and the Uniform Guidance. The paragraph references are to the 2019 edition of the AICPA Audit Guide Government Auditing Standards *and Single Audits*.

Note: The Auditing Standards Board (ASB) has issued a suite of standards that affect the auditor's report. At its April 20, 2020 meeting, the ASB voted to ballot Statement on Auditing Standards (SAS) No. 141, *Amendment to the Effective Dates of SAS Nos. 134–140*, that defers the effective dates of SAS Nos. 134–140. The current effective dates of these SASs are for audits of financial statements for periods ending on or after December 15, 2020. The deferred effective date is for audits of financial statements for periods ending on or after December 15, 2021. Earlier implementation is permitted after the original effective date.

Any new requirements and guidance resulting from these auditing standards will be reflected in a future edition of this checklist. The Governmental Audit Quality Center website will be updated as illustrative auditor's reports become available and can be accessed at https://www.aicpa.org/interestareas/governmentalauditquality/resources/illustrativeauditorsreports.html.

.01 *Government Auditing Standards* (also referred to as the Yellow Book), issued by the Comptroller General of the United States of the U.S. Government Accountability Office (GAO), applies to the audits pertaining to governmental entities, programs, activities, and functions and to government assistance administered by contractors, not-for-profit entities (NFPs), and other nongovernmental entities, when the use of *Government Auditing Standards* is required or is voluntarily adopted. The Single Audit Act Amendments of 1996 (the Single Audit Act) and the Uniform Guidance require a single or program-specific audit for entities that expend $750,000 or more of federal awards in a fiscal year. The Single Audit Act requires single audits and program-specific audits of federal awards to be performed in accordance with *Government Auditing Standards*. Similarly, other laws, regulations, or authoritative sources may require the use of *Government Auditing Standards*.

.02 This checklist has two parts. Section I is for auditor's reports on financial statement audits performed in accordance with *Government Auditing Standards*. (This checklist does not address the performance auditing or attestation standards of *Government Auditing Standards*. It also does not address types of financial audits other than financial statement audits.) Section II contains the additional requirements for auditor's reports on audits performed in accordance with the Single Audit Act and the Uniform Guidance.[1] For audits performed in accordance with the Uniform Guidance, both sections I and II of this checklist should be completed. Illustrative auditor's reports on financial statement audits performed in accordance with *Government Auditing Standards* and illustrative auditor's reports and an illustrative schedule of findings and questioned costs for Uniform Guidance audits are in the AICPA Audit Guide Government Auditing Standards *and Single Audits*.

---

[1] AU-C section 935, *Compliance Audits*, is applicable when an auditor is engaged or required by law or regulation to perform a compliance audit in accordance with (*a*) GAAS, (*b*) standards for financial audits under GAS, and (*c*) a governmental audit requirement that requires an auditor to express an opinion on compliance. This guidance addresses the application of GAAS to a compliance audit and does not apply to the financial statement audit that may be performed in conjunction with a compliance audit.

All AU-C sections can be found in AICPA *Professional Standards*.

© 2020, Association of International Certified Professional Accountants

.03 The OMB issues an annual compliance supplement for conducting single audits. The 2020 *Compliance Supplement* was not available at the time this checklist was being updated. The 2017 and later supplements are available on the OMB's website at https://www.whitehouse.gov/omb/management/office-federal-financial-management/.

.04 The PCAOB establishes standards for audits of *issuers*, as that term is defined by the Sarbanes-Oxley Act of 2002, or whose audit is prescribed by the rules of the SEC. Other entities are referred to as *nonissuers*. Because NFPs are nonissuers, this checklist does not address PCAOB standards. Although uncommon, an auditor may be engaged to follow PCAOB auditing standards in the audit of an NFP. When the audit is not under the jurisdiction of the PCAOB but the entity desires, or is required by an agency, by a regulator, or by contractual agreement, to obtain an audit conducted under PCAOB standards, the AICPA Code of Professional Conduct requires the auditor to also conduct the audit in accordance with GAAS. Statement on Auditing Standards (SAS) No. 131, *Amendment to Statement on Auditing Standards No. 122 Section 700*, Forming an Opinion and Reporting on Financial Statements (AU-C sec. 700B), clarifies the format of the auditor's report that should be issued when the auditor conducts an audit in accordance the standards of the PCAOB, but the audit is not under the jurisdiction of the PCAOB.

.05 If the auditor is engaged to audit and report on the effectiveness of an NFP's internal control over financial reporting in accordance with PCAOB auditing standards, the auditor should modify this checklist considering the guidance in PCAOB standards and *Government Auditing Standards*.

.06 In addition to *Government Auditing Standards*, this checklist is based on the guidance found in the Uniform Guidance. The Uniform Guidance is found in the Code of Federal Regulations and may be updated at any time. To access the current Uniform Guidance regulations go to the electronic Code of Federal Regulations at Part 200 of the eCFR.

.07 Explanation of References:

UG = Title 2 U.S. CFR Part 200, *Uniform Administrative Requirements, Cost Principles, and Audit Requirements for Federal Awards*

GAS = GAO 2018 revision to *Government Auditing Standards*

AU-C = Reference to section number in AICPA *Professional Standards*

AAG = AICPA Audit Guide Government Auditing Standards *and Single Audits*

© 2020, Association of International Certified Professional Accountants

I. Reports on Audits Performed in Accordance With GAS[2]

	Yes	No	N/A

1. In a financial statement audit performed in accordance with GAS, has the auditor issued the following reports:[3]

   a. A report on the entity's financial statements that provides an opinion or disclaimer of opinion on the financial statements?

   [AAG 4.02 and .46]

   b. A report on internal control over financial reporting and on compliance and other matters based on an audit of financial statements performed in accordance with GAS?

   [GAS 6.39; AAG 4.05]

Report on the Financial Statements

2. In addition to the elements listed in the checklist for the auditor's report on the financial statements at part 3, "Auditors' Reports Checklist," does the auditor's report on the financial statements contain

   a. a statement that the audit was conducted in accordance with the standards applicable to financial audits contained in GAS, issued by the Comptroller General of the United States?[4]

   [GAS 6.36; AAG 4.04, .06, and .49–.50]

   b. a statement or a reference to a separate report on internal control over financial reporting and on compliance with certain provisions of laws, regulations, contracts, and grant agreements and other matters prepared in accordance with GAS,[5] which includes

   i. a description of the scope of testing of internal control over financial reporting and compliance and whether the tests performed provided sufficient, appropriate evidence to support opinions on the effectiveness of internal control and on compliance?[6]

---

[2] GAS incorporates by reference AICPA Statements on Auditing Standards. Therefore, auditors performing financial statement audits in accordance with GAS should comply with GAAS, the requirements and guidance found in chapters 1–5 of GAS, and the additional requirements for financial audits found in chapter 6, "Standards for Financial Audits," of GAS. (GAS 6.01; AAG 4.01).

[3] There is no provision in GAS that requires the auditee to prepare financial statements in accordance with accounting principles generally accepted in the United States of America (GAAP). If an auditee prepares financial statements in conformity with a special-purpose framework (sometimes referred to as an other comprehensive basis of accounting), the auditor follows the guidance in AU-C section 800, *Special Considerations — Audits of Financial Statements Prepared in Accordance With Special Purpose Frameworks*. That guidance notes that when forming an opinion and reporting on special purpose financial statements, the auditor should apply the requirements in AU-C section 700B, *Forming an Opinion and Reporting on Financial Statements*.

[4] An auditor in a government entity may be required to perform a nonaudit service that could impair the auditor's independence with respect to a required audit. If the auditor cannot, as a consequence of constitutional or statutory requirements over which the auditor has no control, implement safeguards to reduce the resulting threat to an acceptable level, or decline to perform or terminate a nonaudit service that is incompatible with audit responsibilities, the auditor should disclose the nature of the threat that could not be eliminated or reduced to an acceptable level and modify the generally accepted government auditing standards (GAGAS) compliance statement accordingly. See paragraphs 2.17–.23 of GAS for the discussion of modifications to the GAGAS compliance statement (GAS 3.84; AAG 2.33).

[5] If the reporting on internal control over financial reporting and on compliance and other matters is included in the report on the financial statements, the reference to the separate report is not required. The AICPA Audit Guide Government Auditing Standards *and Single Audits* recommends separate reporting (AAG 4.12 and 4.52).

[6] If auditors issue an opinion on internal control over financial reporting the opinion would satisfy the GAS requirement for reporting on internal control. The guide recommends that the reference to the separate report be modified to indicate that there is such an opinion. (AAG 4.09, 4.54*f*, and footnote 30 of chapter 4).

© 2020, Association of International Certified Professional Accountants

	Yes	*No*	*N/A*

ii.   if a separate report is issued, a reference to the separate report in the report on the financial statements and a statement that the separate report is an integral part of an audit performed in accordance with GAS in considering [*name of entity's*] internal control over financial reporting and compliance?

[GAS 6.42–.43; AAG 4.08, .48*v-w*, and .52]

3.   If the auditor does not follow an applicable standard of GAS, does the scope section of the report disclose the standard that was not followed, the reasons therefore, and how not following the standard affected, or could have affected, the results of the audit?

[GAS 2.19 and .21; AAG 4.50]

4.   If a material organizational unit is not required to have an audit in accordance with GAS, has the scope paragraph of the report on the financial statements been modified to indicate the portion of the entity that was not audited in accordance with GAS?

[AAG 4.79–.80]

Report on Internal Control Over Financial Reporting and on Compliance and Other Matters Based on an Audit Performed in Accordance With GAS

5.   Does the auditor's report on internal control over financial reporting and on compliance and other matters conform to the standard report language illustrated in the AICPA Audit Guide Government Auditing Standards *and Single Audits*, including the appropriate headings?

[Examples 4-3–4-9 in the chapter 4 appendix]

6.   Does the auditor's report on internal control over financial reporting and on compliance and other matters contain

a.   a title that contains the word *independent*?

b.   an appropriate addressee?

c.   a statement that the auditor has audited the financial statements of the entity and a reference to the auditor's report on the financial statements (including the period covered by the report and the date of the auditor's report), and a description of the nature of any opinion modification (for example, a qualified opinion, a modification as to consistency because of a change in accounting principle, or a reference to the report of component auditors)?

d.   a statement that the audit was conducted in accordance with GAAS and an identification of the United States of America as the country of origin of those standards and with the standards applicable to financial audits contained in GAS, issued by the Comptroller General of the United States?

e.   a section with the heading "Internal Control Over Financial Reporting"?

f.   a statement that in planning and performing the audit of the financial statements, the auditor considered the auditee's internal control over financial reporting (internal control) as a basis for designing audit procedures that are appropriate in the circumstances for the purpose of expressing an opinion on the financial statements, but not for the purpose of expressing an opinion on the effectiveness of the auditee's internal control over financial reporting; and accordingly, does not express an opinion on the effectiveness of the auditee's internal control?[7]

---

[7] See footnote 6.

     © 2020, Association of International Certified Professional Accountants

	Yes	No	N/A

g.   the definitions of *deficiency in internal control, significant deficiency,* and *material weakness*?[8]

h.   the following statements if no significant deficiencies or material weaknesses have been identified:

     i.   A statement that the auditor's consideration of internal control was for the limited purpose described in question *6f* and was not designed to identify all deficiencies in internal control that might be material weaknesses or significant deficiencies?

     ii.   A statement that, given the limitations, during the audit the auditor did not identify any deficiencies in internal control that the auditor considers to be material weaknesses, however material weaknesses may exist that have not been identified?[9]

i.   the following four statements if significant deficiencies have been identified:

     i.   A statement that the auditor's consideration of internal control was for the limited purpose described in question *6f* and was not designed to identify all deficiencies in internal control that might be material weaknesses or significant deficiencies, and therefore material weaknesses or significant deficiencies may exist that have not been identified?

     ii.   A statement that given these limitations, during the audit the auditor did not identify any deficiencies in internal control that the auditor considers to be material weaknesses?

     iii.   A statement that the auditor did identify certain deficiencies in internal control over financial reporting that the auditor considers to be significant deficiencies?

     iv.   A description of the significant deficiencies identified, including the title of the schedule in which the findings are reported? (*Note:* Alternatively, the findings may be described in the report.)[10]

j.   The following three statements if material weaknesses have been identified:

     i.   a statement that the auditor's consideration of internal control was for the limited purpose described in question *6f* and was not designed to identify all deficiencies in internal control that might be material weaknesses or significant deficiencies and therefore, material weaknesses or significant deficiencies may exist that have not been identified?

     ii.   a statement that the auditor did identify certain deficiencies in internal control over financial reporting that the auditor considers to be material weaknesses?

---

[8] Although the definitions of *deficiency in internal control* and *material weakness* are required in all reporting, the definition of *significant deficiency* is not required to be included in the report when no significant deficiencies have been identified. However, for clarity purposes, the definition of *significant deficiency* is included in the example reports found in the AICPA Audit Guide Government Auditing Standards *and Single Audits*, regardless of the type of deficiencies identified. The definitions included in the example reports are based on the definitions found in AU-C section 265, *Communicating Internal Control Related Matters Identified in an Audit*.

[9] This wording is based on the requirement in paragraph .16 of AU-C section 265 which states that the auditor should not issue a written communication stating that no significant deficiencies were identified during the audit.

[10] For an audit in accordance with the Uniform Guidance, all findings, including those required to be reported under both GAAS and GAS, should be included in the schedule of findings and questioned costs. Therefore, for such audits, this report should refer to the schedule of findings and questioned costs. See the questions about that schedule in section II of this checklist (AAG 13.37).

© 2020, Association of International Certified Professional Accountants

	Yes	No	N/A

iii. a description of the material weaknesses, including the title of the schedule in which the findings are reported? (*Note:* Alternatively, the findings may be described in this report.) ____ ____ ____

k. the following four statements if material weaknesses and significant deficiencies have been identified:

 i. A statement that the auditor's consideration of internal control was for the limited purpose described in question *6f* and was not designed to identify all deficiencies in internal control that might be material weaknesses or significant deficiencies, and therefore material weaknesses or significant deficiencies may exist that have not been identified? ____ ____ ____

 ii. A statement that the auditor did identify certain deficiencies in internal control over financial reporting that the auditor considers to be material weaknesses and significant deficiencies? ____ ____ ____

 iii. A description of the material weaknesses, including the title of the schedule in which the findings are reported? (*Note:* Alternatively, the findings may be described in the report.)[11] ____ ____ ____

 iv. A description of the significant deficiencies identified, including the title of the schedule in which the findings are reported? (*Note:* Alternatively, the findings may be described in the report.)[12] ____ ____ ____

l. a section with the heading "Compliance and Other Matters"? ____ ____ ____

m. a statement that as part of obtaining reasonable assurance about whether the auditee's financial statements are free from material misstatement, the auditor performed tests of the auditee's compliance with certain provisions of laws, regulations, contracts, and grant agreements, noncompliance with which could have a direct and material effect on the financial statements; however, providing an opinion on compliance with those provisions was not an objective of the audit and that, accordingly, the auditor does not express such an opinion? ____ ____ ____

n. if no instances of noncompliance or other matters have been identified that are required to be reported, a statement that the results of tests disclosed no instances of noncompliance or other matters that are required to be reported under GAS? ____ ____ ____

o. if instances of noncompliance or other matters have been identified that are required to be reported, a statement that the results of the tests disclosed instances of noncompliance or other matters that are required to be reported under GAS, including the title of the schedule in which the findings are reported? (*Note:* Alternatively, the findings may be described in this report.)[13] ____ ____ ____

p. a section with the heading "Purpose of this Report"? ____ ____ ____

---

[11] See footnote 10.

[12] See footnote 10.

[13] Paragraph 4.07 of the guide discusses noncompliance and other matters — certain fraud — for which GAS requires reporting in the auditor's report. Paragraph 4.63 of the guide discusses where to report findings of fraud in the report on internal control over financial reporting and on compliance and other matters.

   © 2020, Association of International Certified Professional Accountants

	Yes	No	N/A

q. a statement that "The purpose of the report is solely to describe the scope of the testing of internal control and compliance and the result of that testing, and not to provide an opinion on the effectiveness of the entity's internal control or on compliance. This report is an integral part of an audit performed in accordance with GAS in considering the entity's internal control and compliance. Accordingly, this communication is not suitable for any other purpose"?

r. the manual or printed signature of the auditor's firm?

s. the auditor's city and state?

t. the date of the auditor's report?

[AAG 4.54]

7. Does the report carry the same date as the report on the financial statements?

[AAG 4.54, footnote 37 in chapter 4]

8. Although not required, if material weaknesses, significant deficiencies, or instances of noncompliance or other matters are identified, has the auditor considered a section following the "Compliance and Other Matters" section with the heading "[*Name of auditee*]'s Response to Findings" that includes the following:

a. a statement that the auditee's response to the findings identified in the audit are described in the accompanying [*include the title of the schedule in which the findings are reported or, if findings and responses are included in the body of the report, "previously"*]?

b. a statement that "[*Name of Entity*]'s response was not subjected to the auditing procedures applied in the audit of the financial statements and, accordingly, the auditor does not express an opinion on it"?

[AAG 4.55]

9. If a material organizational unit is not required to have an audit in accordance with GAS, has the scope paragraph of the report been modified to indicate the portion of the entity that was not audited in accordance with GAS?

[AAG 4.78–.79]

10. If certain pertinent information is prohibited from public disclosure or is excluded from a report because of its confidential or sensitive nature (as it may be by federal, state, or local laws or regulations), does the auditor's report state that certain information has been omitted and the circumstances that makes the omission necessary? (If the report refers to the omitted information, the reference may be general and not specific. If the omitted information is not necessary to meet the audit objectives, the report need not refer to its omission.)

[GAS 6.63; AAG 4.72]

11. Does the language in the compliance and other matters section of the report refer to findings that do or may include fraud? (It is recommended that this language appear in all reports, even if the report does not describe or refer to findings of fraud or even if the only findings of fraud are described in or referred to from the section on internal control over financial reporting.)

[AAG 4.63]

© 2020, Association of International Certified Professional Accountants

	Yes	No	N/A

12. Are findings that relate to both internal control over financial reporting and to compliance reported in or referred to from both the section of the report concerning internal control over financial reporting and in the section of the report concerning compliance and other matters? (The reporting in one section of the report or schedule may be in summary form with a reference to a detailed reporting in the other section.)

    [AAG 4.62]

13. Are findings of fraud reported in or referred to from the compliance and other matters section of the report, unless the primary nature of the finding is a significant deficiency or material weakness in internal control? (Auditors should present or refer to findings of fraud that represent significant deficiencies or material weaknesses in internal control in the internal control section.)

    [AAG 4.63]

14. Do the reported findings include any significant deficiencies or material weaknesses in internal control over financial reporting that the auditor identified based on the audit work performed? Does the report on internal control or compliance include the relevant information about noncompliance and fraud when auditors, based on sufficient, appropriate evidence, identify or suspect (*a*) noncompliance with provisions of laws, regulations, contracts, or grant agreements that has a material effect on the financial statements or other financial data significant to the audit objectives, or (*b*) fraud that is material, either quantitatively or qualitatively to the financial statements or other financial data significant to the audit objectives?[14]

    [GAS 6.40–.41; AAG 4.07]

15. Does each finding include a reference number that meets the numbering format required for Federal Audit Clearinghouse (FAC) submissions (for example, findings identified and reported in the audit of fiscal year 20X1 could be assigned reference numbers 20X1-001, 20X1-002, and so forth)?

    [AAG 4.66]

16. Do the reported findings place the findings in proper perspective (or context) by describing the nature and extent of the issues reported and the work performed that resulted in the finding? (The identified instances should be related to the population or the number of cases examined and be quantified in terms of dollar value or other measures, if appropriate.)

    [GAS 6.51; AAG 4.65]

    a. When reporting instances of fraud or noncompliance with provisions of laws, regulations, contracts, or grant agreements, are the results projected? (If the results cannot be projected, auditors should limit their conclusions appropriately.)

    [GAS 6.51; AAG 4.65]

17. To the extent possible and to achieve audit objectives, do the reported findings present criteria, condition, cause, and effect or potential effect?

    [GAS 4.17–.19, .25–.30, .50, and .52; AAG 4.61]

---

[14] GAS requires this reporting even if the auditor disclaims an opinion on the financial statements (GAS 6.39–.40).

     © 2020, Association of International Certified Professional Accountants

	Yes	No	N/A

18. Does the auditor's report include the views of responsible officials concerning the findings, conclusions, and recommendations, as well as planned corrective actions?[15,16]

   [GAS 6.57; AAG 4.67–.70]

   a. If the auditor receives, in writing, the views of responsible officials, is a copy of the officials' written comments or a summary of the comments received included in the auditor's report?[17]

   b. Does the auditor's report include an evaluation of the comments, as appropriate?

   c. If the entity's views conflict with the report's findings, conclusions, or recommendations, and are not, in the auditor's opinion, valid, does the report state reasons for disagreeing with the comments or planned corrective actions?

   [GAS 6.59; AAG 4.69]

   d. If the audited entity refused to provide comments or is unable to provide comments within a reasonable period of time, does the auditor's report state that the audited entity did not provide comments?

   [GAS 6.60; AAG 4.70]

Other Reporting and Communication Considerations

19. Does a written communication, such as a management letter, communicate identified or suspected noncompliance with provisions of laws, regulations, contracts, or grant agreements and instances of fraud that have an effect on the financial statements that is less than material but warrants the attention of those charged with governance?[18]

   [GAS 6.44 and .48; AAG 4.76 and table 4-1]

   a. Are the discussions worded so that readers can distinguish those matters that are required to be included by GAAS or GAS from matters that are recommendations for improvements or information about "best practices"?

   [AAG 4.77]

   b. Does the communication not include personal identification or other potentially sensitive matters?

   [AAG 4.72–.75]

---

[15] In an audit in accordance with the Uniform Guidance, the auditee is required to prepare and submit a corrective action plan (AAG footnote 41 in chapter 4).

[16] The auditor is required to extend a reasonable effort to obtain and report auditee views and planned corrective actions. GAS does not require the auditor to delay or withhold the release of the report if the auditee does not provide the necessary information on a timely basis. If, however, the auditee refuses to provide comments or is unable to provide the necessary information by the time the report is released, the report should indicate that the audited entity did not provide comments (GAS 6.60; AAG 4.70).

[17] When the responsible officials provide oral comments only, auditors should prepare a summary of the oral comments, provide a copy of the summary to the responsible officials to verify that the comments are accurately represented, and include the summary in their report (GAS 6.58; AAG 4.68).

[18] There is no option for the auditor to report in a management letter, or other written communication, findings that GAS or the Uniform Guidance requires to be reported in the auditor's report or Schedule of Findings and Questioned Costs. (AAG footnote 39 of chapter 4, AAG footnote 28 of chapter 13)

© 2020, Association of International Certified Professional Accountants

	Yes	No	N/A

20. Has the auditor used professional judgment to determine how to communicate to audited entity officials noncompliance with provisions of laws, regulations, contracts, or grant agreements that does not warrant the attention of those charged with governance?[19]

    [GAS 6.44 and .48; AAG 4.76 and table 4-1]

21. Has the auditor reported identified or suspected noncompliance with provisions of laws, regulations, contracts, and grant agreements and instances of fraud directly to parties outside of the audited entity in the situations required by GAS, even if the auditor has resigned or been dismissed from the audit?

    [GAS 6.53–.54 and .56; AAG 4.43–.44]

22. If the auditor is

    a. a government auditor, does the auditor distribute the auditor's reports to those charged with governance, to the appropriate officials of the audited entity, and to the appropriate oversight bodies or organizations requiring or arranging for the audits. As appropriate, auditors should also distribute copies of the reports to other officials who have legal oversight authority or who may be responsible for acting on audit findings and recommendations and to others authorized to receive such reports? (*Note:* Any limitation on report distribution (for example reports containing confidential or sensitive information) should be documented.)

    b. a nongovernment auditor, has the auditor clarified report distribution responsibilities with the engaging party, and if the contracting firm is responsible for the distribution, has an agreement been reached with the party contracting for the audit about which officials or organizations will receive the report and the steps being taken to make the report available to the public? (*Note:* Any limitation on report distribution [for example reports containing confidential or sensitive information] should be documented.)

    [GAS 6.70; AAG 4.71]

23. If the auditor is reporting on restated financial statements, did the auditor's report include an emphasis-of-matter paragraph in the reissued or updated auditor's report that includes

    a. the date of the auditor's previous report?

    b. the type of opinion previously expressed?

    c. the substantive reasons for the different opinion?

    d. that the auditor's opinion on the revised financial statements is different from the auditor's previous opinion?

    [AU-C 560.16c]

    e. notifications to prevent reliance on the auditor's original report by persons or entities that are currently relying or who will rely on the audited financial statements, if considered necessary?[20]

    [AU-C 560.A24]

---

[19] GAAS require that whenever the auditor has identified a fraud or has obtained information that indicates a fraud may exist, the auditor should communicate these matters on a timely basis to the appropriate level of management, even if the matter might be considered inconsequential (AU-C 240.39; AAG 4.29).

[20] Paragraphs .A23–.A26 of AU-C section 560, *Subsequent Events and Subsequently Discovered Facts*, describe considerations relating to an auditor's actions to seek to prevent reliance on the auditor's report.

 © 2020, Association of International Certified Professional Accountants

	Yes	No	N/A

f.   a statement that the previously issued financial statements have been restated for the correction of a material misstatement in the respective period?

[AU-C 708.14]

g.   a reference to the entity's disclosure of the correction of the material misstatement?

[AU-C 708.14]

24.   If financial statement disclosures relating to the restatement to correct a material misstatement in previously issued financial statements are not adequate, does the emphasis-of-matter paragraph address the inadequacy of disclosure, describe the nature of the omitted information; and, if it is practicable to do so, include the omitted information, provided that the auditor has obtained sufficient appropriate audit evidence about the omitted information?

[AU-C 705B.20; AU-C 708.15]

25.   If management does not take the necessary steps to ensure that anyone in receipt of the audited financial statements is informed that the financial statements need to be revised, has the auditor notified management and those charged with governance that the auditor will seek to prevent future reliance on the auditor's report, and if, despite such notification, management or those charged with governance has not taken the necessary steps, has the auditor taken appropriate action to seek to prevent reliance on the auditor's report?

[AU-C 560.15–.18]

26.   When planning the audit, has the auditor asked management of the audited entity to identify previous audits, attestation engagements, and other studies that directly relate to the objectives of the audit, including whether related recommendations have been implemented?

[GAS 6.11; AAG 3.12]

27.   When performing the audit, has the auditor evaluated whether the audited entity has taken appropriate corrective action to address findings and recommendations from previous engagements that could have a significant effect on the financial statements or other financial data significant to the audit objectives?

a.   Has the auditor used this information in assessing risk and determining the nature, timing, and extent of current audit work, and determining the extent to which testing the implementation of the corrective actions is applicable to the current audit objectives?

[GAS 6.11; AAG 3.12]

28.   Has the auditor inquired of management of the audited entity whether any investigations or legal proceedings have been initiated or are in process with respect to the period under audit and evaluated the effect of initiated or in-process investigations or legal proceedings on the current audit?

[GAS 6.12; AAG 3.13]

© 2020, Association of International Certified Professional Accountants

II. Reports on Audits Performed in Accordance With the Uniform Guidance

The 2020 Office of Management and Budget (OMB) *Compliance Supplement* was not available at the time this checklist was being updated. Auditors are cautioned to carefully evaluate the revisions made to the 2020 *Compliance Supplement*. Auditors may refer to the GAQC website for updates and more information regarding the 2020 *Compliance Supplement*.

		Yes	*No*	*N/A*

1. In an audit performed in accordance with the Uniform Guidance, has the auditor issued the following reports in addition to those in section I of this checklist:[21]

    a. A report on the supplementary schedule of expenditures of federal awards that provides an opinion (or disclaimer of opinion) as to whether the schedule is presented fairly in all material respects in relation to the financial statements as a whole?   ____ ____ ____

    b. A report on compliance for each major program and on internal control over compliance in accordance with the Uniform Guidance that provides an opinion (or disclaimer of opinion) as to whether the audited entity complied with federal statutes, regulations, and the terms and conditions of federal awards that could have a direct and material effect on each major program, and, where applicable, a reference to the separate schedule of findings and questioned costs?   ____ ____ ____

    c. A schedule of findings and questioned costs?   ____ ____ ____

    [UG 200.515; AAG 13.06]

Report on the Supplementary Schedule of Expenditures of Federal Awards[22]

2. Is the report on the schedule of expenditures included in (*a*) an other-matter paragraph presented in accordance with AU-C section 706B, *Emphasis-of-Matter Paragraphs and Other-Matter Paragraphs in the Independent Auditor's Report*, or (*b*) a separate report on the schedule? (**Note:** Reporting using an other-matter paragraph is applicable when reporting on the schedule of expenditures of federal awards in the auditor's report on the financial statements. Otherwise, the reporting on the schedule of expenditures of federal awards may be included in the report on compliance and on internal control over compliance required under the Uniform Guidance, or in a separate report.)[23]   ____ ____ ____

    [AAG 13.11]

3. When the schedule of expenditures is presented with the financial statements, does the report on the schedule appear in

    a. an other-matter paragraph following the opinion paragraph in the auditor's report on the financial statements?   ____ ____ ____

    b. in a separate report on the schedule?   ____ ____ ____

    [AAG example 4-2, 13.11]

---

[21] Because of the requirements of GAS, the auditor also has other reporting and communication responsibilities in a Uniform Guidance audit. See the questions in the section titled "Other Reporting and Communication Considerations" in section I of this checklist.

[22] AU-C section 725, *Supplementary Information in Relation to the Financial Statements as a Whole*, provides requirements and guidance related to issuing an "in relation to" opinion on the schedule of expenditures of federal awards. For more information on the requirements under AU-C section 725, including illustrative report language, see the AICPA Audit Guide Government Auditing Standards *and Single Audits*.

[23] Paragraph 13.13 of the guide recommends that, when possible, the auditor report on the schedule of expenditures of federal awards as supplementary information in the report on the financial statements.

          © **2020, Association of International Certified Professional Accountants**

	Yes	No	N/A

4. Does the report on the schedule of expenditures include the following elements:

   a. A statement that the audit was conducted for the purpose of forming an opinion on the financial statements as a whole? ____ ____ ____

   b. A statement that the schedule is presented for purposes of additional analysis and is not a required part of the financial statements? ____ ____ ____

   c. A statement that the schedule of expenditures of federal awards is the responsibility of management and was derived from, and relates directly to, the underlying accounting and other records used to prepare the financial statements? ____ ____ ____

   d. A statement that the schedule has been subjected to the auditing procedures applied in the audit of the financial statements and certain additional procedures, including comparing and reconciling such information directly to the underlying accounting and other records used to prepare the financial statements or to the financial statements themselves and other additional procedures, in accordance with GAAS? ____ ____ ____

   e. If an unmodified opinion was issued on the financial statements and the auditor has concluded that the schedule is fairly stated, in all material respects, in relation to the financial statements as a whole, a statement that, in the auditor's opinion, the schedule of expenditures of federal awards is fairly stated, in all material respects, in relation to the financial statements as a whole? ____ ____ ____

   f. If a qualified opinion was issued on the financial statements and the qualification has an effect on the schedule of expenditures of federal awards, a statement that, in the auditor's opinion, except for the effects on the schedule of expenditures of federal awards of (refer to the paragraph in the auditor's report explaining the qualification), such information is fairly stated, in all material respects, in relation to the financial statements as a whole? ____ ____ ____

   [AAG example 4-2, 13.11, and examples 13-1–13-6]

5. When the schedule of expenditures of federal awards is not presented with the audited financial statements, is the "in relation to" opinion included in either the report on compliance and on internal control over compliance required by the Uniform Guidance or in a separate report?[24] ____ ____ ____

   [AAG 13.12 and examples 13-1–13-6]

6. When reporting separately on the schedule of expenditures of federal awards, does the report include, in addition to the elements in part II question 4, all of the following elements:

   a. A reference to the report on the financial statements? ____ ____ ____

   b. The date of the report on the financial statements? ____ ____ ____

   c. The nature of the opinion expressed on the financial statements? ____ ____ ____

   d. Any report modifications? ____ ____ ____

   [AAG 13.12 and examples 13-1–13-6]

---

[24] An in-relation-to opinion may not be issued if an auditor is engaged to issue a stand-alone opinion on the schedule of expenditures of federal awards, either as part of the report issued to meet the requirements of the Uniform Guidance or separately, and not perform the financial statement audit. (AAG 13.20)

© 2020, Association of International Certified Professional Accountants

	Yes	No	N/A

7. When the auditor's report on the audited financial statements contains an adverse or a disclaimer of opinion and the auditor has been engaged to report on whether the schedule is fairly stated, in all material respects, in relation to the financial statements as a whole, the auditor is precluded from expressing an opinion on the schedule. In this situation, has the auditor

    a. withdrawn from the engagement to report on the schedule, when permitted by law or regulation? ____ ____ ____

    b. if the auditor chose not to withdraw, does the auditor's report on the schedule state that because of the significance of the matter disclosed in the auditor's report, it is inappropriate to, and the auditor does not, express an opinion on the schedule? ____ ____ ____

     [AAG 13.14–.15]

8. Is the date of the auditor's report on the schedule the same date or subsequent to the date on which the auditor completed the procedures described in AU-C section 725, *Supplementary Information in Relation to the Financial Statements as a Whole*? ____ ____ ____

    [AAG 13.16–.19]

9. If the auditor concludes, on the basis of procedures performed, that the schedule is materially misstated in relation to the financial statements as a whole, has the auditor discussed the matter with management and proposed appropriate revision of the schedule? ____ ____ ____

    [AAG 13.14]

10. If the auditor has concluded, on the basis of procedures performed, that the schedule is materially misstated in relation to the financial statements as a whole, has the auditor

    a. modified the auditor's opinion on the schedule and described the misstatement in the auditor's report? ____ ____ ____

    b. in the case when a separate report is issued on the schedule, withheld the auditor's report on the schedule? ____ ____ ____

     [AAG 13.14]

11. If the report on the financial statements refers to the work of component auditors, has the auditor considered the need to refer to the major federal programs audited by component auditors in the report on the schedule? ____ ____ ____

    [AAG 13.32]

Report on Compliance With Requirements That Could Have a Direct and Material Effect on Each Major Program and on Internal Control Over Compliance in Accordance With the Uniform Guidance

12. Does the report conform to the standard report language illustrated in the AAG? ____ ____ ____

    [AAG examples 13-1–13-6]

13. Does the report contain the following elements:

    a. A title that includes the word *independent*? ____ ____ ____

    b. An addressee appropriate for the circumstances of the engagement? ____ ____ ____

    c. A section titled "Report on Compliance for Each Major Federal Program"? ____ ____ ____

     © 2020, Association of International Certified Professional Accountants

	Yes	No	N/A

d. An introductory paragraph that includes the following:

    i. A statement that the auditor has audited the auditee's compliance with the types of compliance requirements described in the *OMB Compliance Supplement* that could have a direct and material effect on each of its major federal programs?

    ii. Identification of the period covered by the report?

    iii. A statement that the auditee's major federal programs are identified in the summary of auditor's results section of the accompanying schedule of findings and questioned costs?

e. A subheading titled "Management's Responsibility" that includes a statement that compliance with the requirements of federal statutes, regulations, and the terms and conditions of federal awards applicable to each of the auditee's federal programs is the responsibility of the auditee's management?

f. A subheading titled "Auditor's Responsibility" that includes the following:

    i. A statement that the auditor's responsibility is to express an opinion on compliance for each of the entity's major federal programs based on the audit of the types of compliance requirements?

    ii. A statement that the compliance audit was conducted in accordance with auditing standards generally accepted in the United States of America, the standards applicable to financial audits contained in GAS issued by the Comptroller General of the United States and the Uniform Guidance?

    iii. A statement that those standards (identified in item ii of this question) and the Uniform Guidance require that the auditor plan and perform the audit to obtain reasonable assurance about whether noncompliance with the types of compliance requirements that could have a direct and material effect on a major federal program occurred?

    iv. A statement that an audit includes examining, on a test basis, evidence about the entity's compliance with those requirements and performing such other procedures as the auditor considered necessary in the circumstances?

    v. A statement that the auditor believes that the compliance audit provides a reasonable basis for the auditor's opinion?

    vi. A statement that the compliance audit does not provide a legal determination of the auditee's compliance with those requirements?

g. If the auditor is expressing an unmodified opinion on all major programs, a subheading titled "Opinion on Each Major Federal Program" that contains a statement that in the auditor's opinion the auditee complied, in all material respects, with the types of compliance requirements that could have a direct and material effect on each of its major federal programs for the year ended [*specify date*]?

© 2020, Association of International Certified Professional Accountants

	Yes	*No*	*N/A*

h. If instances of noncompliance for a major program are noted that result in an opinion qualification, a subheading titled, "Basis for Qualified Opinion on [*Name of Major Federal Program*] that includes the following:

   i. A statement that, as described in the accompanying schedule of findings and questioned costs, the auditee did not comply with requirements regarding [*identify the major federal program*]?   ____ ____ ____

   ii. The associated finding number(s) matched to the type(s) of compliance requirements?   ____ ____ ____

   iii. A statement that compliance with such requirements is necessary, in the auditor's opinion, for the auditee to comply with the requirements applicable to the program(s)?   ____ ____ ____

i. If instances of noncompliance are noted that result in an opinion qualification for one or more major programs, is there

   i. a subheading with an appropriate title (for example, "Qualified Opinion on [*Name of Major Federal Program*]") that includes the auditor's opinion that, except for the noncompliance described in the Basis for Qualification paragraph, the auditee complied, in all material respects, with the types of compliance requirements that could have a direct and material effect on [*name of major federal program*] for the period being audited?   ____ ____ ____

   ii. a subheading with an appropriate title (for example, "Unmodified Opinion on Each of the Other Major Federal Programs") if there are other major programs receiving an unmodified opinion, to be more clear about the programs receiving an unmodified opinion?   ____ ____ ____

j. If other noncompliance is identified that does not result in a modified opinion but that is required to be reported in accordance with the Uniform Guidance, a subheading titled "Other Matters" containing all of the following:

   i. A reference to the schedule of findings and questioned costs in which the instances of noncompliance are described, including the reference number(s) of the finding(s)?   ____ ____ ____

   ii. A statement that the auditor's opinion on each major federal program is not modified with respect to the matters?   ____ ____ ____

k. A section heading "Report on Internal Control Over Compliance" that includes the following statements and definitions:

   i. A statement that the auditee's management is responsible for establishing and maintaining effective internal control over compliance with the types of compliance requirements?   ____ ____ ____

   ii. A statement that in planning and performing the compliance audit, the auditor considered the auditee's internal control over compliance with the types of requirements that could have a direct and material effect on each major federal program to determine the auditing procedures that are appropriate in the circumstances for the purpose of expressing an opinion on compliance for each major federal program and to test and report on internal control over compliance in accordance with the Uniform Guidance, but not for the purpose of expressing an opinion on the effectiveness of internal control over compliance?   ____ ____ ____

	Yes	No	N/A

iii. A statement that the auditor is not expressing an opinion on the effectiveness of internal control over compliance?

iv. The definitions of *deficiency in internal control over compliance, material weakness in internal control over compliance,* and *significant deficiency in internal control over compliance*?[25]

v. A statement that the auditor's consideration of internal control over compliance was for the limited purpose described in item ii of this question and was not designed to identify all deficiencies in internal control over compliance that might be material weaknesses or significant deficiencies?

vi. If no material weaknesses in internal control over compliance were identified, a statement that the auditor did not identify any deficiencies in internal control over compliance that are considered to be material weaknesses?

vii. A statement that material weaknesses may exist that have not been identified? (*Note:* For situations where significant deficiencies or material weaknesses are identified, this statement is revised to indicate that material weaknesses or significant deficiencies may exist that have not been identified.)

viii. If significant deficiencies in internal control over compliance were identified, a statement that no deficiencies in internal control over compliance were identified that are considered to be material weaknesses, however deficiencies in internal control over compliance were identified that are considered to be significant deficiencies, and a description of the significant deficiencies in internal control over compliance or a reference to the accompanying schedule of findings and questioned costs, including the reference number(s) of the finding(s)?

ix. If material weaknesses in internal control over compliance were identified, a statement that deficiencies in internal control over compliance were identified that are considered to be material weaknesses and a description of the material weaknesses in internal control over compliance or a reference to the accompanying schedule of findings and questioned costs, including the reference number(s) of the finding(s)?

x. A separate paragraph at the end of the section stating that the purpose of the report on internal control over compliance is solely to describe the scope of our testing of internal control over compliance and the result of that testing based on the requirements of the Uniform Guidance. Accordingly, this report is not suitable for any other purpose?[26]

---

[25] Although the definitions of *deficiency in internal control over compliance* and *material weakness in internal control over compliance* are required in all reporting, the definition of *significant deficiency in internal control over compliance* is not required to be included in the report when no significant deficiencies in internal control over compliance have been identified. However, for clarity purposes, the definition of *significant deficiency in internal control over compliance* is included in the example reports found in the AICPA Audit Guide Government Auditing Standards *and Single Audits,* regardless of the type of deficiencies identified. The definitions included in the example reports are based on the definitions found in AU-C section 935.

[26] This paragraph of the report conforms to paragraph .11 of AU-C section 905, *Alert That Restricts the Use of the Auditor's Written Communication,* which modifies the alert language used for compliance audits performed under GAS. This language should only be included in the internal control over compliance section of combined reports on the entity's compliance and internal control over compliance in light of the fact that it is the nature of the reporting on internal control over compliance that triggers the required use of alert language (see paragraph .06c of AU-C section 905). If the auditor issues separate reports on the entity's compliance and its internal control over compliance, this alert should be included in the report on internal control over compliance but would not be included in the report on compliance.

© 2020, Association of International Certified Professional Accountants

	Yes	No	N/A

l.   The manual or printed signature of the auditor's firm?   ____ ____ ____

m.   The city and state where the auditor practices?   ____ ____ ____

n.   The date of the auditor's report?   ____ ____ ____

     [AAG 13.26]

14. Although not required, if material weaknesses, significant deficiencies, or instances of noncompliance or other matters are identified, has the auditor considered a paragraph in the auditor's reporting on compliance and the auditor's reporting on internal control over compliance, as applicable, containing the following:

     a.   a statement that the auditee's response to the findings identified in the audit are described in the accompanying schedule of findings and questioned costs?   ____ ____ ____

     b.   a statement that "[*Name of Entity*]'s response was not subjected to the auditing procedures applied in the audit of compliance and, accordingly, the auditor does not express an opinion on the response"?   ____ ____ ____

     [AAG 13.27]

15. If the compliance audit detects material instances of noncompliance related to a major program, does the auditor's report express a qualified or adverse opinion?   ____ ____ ____

     [AAG 13.22]

16. If there were scope limitations on the auditor's testing of the auditee's compliance with federal statutes, regulations, and the terms and conditions of federal awards,

     a.   have those limitations been considered in the opinion on compliance with requirements applicable to each major program?   ____ ____ ____

     b.   and if the scope limitations require the auditor to disclaim an opinion on compliance, does the report contain a separate opinion paragraph stating that because of the significance of the matter(s) described in the basis for disclaimer of opinion paragraph, the auditor has not been able to obtain sufficient appropriate audit evidence to provide a basis for an audit opinion, and the auditor does not express an opinion?   ____ ____ ____

     [AAG 13.23–.25]

17. Have the cumulative effects of all instances of noncompliance with federal programs and scope limitations been considered in the opinion on the financial statements?   ____ ____ ____

     [AAG 13.22–.23]

18. Is the report dated the same as or later than the date of the auditor's report on the financial statements (the date being determined by when the auditor has obtained sufficient appropriate audit evidence to support the report on the audit of compliance)?   ____ ____ ____

     a.   If the report is dated later than the date of the auditor's report on the financial statements, have appropriate subsequent events procedures been performed?   ____ ____ ____

     [AAG 13.29]

 © **2020, Association of International Certified Professional Accountants**

	Yes	No	N/A

19. If the audit of federal awards does not encompass the entirety of the auditee's operations expending federal awards, are the operations that are not included identified in a separate paragraph following the first paragraph of the report?

    [AAG 13.33]

20. If the report on the financial statements refers to the work of component auditors, has the auditor considered the need to refer to the major federal programs audited by component auditors in the report on compliance and on internal control over compliance?

    [AAG 4.85, 13.32]

Schedule of Findings and Questioned Costs

21. Do the component sections of the schedule conform to the example schedule illustrated in the AAG?

    [AAG example 13-7]

22. Is the schedule presented even if there are no findings to report? (In a situation in which there are no findings or questioned costs, the auditor should prepare the summary of auditor's results section of the schedule and either omit the other sections or include them, indicating that no matters were reported.)

    [AAG 13.47]

23. Does the report contain the following three sections:

    a. A summary of the auditor's results?

    b. Findings related to the financial statements that are required to be reported in accordance with GAS? (See the questions about those findings in section I of this checklist.)

    c. Findings and questioned costs for federal awards?

       [AAG 13.34]

24. Does the summary of auditor's results include

    a. the type of report the auditor issued on whether the financial statements were prepared in accordance with GAAP (that is, unmodified opinion, qualified opinion, adverse opinion, or disclaimer of opinion)?

    b. where applicable, a statement that significant deficiencies or material weaknesses in internal control were disclosed by the audit of the financial statements?

    c. a statement on whether the audit disclosed any noncompliance that is material to the financial statements?

    d. where applicable, a statement that significant deficiencies and material weaknesses in the internal control over major programs were disclosed by the audit?

    e. the type of report the auditor issued on compliance for major programs (that is, unmodified opinion, qualified opinion, adverse opinion, or disclaimer of opinion)? (If the audit report for one or more major programs is modified, indicate the type of report issued for each program.)

    f. a statement on whether the audit disclosed any audit findings that the auditor is required to report under the Uniform Guidance? (See section II question 25.)

	Yes	No	N/A

g. an identification of major programs? (In the case of a cluster of programs, only the cluster name as shown on the schedule of expenditures of federal awards is required.) ____ ____ ____

h. the dollar threshold used to distinguish between type A and type B programs? ____ ____ ____

i. a statement on whether the auditee qualified as a low-risk auditee? ____ ____ ____

[AAG 13.35]

25. Are the following reported as audit findings related to federal awards?

[UG 200.516(a); AAG 13.39 and table 13-2]

a. Significant deficiencies and material weaknesses in internal control over major programs? ____ ____ ____

b. Material noncompliance with federal statutes, regulations, or the terms and conditions of federal awards related to a major program? ____ ____ ____

c. Known questioned costs that are greater than $25,000 for a type of compliance requirement for a major program? ____ ____ ____

d. Known questioned costs when likely questioned costs are greater than $25,000 for a type of compliance requirement for a major program? ____ ____ ____

e. Known questioned costs that are greater than $25,000 for programs that are not audited as major? ____ ____ ____

f. The circumstances concerning why the opinion in the auditor's report on compliance for each major program is other than unmodified, if not otherwise reported as an audit finding? ____ ____ ____

g. Known or likely fraud affecting a federal award, if not otherwise reported as an audit finding? (An audit finding is not required if the fraud was reported outside the entity as required by GAS.) ____ ____ ____

h. Instances of material misrepresentation by the auditee of the status of any prior audit findings? ____ ____ ____

[AAG 13.53]

i. Abuse involving federal awards that is quantitatively or qualitatively material to a major program? ____ ____ ____

[AAG 13.41]

26. Does the audit finding detail include

a. a reference number that meets the numbering format required for FAC submissions (for example, findings identified and reported in the audit of fiscal year 20X1 would be assigned reference numbers 20X1-001, 20X1-002, and so forth)? ____ ____ ____

[UG 200.516(c); AAG 13.46]

b. identification of the federal program and specific federal award, including Catalog of Federal Domestic Assistance, or CFDA, title and number, federal award identification number and year, name of the federal agency, and name of the applicable pass-through entity?[27] ____ ____ ____

---

[27] When information such as the Catalog of Federal Domestic Assistance (CFDA) title and number or the federal award number is not available, the auditor should provide the best information available to describe the federal award (chapter 7, "Schedule of Expenditures of Federal Awards," of the guide discusses an alternative for presentation if a CFDA number is not available). (UG 200.516(b)(1); AAG 13.42*a*)

 © 2020, Association of International Certified Professional Accountants

	Yes	No	N/A

  c. the criteria or specific requirement upon which the audit finding is based, including the federal statutes, regulations, or the terms and conditions of the federal awards?   _____ _____ _____

  d. the condition found, including facts that support the deficiency identified in the audit finding?   _____ _____ _____

  e. a statement of cause that identifies the reason or explanation for the condition or factors responsible for the difference between the situation that exists (condition) and the required or desired state (criteria)?[28]   _____ _____ _____

  f. the possible asserted effect to provide sufficient information to the auditee and federal agency, or pass-through entity in the case of a subrecipient, to permit them to determine the cause and effect to facilitate prompt and proper corrective action?   _____ _____ _____

  g. identification of questioned costs and how they were computed?   _____ _____ _____

  h. information to provide a proper perspective for judging the prevalence and consequences of the audit findings?[29]   _____ _____ _____

  i. identification of whether the audit finding was a repeat of a finding in the immediately prior audit and if so any applicable prior audit finding numbers?   _____ _____ _____

  j. recommendations to prevent future occurrences of the deficiency identified in the finding?   _____ _____ _____

  k. views of responsible officials of the auditee?[30]   _____ _____ _____

  [UG 200.516(b); AAG 13.42]

27. Do the audit findings not include protected personally identifiable information?   _____ _____ _____

  [UG 200.512(a)(2); AAG 13.42, 13.48]

28. Do the audit findings related to federal awards also meet the presentation requirements of GAS? (See the questions about those presentation requirements in section I of this checklist.)   _____ _____ _____

  [AAG 13.43]

29. Are audit findings and questioned costs that relate to federal awards

  a. presented as one finding if findings (for example, internal control findings, compliance findings, questioned costs, or fraud) relate to the same issue?   _____ _____ _____

  b. organized by federal agency or pass-through entity, where practical?   _____ _____ _____

  [UG 200.515(d)(3)(i); AAG 13.35c]

---

[28] The cause of a finding may relate to one or more underlying internal control deficiencies. Depending on the magnitude of impact, likelihood of occurrence, and nature of the deficiency, the deficiency could be a significant deficiency or material weakness in a financial audit. Considering internal control in the context of a comprehensive internal control framework can help auditors to determine whether underlying internal control deficiencies exist as a root cause of findings. Identifying these deficiencies can help provide the basis for developing meaningful recommendations for corrective actions.

[29] Where appropriate, the instances identified should be related to the universe and the number of cases examined and be quantified in terms of the dollar value. The auditor should (best practice) report whether the sampling was a statistically valid sample. (UG 200.516(b)(7); AAG 13.42g).

[30] The auditee must prepare, in a document separate from the schedule of findings and questioned costs, a corrective action plan to address each audit finding included in the current year auditor's report. The corrective action plan must include findings relating to the financial statements required to be reported in accordance with *Government Auditing Standards* (UG 200.511(c); AAG 13.56).

© 2020, Association of International Certified Professional Accountants

	Yes	No	N/A

30. Are findings that relate to both the financial statements and federal awards reported in both sections of the schedule? (An alternative is to report the finding in one section of the schedule in summary form, with a reference to a detailed reporting in the other section of the schedule.)

     [UG 200.515(d)(3)(ii); AAG 13.35c]

Data Collection Form[31,32]

31. Has the auditor completed the applicable date elements of the online data collection form?

     [AAG 13.60]

32. Has the auditor electronically signed the auditor statement and dated it as of the date on which the auditor completes the form?

     [AAG 13.60]

33. Does the information on the data collection form that is required to be completed by the auditor agree to the information in the auditor's reports and the summary of auditor's results in the schedule of findings and questioned costs?

     [Federal Audit Clearinghouse, Data Collection Form, No. SF-SAC; AAG 13.60]

34. Has the auditor ensured that their part of the reporting package does not include protected personally identifiable information or other sensitive information?

     [UG 200.512(a)(2); AAG 13.61]

Note

When an auditee expends federal awards under only one federal program (excluding research and development) and the federal program's federal statutes, regulations, or terms and conditions do not require a financial statement audit of the auditee, the auditee may elect to have a program-specific audit. A program-specific audit may not be elected for research and development unless all federal awards expended were received from the same federal agency (or the same federal agency and the same pass-through entity) and that federal agency (or pass-through entity, in the case of a subrecipient) approves a program-specific audit in advance.

[UG 200.501(c); AAG 14.02]

Program-Specific Audits

35. If a program-specific audit guide is available and current with regard to the program's compliance requirements, has the auditor issued the reports required by the guide?

     [UG 200.507(a); AAG 14.04]

---

[31] The auditee must submit a data collection form (Form SF-SAC) that states whether the audit was completed in accordance with the Uniform Guidance and provides information about the auditee, its federal programs, and the results of the audit (UG 200.512(d)).

[32] The data collection form and related instructions are available from the Federal Audit Clearinghouse's (FAC's) website at https://harvester.census.gov/facweb/. The form number is SF-SAC. The FAC requires electronic submission of the data collection form via an online Internet Data Entry System. The Office of Management and Budget periodically revises the data collection form and its accompanying instructions. (AAG 13.57–.59).

       © 2020, Association of International Certified Professional Accountants

	Yes	No	N/A

36. If a program-specific audit guide is not available or not current with regard to the program's compliance requirements, has the auditor issued the following reports:[33, 34]

    a. A report on the federal program's financial statements that provides an opinion or disclaimer of opinion on the financial statements? _____ _____ _____

    b. A report on compliance with requirements that could have a direct and material effect on the federal program and on the internal control over compliance in accordance with the program-specific audit option under the Uniform Guidance? _____ _____ _____

    c. A schedule of findings and questioned costs for the program? _____ _____ _____

    [UG 200.507(b)(4); AAG 14.09–.11]

37. Do the reports conform to the standard report language illustrated in the AAG? _____ _____ _____

    [AAG examples 14-1–14-2]

---

[34] If the financial statement(s) of the program present only the activity of the federal program, the auditor is not required to issue a separate report to meet the reporting requirements of GAS. However, the auditor always has the option of issuing a separate GAS report (in addition to the reports required as part of the program-specific audit) (AAG 14.11).

[34] See footnote 21.

© 2020, Association of International Certified Professional Accountants

Part 5

Accountants' Reports on Compiled Financial Statements or Information or Reviewed Financial Statements Checklist

.01 This checklist has been developed by the staff of the Accounting and Auditing Publications Team of the AICPA as a nonauthoritative practice aid.

.02 The AICPA Guide *Preparation, Compilation, and Review Engagements* (available at www.aicpastore.com), features information on implementing the Statements on Standards for Accounting and Review Services (SSARSs) and includes illustrative engagement and representation letters, sample compilation and review reports, detailed illustrations, and case studies. Additionally, the AICPA Compilation and Review Alert *Developments in Preparation, Compilation, and Review Engagements* (available at www.aicpastore.com) is published annually to provide CPAs with an update on recent practice issues and professional standards that affect compilation and review engagements. The guide and alert are *interpretive publications*, as defined in AR-C section 60, *General Principles for Engagements Performed in Accordance With Statements on Standards for Accounting and Review Services*.[1] Interpretive publications have no authoritative status; however, they may help the accountant understand and apply the SSARSs.

.03 SSARS No. 25, *Materiality in a Review of Financial Statements and Adverse Conclusions*, issued in February 2020, amends AR-C section 60, AR-C section 70, *Preparation of Financial Statements*; AR-C section 80, *Compilation Engagements*; and AR-C section 90, *Review of Financial Statements*. SSARS No. 25 further converges AR-C section 90 with International Standard on Review Engagements (ISRE) 2400 (Revised), *Engagements to Review Historical Financial Statements*, and minimizes differences with the auditing standards regarding concepts that are consistent regardless of the level of service performed on the financial statements. Significant changes include an explicit requirement to determine materiality, permission to express an adverse review conclusion when financial statements are materially and pervasively misstated, and a requirement that the accountant's review report include a statement that the accountant is required to be independent of the entity and to meet the accountant's other ethical responsibilities. The revisions in SSARS No. 25 are effective for compilations and reviews of financial statements for periods ending on or after December 15, 2021. Early implementation is permitted. This checklist has been updated for SSARS No. 25.

.04 This checklist is not intended to address all the considerations if an auditor is engaged to compile or review special-purpose financial statements, which are prepared to comply with a contractual agreement or regulatory provision that specifies a special basis of presentation. In most circumstances, these financial statements are intended solely for the use of the parties to the agreement, regulatory bodies, or other specified parties. For compilations performed before the adoption of SSARS No. 25, refer to paragraphs .18–.21 of AR-C section 80A, *Compilation Engagements*, and paragraphs .40–.44 of AR-C section 90A for guidance about how the accountant should modify the standard compilation or review report when reporting on these special-purpose financial statements. For compilations performed after the adoption of SSARS No. 25, refer to paragraphs .18–.21 of AR-C section 80, *Compilation Engagements*, and paragraphs .74–.78 of AR-C section 90 for guidance about how the accountant should modify the standard compilation or review report when reporting on these special-purpose financial statements. This checklist does not address standards for reports if financial statements include required supplementary information; generally accepted accounting principles do not currently require supplementary information in the statements of not-for-profit entities (NFPs).

.05 AR-C section 100, which is not included in this checklist, provides requirements and guidance when an accountant is engaged to perform a compilation or review in either of the following circumstances:

---

[1] All AR-C sections can be found in AICPA *Professional Standards*.

© 2020, Association of International Certified Professional Accountants

- The financial statements have been prepared in accordance with a financial reporting framework generally accepted in another country.

- The compilation or review is to be performed in accordance with both SSARSs and another set of compilation or review standards.

.06 This checklist is divided into three parts. Section I, "Checklist Questionnaire for Compiled Financial Statements, Prospective Financial Information, Pro Forma Financial Information, and Other Historical Financial Information Using AR-C (Clarified) Standards," should be used by accountants engaged to report on compiled financial statements using the AR-C standards. Section II, "Checklist Questionnaire for Review Engagements Using AR-C (Clarified) Standards Prior to Adoption of SSARS No. 25," should be used if the accountant performs a review of financial statements using the AR-C standards prior to the adoption of SSARS No. 25. Section III, "Checklist Questionnaire for Review Engagements Using AR-C (Clarified) Standards After the Adoption of SSARS No. 25," should be used if the accountant performs a review of financial statements using the AR-C standards after the adoption of SSARS No. 25.

.07 Explanation of References:

AR-C = Reference to the section number of the clarified standards in AICPA *Professional Standards*

I. Checklist Questionnaire for Compiled Financial Statements, Prospective Financial Information, Pro Forma Financial Information, and Other Historical Financial Information Using AR-C (Clarified) Standards

	Yes	*No*	*N/A*

The Accountant's Compilation Report

Basic Elements of the Report

1. Is the report in writing?

    [AR-C 80A.17]
    [AR-C 80.17]

2. Does the compilation report contain the following elements:

    a. A statement that management is responsible for the financial statements or other financial information?

    b. The financial statements or other financial information that have (has) been subjected to the compilation engagement?

    c. The entity whose financial statements or other financial information have (has) been subjected to the compilation engagement?

    d. The date or period covered by the financial statements or other financial information?

    e. A statement that the accountant performed the compilation engagement in accordance with SSARSs promulgated by the Accounting and Review Services Committee (ARSC) of the AICPA?

    f. A statement that the accountant did not audit or review the financial statements or other financial information nor was the accountant required to perform any procedures to verify the accuracy or completeness of the information provided by management and, accordingly, does not express an opinion, a conclusion, nor provide any assurance on the financial statements or other financial information?

© 2020, Association of International Certified Professional Accountants

	Yes	No	N/A

g. The signature of the accountant or the accountant's firm?

h. The city and state where the accountant practices, which may be indicated on letterhead that contains the issuing office's city and state?

i. The date of the report, which should be the date that the accountant has completed the procedures required by AR-C section 80A or AR-C section 80, as applicable?

[AR-C 80A.17, 80A.24, and 80A.26–.A27] [AR-C 80.17, 80.A24, and 80.A26–.A27]

Reporting When the Accountant is Not Independent

3. If the accountant is not independent with respect to the entity, has the accountant indicated the accountant's lack of independence in a final paragraph of the accountant's compilation report?

[AR-C 80A.22 and 80A.A33–.A35]
[AR-C 80.22 and 80.A37–.A39]

4. If the accountant elects to disclose a description about the reasons the accountant's independence is impaired, are all such reasons in the description?

[AR-C 80A.23]
[AR-C 80.23]

Reporting on Prospective Financial Information

Note

The summary of significant assumptions is essential to the user's understanding of prospective financial information. Accordingly, the accountant should not issue a compilation report on prospective financial information that excludes disclosure of the summary of significant assumptions. Also, the accountant should not issue a compilation report on a financial projection that excludes either (*a*) an identification of the hypothetical assumptions or (*b*) a description of the limitations on the usefulness of the presentation. [AR-C 80A.24 and AR-C 80.24]

---

5. In addition to the reporting elements required by question 2, has the accountant included the following in the accountant's compilation report on prospective financial information:

a. A statement that the forecasted or projected results may not be achieved?

b. A statement that the accountant assumes no responsibility to update the report for events and circumstances occurring after the date of the report?

[AR-C 80A.25]
[AR-C 80.25]

Reporting on Pro Forma Financial Information

Note

For purposes of this section, the following term has the meaning attributed as follows:

Pro forma financial information. A presentation that shows what the significant effects on historical financial information might have been had a consummated or proposed transaction (or event) occurred at an earlier date. [AR-C 120.04 and .A2–.A5]

© 2020, Association of International Certified Professional Accountants

	Yes	No	N/A

6.   In addition to the reporting elements required by question 2, has the accountant included the following in the accountant's compilation report on pro forma financial information:

    a.   A reference to the financial statements from which the historical financial information is derived and a statement as to whether such financial statements were subjected to an audit, a review, or a compilation engagement? ____ ____ ____

    b.   A reference to any modification of the audit, review, or compilation report on the historical financial information? ____ ____ ____

    c.   A description of the nature and limitations of pro forma financial information? ____ ____ ____

    [AR-C 120.14]

Financial Statements That Omit Substantially All Disclosures

Note

The accountant should not issue an accountant's compilation report on financial statements that omit substantially all disclosures required by the applicable financial reporting framework unless the omission of substantially all disclosures is not, to the accountant's knowledge, undertaken with the intention of misleading those who might reasonably be expected to use such financial statements. [AR-C 80A.26]

As amended by SSARS No. 25: The accountant should not issue an accountant's compilation report on financial statements that omit substantially all disclosures required by the applicable financial reporting framework if, in the accountant's professional judgment, such financial statements would be misleading to users of the financial statements. [AR-C 80.26]

---

7.   When reporting on financial statements that omit substantially all disclosures required by the applicable financial reporting framework, has the accountant included a separate paragraph in the accountant's compilation report that includes the following elements:

    a.   A statement that management has elected to omit substantially all the disclosures (and the statement of cash flows, if applicable) required by the applicable financial reporting framework (or ordinarily included in the financial statements if the financial statements are prepared in accordance with a special purpose framework)? ____ ____ ____

    b.   A statement that if the omitted disclosures (and the statement of cash flows, if applicable) were included in the financial statements, they might influence the user's conclusions about the entity's financial position, results of operations, and cash flows (or the equivalent for presentations other than GAAP)? ____ ____ ____

    c.   A statement that, accordingly, the financial statements are not designed for those who are not informed about such matters? ____ ____ ____

    [AR-C 80A.27 and 80A.A36–.A37]
    [AR-C 80.27 and 80.A40–.A41]

Yes   _No_   _N/A_

Reporting Known Departures From the Applicable Financial Reporting Framework

Note

If the accountant becomes aware of a departure from the applicable financial reporting framework (including inadequate disclosure) that is material to the financial statements and the financial statements are not revised, the accountant should consider whether modification of the standard report is adequate to disclose the departure. [AR-C 80A.29 and AR-C 80.29]

The accountant should not modify the compilation report to include a statement that the financial statements are not in conformity with the applicable financial reporting framework. If the accountant believes that modification of the compilation report is not adequate to indicate the deficiencies in the financial statements as a whole, then the accountant should withdraw from the engagement and provide no further services with respect to those financial statements. [AR-C 80A.32–.33 and AR-C 80.32–.33]

8.   If the accountant concludes that modification of the standard report is adequate, is the departure disclosed in a separate paragraph of the report?

[AR-C 80A.30]
[AR-C 80.30]

9.   Are the effects of the departure on the financial statements disclosed if such effects have been determined by management or are readily known to the accountant as the result of the accountant's procedures?

[AR-C 80A.30]
[AR-C 80.30]

10. If the effects of the departure have not been determined by management or are not readily known to the accountant as a result of the accountant's procedures, has the accountant stated in the report that such determination has not been made by management?

[AR-C 80A.31]
[AR-C 80.31]

Supplementary Information That Accompanies Financial Statements and the Accountant's Compilation Report Thereon

Note

Although not required to perform a compilation engagement on supplementary information that accompanies financial statements and the accountant's compilation report thereon, nothing precludes the accountant from performing a compilation engagement on such information if engaged to do so.

11. If supplementary information accompanies financial statements and the accountant's compilation report thereon, has the accountant clearly indicated the degree of responsibility, if any, the accountant is taking with respect to such information in either (_a_) an other-matter paragraph in the accountant's compilation report on the financial statements or (_b_) a separate report on the supplementary information?

[AR-C 80A.34]
[AR-C 80.34]

	Yes	No	N/A

12. If the accountant has performed a compilation engagement with respect to both the financial statements and the supplementary information, has the accountant included an other-matter paragraph in the accountant's compilation report or issued a separate report on the supplementary information that states the following:

a.	The information is presented for purposes of additional analysis and is not a required part of the basic financial statements?	____	____	____
b.	The information is the representation of management?	____	____	____
c.	The information was subject to the compilation engagement?	____	____	____
d.	The accountant has not audited or reviewed the information and, accordingly, does not express an opinion, a conclusion, nor provide any assurance on such information?	____	____	____

[AR-C 80A.35, 80A.A41, and 80A.A43]
[AR-C 80.35, 80.A45, and 80.A47]

13. When the accountant has performed a compilation engagement with respect to the financial statements but the supplementary information was not subject to the compilation engagement, has the accountant included an other-matter paragraph in the accountant's compilation report on the financial statements or issued a separate report on the supplementary information that states the following:

a.	The information is presented for purposes of additional analysis and is not a required part of the basic financial statements?	____	____	____
b.	The information is the representation of management?	____	____	____
c.	The information was not subject to the compilation engagement and, accordingly, the accountant does not express an opinion, a conclusion, nor provide any assurance on such information?	____	____	____

[AR-C 80A.36 and 80A.A42–.A43]
[AR-C 80.36 and 80.A46–.A47]

II. Checklist Questionnaire for Review Engagements Using AR-C (Clarified) Standards Prior to the Adoption of SSARS No. 25

	Yes	No	N/A

Note

The accountant must be independent of the entity when performing a review of financial statements in accordance with SSARSs. If, during the performance of the review engagement, the accountant determines that the accountant's independence is impaired, then the accountant should withdraw from the review engagement. [AR-C 90A.07]

Basic Elements of the Report

1. Is the accountant's review report in writing?

   [AR-C 90A.38 and 90A.A62–.A64]

2. Does the written review report include the following:

   a. A title that includes the word *independent* to clearly indicate that it is the report of an independent accountant?

   b. An addressee, as appropriate for the circumstances of the engagement?

   c. An introductory paragraph that

      i. identifies the entity whose financial statements have been reviewed?

      ii. states that the financial statements identified in the report were reviewed?

      iii. identifies the financial statements?

      iv. specifies the date or period covered by each financial statement?

      v. includes a statement that a review includes primarily applying analytical procedures to management's financial data and making inquiries of management?

      vi. includes a statement that a review is substantially less in scope than an audit, the objective of which is the expression of an opinion regarding the financial statements as a whole, and that, accordingly, the accountant does not express such an opinion?

      [AR-C 90A.39 and 90A.A81]

   d. A section with the heading "Management's Responsibility for the Financial Statements" that includes an explanation that management is responsible for the preparation and fair presentation of the financial statements in accordance with the applicable financial reporting framework; this responsibility includes the design, implementation, and maintenance of internal control relevant to the preparation and fair presentation of financial statements that are free from material misstatement whether due to fraud or error?

      [AR-C 90A.39 and 90A.A74]

   e. A section with the heading "Accountant's Responsibility" that includes the following statements:

      i. That the accountant's responsibility is to conduct the review engagement in accordance with SSARSs promulgated by the ARSC of the AICPA?

© 2020, Association of International Certified Professional Accountants

ii. An explanation that those standards require that the accountant perform the procedures to obtain limited assurance as a basis for reporting whether the accountant is aware of any material modifications that should be made to the financial statements for them to be in accordance with the applicable financial reporting framework?

iii. That the accountant believes that the results of the accountant's procedures provide a reasonable basis for the accountant's conclusion?

[AR-C 90A.39 and 90A.A75–.A77]

f. A concluding section with an appropriate heading that includes a statement about whether the accountant is aware of any material modifications that should be made to the accompanying financial statements for them to be in accordance with the applicable financial reporting framework?

g. Identification of the country of origin of the accounting principles, if applicable?

h. The signature of the accountant or the accountant's firm?

i. The city and state where the accountant practices?

[AR-C 90A.39, 90A.A50, and 90A.A78]

j. The date of the review report, which should be no earlier than the date on which the accountant completed procedures sufficient to obtain limited assurance as a basis for reporting whether the accountant is aware of any material modifications that should be made to the financial statements for them to be in accordance with the applicable financial reporting framework?

[AR-C 90A.39 and 90A.A79–.A80]

Comparative Financial Statements

3. When comparative financial statements are presented, does the accountant's report refer to each period for which financial statements are presented?

[AR-C 90A.45 and 90A.A87–.A88]

4. When reporting on all periods presented, has the continuing accountant updated the report on one or more prior periods presented on a comparative basis with those of the current period?

[AR-C 90A.46 and 90A.A89]

5. If the accountant's report on the financial statements of the prior period contains a changed reference to a departure from the applicable financial reporting framework, does the accountant's review report include an other-matter paragraph indicating the following:

a. The date of the accountant's previous review report?

b. The circumstances or events that caused the reference to be changed?

c. If applicable, that the financial statements of the prior period have been changed?

[AR-C 90A.49 and 90A.A90]

                    © 2020, Association of International Certified Professional Accountants

	Yes	*No*	*N/A*

6.   If the prior period financial statements were audited and the auditor's report on the prior period financial statements is not reissued, does the review report on the current period financial statements include an other-matter paragraph indicating the following:

   a.   That the financial statements of the prior period were previously audited? ____ ____ ____

   b.   The date of the auditor's report on the prior period financial statements? ____ ____ ____

   c.   The type of opinion issued on the prior period financial statements? ____ ____ ____

   d.   If the opinion was modified, the substantive reasons for the modification? ____ ____ ____

   e.   That no auditing procedures were performed after the date of the previous report? ____ ____ ____

   [AR-C 90A.50]

Emphasis of Matter

7.   If the accountant considers it necessary to draw users' attention to a matter appropriately presented or disclosed in the financial statements that, in the accountant's professional judgment, is of such importance that it is fundamental to users' understanding of the financial statements, does the accountant's review report include an emphasis-of-matter paragraph (provided that the accountant does not believe that the financial statements may be materially misstated)? ____ ____ ____

   [AR-C 90A.52 and 90A.A95–.A97]

8.   Does the emphasis-of-matter paragraph refer only to information presented or disclosed in the financial statements? ____ ____ ____

   [AR-C 90A.52 and 90A.A97]

9.   When the accountant includes an emphasis-of-matter paragraph in the accountant's review report, does that paragraph

   a.   appear immediately after the accountant's conclusion paragraph in the accountant's review report? ____ ____ ____

   b.   have a heading "Emphasis of a Matter" or other appropriate heading? ____ ____ ____

   c.   provide a clear reference to the matter being emphasized and to where relevant disclosures that fully describe the matter can be found in the financial statements? ____ ____ ____

   d.   indicate that the accountant's conclusion is not modified with respect to the matter emphasized? ____ ____ ____

   [AR-C 90A.53 and 90A.A98–.A99]

© 2020, Association of International Certified Professional Accountants

	Yes	No	N/A

Other-Matter Paragraphs in the Accountant's Review Report

10.   If the accountant considers it necessary to communicate a matter other than those that are presented or disclosed in the financial statements and, in the accountant's professional judgment, that matter is relevant to the users' understanding of the review, the accountant's responsibilities, or the accountant's review report, does the accountant's review report include a paragraph with the heading "Other Matter" or other appropriate heading?

        [AR-C 90A.54, 90A.A98, and 90A.A100–.A102]

11.   Does the other-matter paragraph appear immediately after the accountant's conclusion paragraph and any emphasis-of-matter paragraph?

        [AR-C 90A.54]

Known Departures From the Applicable Financial Reporting Framework

---

Note

If the accountant believes that modification of the standard report is not adequate to indicate the deficiencies in the financial statements as a whole, then the accountant should withdraw from the review engagement. The accountant should not modify the standard report to include a statement that the financial statements are not in accordance with the applicable financial reporting framework. [AR-C 90A.59–.60 and 90A.A106–.A109]

---

12.   When the accountant becomes aware of a departure from the applicable financial reporting framework (including inadequate disclosure) and that departure is material to the financial statements, if the financial statements are not revised and the accountant concludes that modification of the standard report is adequate to disclose the departure

    a.   is the departure disclosed in a separate paragraph of the report under the heading "Known Departures From the [*identify the applicable financial reporting framework*]"?

    b.   are the effects of the departure on the financial statements disclosed if such effects have been determined by management or are known to the accountant as the result of the accountant's procedures?

    c.   if the effects of the departure have not been determined by management or are not known to the accountant as a result of the accountant's procedures, does the accountant's review report state that such determination has not been made?

        [AR-C 90A.56–.58, 90A.A105, and 90A.A110]

Alert That Restricts the Use of the Accountant's Review Report

---

Note

An accountant's review report should include an alert, in a separate paragraph, that restricts its use when the subject matter of the accountant's review report is based on measurement or disclosure criteria that are (*a*) determined by the accountant to be suitable only for a limited number of users who can be presumed to have an adequate understanding of the criteria or (*b*) available only to the specified parties. [AR-C 90A.61]

© 2020, Association of International Certified Professional Accountants

	Yes	No	N/A

13. Does the required alert appear in a separate paragraph of the accountant's review report?

 [AR-C 90A.61 and 90A.A111–.A113]

14. If the accountant's report is restricted, does the alert

 a. state that the accountant's review report is intended solely for the information and use of the specified parties?

 b. identify the specified parties for whom use is intended?

 c. state that the accountant's review report is not intended to be, and should not be, used by anyone other than the specified parties?

 [AR-C 90A.62 and 90A.A114]

15. If the accountant's report is restricted and other parties are added after the release of the accountant's review report, did the accountant either (a) amend the accountant's review report to add the other parties and, in such circumstances, not change the original date of the accountant's review report or (b) provide a written acknowledgment to management and the other parties that such parties have been added as specified parties and state in the acknowledgment that no procedures were performed subsequent to the original date of the accountant's review report?

 [AR-C 90A.64]

The Accountant's Consideration of an Entity's Ability to Continue as a Going Concern

---

Note

If adequate disclosure about an entity's ability to continue as a going concern for a reasonable period of time is not made in the financial statements, the accountant should apply paragraphs .56–.60 of AR-C 90A regarding known departures from the applicable financial reporting framework. [AR-C 90A.69] See question 12.

---

16. If, after considering conditions or events and management's plans, the accountant concludes that substantial doubt about the entity's ability to continue as a going concern for a reasonable period of time remains, does the accountant's review report include an emphasis of-matter paragraph?

 [AR-C 90A.64 and 90A.A124–.A126]

17. If an emphasis-of-matter paragraph about the entity's ability to continue as a going concern for a reasonable period of time is included, does the paragraph

 a. use terms consistent with those included in the applicable financial reporting framework?

 b. not use conditional language concerning the existence of substantial doubt about the entity's ability to continue as a going concern for a reasonable period of time?

 [AR-C 90A.68 and 90A.A123–.A126]

	Yes	No	N/A

Subsequent Events and Subsequently Discovered Facts

Note

This checklist only addresses subsequently discovered facts that become known before the report release date. Paragraphs .75–.78 of AR-C 90A provide guidance for situations in which a subsequently discovered fact becomes known to the accountant after the report release date.

---

18. If, after considering the evidence or information of subsequent events that require adjustment of, or disclosure in, the financial statements and management's consideration of whether each such event is appropriately reflected in the financial statements in accordance with the applicable financial reporting framework, the accountant determines that the subsequent event is not adequately accounted for in the financial statements or disclosed in the notes, has the accountant followed the guidance in paragraphs .56–.60 of AR-C section 90A for known departures from the applicable financial reporting framework?

    [AR-C 90A.71]

19. If a subsequently discovered fact becomes known to the accountant before the report release date and management revises the financial statements, has the accountant performed the review procedures necessary in the circumstances on the revision and either (*a*) dated the accountant's review report as of a later date or (*b*) included an additional date in the accountant's review report on the revised financial statements that is limited to the revision (that is, dual-date the accountant's review report for that revision), thereby indicating that the accountant's review procedures subsequent to the original date of the accountant's review report are limited solely to the revision of the financial statements described in the relevant note to the financial statements?

    [AR-C 90A.73]

20. If a subsequently discovered fact becomes known to the accountant before the report release date and management does not revise the financial statements in circumstances when the accountant believes they need to be revised, has the accountant modified the accountant's review report, as appropriate?

    [AR-C 90A.74]

Reference to the Work of Other Accountants in an Accountant's Review Report

---

Note

Reference to the audit or review of other accountants in the accountant's review report on the reporting entity should not be made if the other accountants issued an auditor's or an accountant's review report that includes an alert that restricts the use of such report. [AR-C 90A.80]

---

21. If other accountants audited or reviewed the financial statements of significant components, such as consolidated and unconsolidated subsidiaries and investees, and the accountant of the reporting entity decides not to assume responsibility for the audit or review performed by the other accountants, does the accountant's review report include all of the following:

    a. A clear indication that the accountant used the work of other accountants?

	Yes	No	N/A

    b.   An indication of the magnitude of the portion of the financial statements audited or reviewed by the other accountants?

       [AR-C 90A.79–.80 and 90A.A135–.A137]

22.   If the component's financial statements are prepared using a different financial reporting framework from that used for the financial statements of the reporting entity, and reference to the review or audit of the other accountants is made in the review report of the accountant of the reporting entity, has the accountant of the reporting entity performed the procedures in paragraph .82 of AR-C 90A?

       [AR-C 90A.82]

Supplementary Information That Accompanies Reviewed Financial Statements

23.   When supplementary information accompanies reviewed financial statements and the accountant's review report thereon, has the accountant clearly indicated the degree of responsibility, if any, the accountant is taking with respect to such information in either an other-matter paragraph or a separate report on the supplementary information?

       [AR-C 90A.83]

24.   When the accountant has subjected the supplementary information to review procedures applied in the accountant's review of the basic financial statements, does the other-matter paragraph in the accountant's review report on the financial statements or the separate report on the supplementary information state the following:

    a.   That the supplementary information is presented for purposes of additional analysis and is not a required part of the basic financial statements?

    b.   That the supplementary information is the responsibility of management and was derived from, and relates directly to, the underlying accounting and other records used to prepare the financial statements?

    c.   That the supplementary information has been subjected to the review procedures applied in the accountant's review of the basic financial statements?

    d.   Whether the accountant is aware of any material modifications that should be made to the supplementary information?

    e.   That the accountant has not audited the supplementary information and does not express an opinion on such information?

       [AR-C 90A.84, 90A.A142, and 90A.A144]

25.   When the accountant has not subjected supplementary information to review procedures applied in the accountant's review of the basic financial statements, does the other-matter paragraph in the accountant's review report on the financial statements or the separate report on the supplementary information state the following:

    a.   That the supplementary information is presented for purposes of additional analysis and is not a required part of the basic financial statements?

© 2020, Association of International Certified Professional Accountants

			Yes	No	N/A

b.   That the supplementary information is the responsibility of management?

c.   That the accountant has not audited or reviewed the supplementary information and, accordingly, does not express an opinion, a conclusion, nor provide any assurance on such information?

[AR-C 90A.85 and 90A.A143–.144]

Change in Engagement From Audit to Review

26.   During the audit, did the client permit the auditor to contact legal counsel? (*Note:* If the answer is "no," the accountant, except in rare circumstances, is precluded from accepting an engagement to review those financial statements.)

[AR-C 90A.93]

27.   If an audit engagement is changed to a review, does the report omit reference to (*a*) the original engagement, (*b*) any audit procedures that may have been performed, and (*c*) any scope limitation that resulted in the changed engagement?

[AR-C 90A.92]

III. Checklist Questionnaire for Review Engagements Using AR-C (Clarified) Standards After the Adoption of SSARS No. 25

	Yes	No	N/A

Note

The accountant must be independent of the entity when performing a review of financial statements in accordance with SSARSs. If, during the performance of the review engagement, the accountant determines that the accountant's independence is impaired, then the accountant should withdraw from the review engagement. [AR-C 90.10]

Basic Elements of the Report

1.   Is the accountant's review report in writing?

[AR-C 90.75 and 90.A107–.A109]

2.   Does the written review report include the following:

a.   A title that includes the word *independent* to clearly indicate that it is the report of an independent accountant for a review engagement?

b.   An addressee, based on the circumstances of the engagement?

c.   An introductory paragraph that

   i.   identifies the entity whose financial statements have been reviewed?

   ii.   states that the financial statements identified in the report were reviewed?

   iii.   identifies the financial statements?

   iv.   specifies the date or period covered by each financial statement?

    © 2020, Association of International Certified Professional Accountants

v.   includes a statement that a review includes primarily applying analytical procedures to management's financial data and making inquiries of management?

vi.   includes a statement that a review is substantially less in scope than an audit, the objective of which is the expression of an opinion regarding the financial statements as a whole, and that, accordingly, the accountant does not express such an opinion?

[AR-C 90.76 and 90.A102, 90.A104–.A106, and 90.A115]

d.   A section with the heading "Management's Responsibility for the Financial Statements" that includes an explanation that management is responsible for the preparation and fair presentation of the financial statements in accordance with the applicable financial reporting framework; this responsibility includes the design, implementation, and maintenance of internal control relevant to the preparation and fair presentation of financial statements that are free from material misstatement whether due to fraud or error?

[AR-C 90.76 and 90.A107]

e.   A section with the heading "Accountant's Responsibility" that includes the following statements:

i.   That the accountant's responsibility is to conduct the review engagement in accordance with SSARSs promulgated by the Accounting and Review Services Committee (ARSC) of the AICPA?

ii.   An explanation that those standards require that the accountant perform the procedures to obtain limited assurance as a basis for reporting whether the accountant is aware of any material modifications that should be made to the financial statements for them to be in accordance with the applicable financial reporting framework?

iii.   That the accountant believes that the results of the accountant's procedures provide a reasonable basis for the accountant's conclusion?

iv.   The accountant is required to be independent of the entity and to meet the accountant's other ethical responsibilities, in accordance with the relevant ethical requirements relating to the review?

[AR-C 90.76 and 90.A108–.A110]

f.   A concluding section with an appropriate heading that includes the accountant's conclusion on the financial statements in accordance with paragraphs .67–.74 of AR-C section 90, as appropriate? Complete questions 15-20.

[AR-C 90.76]

g.   Identification of the country of origin of the accounting principles, if applicable?

[AR-C 90.76]

h.   When the accountant's conclusion on the financial statements is modified:

      i.   a paragraph, under the appropriate heading, that contains the accountant's modified conclusion in accordance with paragraphs .69–.74 of AR-C section 90, as appropriate? Complete questions 16–19.

      ii.   a paragraph, under an appropriate heading, that provides a description of the matter or matters giving rise to the modification? Complete question 20.

          [AR-C 90.76 and 90.A119]

i.   The signature of the accountant or the accountant's firm?

      [AR-C 90.76]

j.   The city and state where the accountant practices?

      [AR-C 90.76 and 90.A120]

k.   The date of the review report, which should be no earlier than the date on which the accountant has obtained sufficient appropriate review evidence as the basis for the accountant's conclusion on the financial statements, including being satisfied that:

      i.   all the statements that the financial statements comprise, including the related notes, have been prepared and

      ii.   management has asserted that it has taken responsibility for those financial statements

          [AR-C 90.76 and 90.A121-.A122]

Comparative Financial Statements

3. When comparative financial statements are presented, does the accountant's report refer to each period for which financial statements are presented?

    [AR-C 90.82 and 90.A133–.A134]

4. When reporting on all periods presented, has the continuing accountant updated the report on one or more prior periods presented on a comparative basis with those of the current period?

    [AR-C 90.83 and 90.A135]

5. If the accountant's report on the financial statements of the prior period contains a changed reference to a departure from the applicable financial reporting framework, does the accountant's review report include an other-matter paragraph indicating the following:

    a.   The date of the accountant's previous review report?

    b.   The circumstances or events that caused the reference to be changed?

    c.   If applicable, that the financial statements of the prior period have been changed?

        [AR-C 90.86 and 90.A136]

6. If the prior period financial statements were audited and the auditor's report on the prior period financial statements is not reissued, does the review report on the current period financial statements include an other-matter paragraph indicating the following:

	Yes	No	N/A

a. That the financial statements of the prior period were previously audited?

b. The date of the auditor's report on the prior period financial statements?

c. The type of opinion issued on the prior period financial statements?

d. If the opinion was modified, the substantive reasons for the modification?

e. That no auditing procedures were performed after the date of the previous report?

[AR-C 90.87]

Emphasis of Matter Paragraphs in the Accountant's Review Report

7. If the accountant considers it necessary to draw users' attention to a matter appropriately presented or disclosed in the financial statements that, in the accountant's professional judgment, is of such importance that it is fundamental to users' understanding of the financial statements, does the accountant's review report include an emphasis-of-matter paragraph (provided that the accountant has obtained sufficient appropriate review evidence to conclude that the accountant is not aware of any material modifications that should be made to the financial statements with respect to such matter)?

[AR-C 90.89 and 90.A141–.A143]

8. Does the emphasis-of-matter paragraph refer only to information presented or disclosed in the financial statements?

[AR-C 90.89 and 90.A143]

9. When the accountant includes an emphasis-of-matter paragraph in the accountant's review report, does that paragraph

a. Include the paragraph within a separate section of the accountant's review report with a heading "Emphasis of a Matter" or other appropriate heading?

b. include a clear reference to the matter being emphasized and to where relevant disclosures that fully describe the matter can be found in the financial statements?

c. indicate that the accountant's conclusion is not modified with respect to the matter emphasized?

[AR-C 90.90 and 90.A144–.A146]

Other-Matter Paragraphs in the Accountant's Review Report

10. If the accountant considers it necessary to communicate a matter other than those that are presented or disclosed in the financial statements and, in the accountant's professional judgment, that matter is relevant to the users' understanding of the review, the accountant's responsibilities, or the accountant's review report, does the accountant's review report include an other-matter paragraph?

[AR-C 90.91]

11. Does the other-matter paragraph appear within a separate section of the accountant's review report with the heading "Other Matter" or other appropriate heading?

[AR-C 90.92, 90.A141, 90.A144, and 90.A147–.A149]

© 2020, Association of International Certified Professional Accountants

	Yes	No	N/A

Correction of a Material Misstatement in Previously Issued Financial Statements

12. If the financial statements are restated to correct a material misstatement in previously issued financial statements, does the accountant's review report include an emphasis-of-matter paragraph?

    [AR-C 90.94, 90.A152–.A154]

13. Does the emphasis-of-matter paragraph for question 12 include:

    a. a statement that the previously issued financial statements have been restated for the correction of a material misstatement in the respective period?

    b. a reference to the entity's disclosure of the correction of the material misstatement?

    [AR-C 90.95 and 90.A155]

14. If the financial statement disclosures relating to the restatement to correct a material misstatement in previously issued financial statements are not adequate, does the accountant express a "Qualified Conclusion" or "Adverse Conclusion," as appropriate?

    [AR-C 90.96]

Form of the Conclusion

15. When the accountant expresses an unmodified conclusion, does the accountant's review report include a separate paragraph titled "Accountant's Conclusion" that states "Based on my (our) review, I am (we are) not aware of any material modifications that should be made to the accompanying financial statements for them to be in accordance with [the applicable financial reporting framework]" unless required by law or regulation?

    [AR-C 90.68]

16. If the accountant determines, based on the procedures performed and the review evidence obtained, or otherwise determines that the financial statements are materially misstated, does the accountant express:

    a. a qualified conclusion, if the accountant concludes that the effects of the matter or matters giving rise to the modification are material but not pervasive to the financial statements?

    b. an adverse conclusion, when the effects of the matter or matters giving rise to the modification are both material and pervasive to the financial statements?

    [AR-C 90.71 and 90.A106]

17. When the accountant modifies the conclusion expressed on the financial statements, does the accountant's review report

    a. replace the heading "Accountant's Conclusion" with the heading "Qualified Conclusion" or "Adverse Conclusion," as appropriate, for the conclusion paragraph in the accountant's review report?

       © 2020, Association of International Certified Professional Accountants

	Yes	*No*	*N/A*

b.   provide a description of the matter giving rise to the modification, under an appropriate heading (for example, "Basis for Qualified Conclusion," or "Basis for Adverse Conclusion," as appropriate), in a separate paragraph in the accountant's review report immediately before the conclusion paragraph?

[AR-C 90.70]

18.   When the accountant expresses a qualified conclusion on the financial statements because of a material misstatement, does the accountant's review report state, unless otherwise required by law or regulation, that "Based on my (our) review, except for the effects of the matter(s) described in the Basis for Qualified Conclusion paragraph, I am (we are) not aware of any material modifications that should be made to the accompanying financial statements in order for them to be in accordance with [the applicable financial reporting framework]"?

[AR-C 90.72]

19.   When the accountant expresses an adverse conclusion on the financial statements, does the accountant's review report state, unless otherwise required by law or regulation, that "Based on my (our) review, due to the significance of the matter(s) described in the Basis for Adverse Conclusion paragraph, the financial statements are not in accordance with [the applicable financial reporting framework]"?

[AR-C 90.73]

20.   Does the "Basis for Qualified Conclusion" or "Basis for Adverse Conclusion" paragraph, as appropriate:

a.   describe and quantify the financial effects of the material misstatement if the misstatement relates to specific amounts in the financial statements (including quantitative disclosures) if the effects of the departure on the financial statements have been determined by management or are known to the accountant as a result of the accountant's procedures?

b.   state in the report that a determination of the effects has not been made by management if that is the fact and the effects are not known to the accountant as a result of the accountant's procedures?

c.   explain how disclosure(s) are misstated if the material misstatement relates to narrative disclosure(s)?

d.   describe the nature of omitted information if the material misstatement relates to the nondisclosure of information required to be disclosed and include the omitted disclosure(s) when practicable to do so?

[AR-C 90.74]

© 2020, Association of International Certified Professional Accountants

Yes   *No*   *N/A*

Other Reporting Responsibilities

21. If the accountant is requested to address other reporting responsibilities in the accountant's review report on the financial statements (in addition to the accountant's responsibilities to report on the financial statements, are those other reporting responsibilities addressed by the accountant in a separate section of the accountant's review report, under the heading "Report on Other Legal and Regulatory Requirements," or otherwise, as appropriate to the content of the section, following the section of the report titled "Report on the Financial Statements?"   ____   ____   ____

   [AR-C 90.97 and 90.A156]

Alert That Restricts the Use of the Accountant's Review Report

---

Note

An accountant's review report should include an alert, in a separate paragraph, that restricts its use when the subject matter of the accountant's review report is based on (*a*) measurement or disclosure criteria that are determined by the accountant to be suitable only for a limited number of users who can be presumed to have an adequate understanding of the criteria or (*b*) measurement or disclosure criteria that available only to the specified parties. [AR-C 90.103 and 90.A163–.A165]

---

22. Does the required alert appear in a separate paragraph of the accountant's review report?   ____   ____   ____

   [AR-C 90.103 and 90.A163–.A165]

23. If the accountant's report is restricted, does the alert

   a. state that the accountant's review report is intended solely for the information and use of the specified parties?   ____   ____   ____

   b. identify the specified parties for whom use is intended?   ____   ____   ____

   c. state that the accountant's review report is not intended to be, and should not be, used by anyone other than the specified parties?   ____   ____   ____

   [AR-C 90.104 and 90.A166]

24. If the accountant's report is restricted and other parties are added after the release of the accountant's review report, did the accountant either (*a*) amend the accountant's review report to add the other parties and, in such circumstances, not change the original date of the accountant's review report or (*b*) provide a written acknowledgment to management and the other parties that such parties have been added as specified parties and state in the acknowledgment that no procedures were performed subsequent to the original date of the accountant's review report?   ____   ____   ____

   [AR-C 90.106]

When Substantial Doubt Exists About the Entity's Ability to Continue as a Going Concern

25. If, after considering conditions or events and management's plans, the accountant concludes that substantial doubt about the entity's ability to continue as a going concern for a reasonable period of time remains, does the accountant's review report include a separate section with the heading "Substantial Doubt About the Entity's Ability to Continue as a Going Concern?"   ____   ____   ____

   [AR-C 90.109 and 90.A175–.A182]

	Yes	No	N/A

26. If a "Substantial Doubt About the Entity's Ability to Continue as a Going Concern" is included, does the paragraph

    a.   draw attention to the note in the financial statements that discloses the conditions or events identified and management's plans that deal with these conditions or events and that these conditions or events indicate that substantial doubt exists about the entity's ability to continue as a going concern for a reasonable period of time?   ____ ____ ____

    b.   state that the accountant's conclusion is not modified with respect to the matter?   ____ ____ ____

    c.   use terms consistent with those included in the applicable financial reporting framework?   ____ ____ ____

    d.   not use conditional language concerning the existence of substantial doubt about the entity's ability to continue as a going concern for a reasonable period of time?   ____ ____ ____

    [AR-C 90.109–.110 and 90.A175–.A182]

27. If adequate disclosure about an entity's ability to continue as a going concern for a reasonable period of time is not made in the financial statements, does the accountant's review report:

    a.   include a qualified or adverse conclusion, as appropriate?   ____ ____ ____

    b.   state in the "Basis for Qualified (Adverse) Conclusion" section of the accountant's review report, that either (1) substantial doubt exists about the entity's ability to continue as a going concern and that the financial statements do not adequately disclose this matter or (2) substantial doubt about the entity's ability to continue as a going concern has been alleviated by management's plans but the financial statements do not adequately disclose this matter, as appropriate?   ____ ____ ____

    [AR-C 90.111]

Reference to the Work of Other Accountants in an Accountant's Review Report

---

Note

Reference to the audit or review of other accountants in the accountant's review report on the reporting entity should not be made if the other accountants issued an auditor's or an accountant's review report that includes an alert that restricts the use of such report. [AR-C 90.123]

---

28. If other accountants audited or reviewed the financial statements of significant components, such as consolidated and unconsolidated subsidiaries and investees, and the accountant of the reporting entity decides not to assume responsibility for the audit or review performed by the other accountants, does the accountant's review report include all of the following:

    a.   A clear indication that the accountant used the work of other accountants?   ____ ____ ____

    b.   An indication of the magnitude of the portion of the financial statements audited or reviewed by the other accountants?   ____ ____ ____

    [AR-C 90.122 and 90.A191–.A193]

© 2020, Association of International Certified Professional Accountants

	Yes	*No*	*N/A*

29. If the component's financial statements are prepared using a different financial reporting framework from that used for the financial statements of the reporting entity, and reference to the review or audit of the other accountants is made in the review report of the accountant of the reporting entity, has the accountant of the reporting entity performed the procedures in paragraph .125 of AR-C 90?   ____   ____   ____

   [AR-C 90.125]

Subsequent Events and Subsequently Discovered Facts That Become Known to the Accountant Before the Report Release Date

---

Note

This checklist only addresses subsequently discovered facts that become known before the report release date. Paragraphs .54–.57 of AR-C 90 provide guidance for situations in which a subsequently discovered fact becomes known to the accountant after the report release date.

---

30. If the accountant determines that a subsequent event is not adequately accounted for in the financial statements or disclosed in the notes, has the accountant issued a modified conclusion in accordance with paragraphs .69–.72 of AU-C 90? Complete questions 16–20.   ____   ____   ____

   [AR-C 90.50]

31. If a subsequently discovered fact becomes known to the accountant before the report release date and management revises the financial statements, has the accountant performed the review procedures necessary in the circumstances on the revision and either (*a*) dated the accountant's review report as of a later date or (*b*) included an additional date in the accountant's review report on the revised financial statements that is limited to the revision (that is, dual-date the accountant's review report for that revision), thereby indicating that the accountant's review procedures subsequent to the original date of the accountant's review report are limited solely to the revision of the financial statements described in the relevant note to the financial statements?   ____   ____   ____

   [AR-C 90.52]

32. If a subsequently discovered fact becomes known to the accountant before the report release date and management does not revise the financial statements in circumstances when the accountant believes they need to be revised, has the accountant modified the accountant's review report, or withdrawn from the engagement, as appropriate?   ____   ____   ____

   [AR-C 90.53 and 90.76]

Supplementary Information That Accompanies Reviewed Financial Statements

33. When supplementary information accompanies reviewed financial statements and the accountant's review report thereon, has the accountant clearly indicated the degree of responsibility, if any, the accountant is taking with respect to such information in either an other-matter paragraph or a separate report on the supplementary information?   ____   ____   ____

   [AR-C 90.126]

      © 2020, Association of International Certified Professional Accountants

34. When the accountant has subjected the supplementary information to review procedures applied in the accountant's review of the basic financial statements, does the other-matter paragraph in the accountant's review report on the financial statements or the separate report on the supplementary information state the following:

   a. That the supplementary information is presented for purposes of additional analysis and is not a required part of the basic financial statements?

   b. That the supplementary information is the responsibility of management and was derived from, and relates directly to, the underlying accounting and other records used to prepare the financial statements?

   c. That the supplementary information has been subjected to the review procedures applied in the accountant's review of the basic financial statements?

   d. Whether the accountant is aware of any material modifications that should be made to the supplementary information?

   e. That the accountant has not audited the supplementary information and does not express an opinion on such information?

       [AR-C 90.127, 90.A198, and 90.A200]

35. When the accountant has not subjected supplementary information to review procedures applied in the accountant's review of the basic financial statements, does the other-matter paragraph in the accountant's review report on the financial statements or the separate report on the supplementary information state the following:

   a. That the supplementary information is presented for purposes of additional analysis and is not a required part of the basic financial statements?

   b. That the supplementary information is the responsibility of management?

   c. That the accountant has not audited or reviewed the supplementary information and, accordingly, does not express an opinion, a conclusion, nor provide any assurance on such information?

       [AR-C 90.128 and 90.A199–.A200]

Change in Engagement From Audit to Review

36. During the audit, did the client permit the auditor to contact legal counsel? (*Note:* If the answer is "no," the accountant, except in rare circumstances, is precluded from accepting an engagement to review those financial statements.)

    [AR-C 90.136]

37. If an audit engagement is changed to a review, does the accountant's review report omit reference to (*a*) the original engagement, (*b*) any audit procedures that may have been performed, and (*c*) any scope limitation that resulted in the changed engagement?

    [AR-C 90.135]

Part 6
Illustrative Financial Statements, Notes, and Auditor's Report

.01 The following illustrative auditor's report and financial statements demonstrate financial statement formats and disclosures appropriate for not-for-profit entities (NFPs). These illustrations are not intended to represent the *only* appropriate presentation and disclosure formats, however. NFPs are urged to develop financial statement formats that are appropriate for their individual circumstances and are consistent with the accounting and reporting practices promulgated. Furthermore, the illustrative financial statements do not include all disclosures and presentation items promulgated.

.02

The following auditor's report does not illustrate the new reporting standards in AU-C section 700, *Forming an Opinion and Reporting on Financial Statements*.[1] For eight illustrative auditor's reports that comply with the new reporting standards, refer to the exhibit in AU-C section 700.

Independent Auditor's Report

The Board of Directors

STEM to STEAM and Beyond, Inc.

Report on the Financial Statements

We have audited the accompanying statement of financial position of STEM to STEAM and Beyond, Inc. (the Organization), as of June 30, 20X1, and the related statements of activities, cash flows, and functional expenses for the year then ended, and the related notes to the financial statements.

Management's Responsibility for the Financial Statements

Management is responsible for the preparation and fair presentation of these financial statements in accordance with accounting principles generally accepted in the United States of America; this includes the design, implementation, and maintenance of internal control relevant to the preparation and fair presentation of financial statements that are free from material misstatement, whether due to fraud or error.

Auditor's Responsibility

Our responsibility is to express an opinion on these financial statements based on our audit. We conducted our audit in accordance with auditing standards generally accepted in the United States. Those standards require that we plan and perform the audit to obtain reasonable assurance about whether the financial statements are free of material misstatement.

An audit involves performing procedures to obtain audit evidence about the amounts and disclosures in the financial statements. The procedures selected depend on the auditor's judgment, including the assessment of the risks of material misstatement of the financial statements, whether due to fraud or error. In making those risk assessments, the auditor considers internal control relevant to the entity's preparation and fair presentation of the financial statements in order to design audit procedures that are appropriate in the circumstances, but not for the purpose of expressing an opinion on the effectiveness of the entity's internal control. Accordingly, we express no such opinion. An audit also includes evaluating the appropriateness of accounting policies used and the reasonableness of significant accounting estimates made by management, as well as evaluating the overall presentation of the financial statements.

---

[1] All AU-C sections can be found in AICPA *Professional Standards*.

© 2020, Association of International Certified Professional Accountants

We believe that the audit evidence we have obtained is sufficient and appropriate to provide a basis for our audit opinion.

Opinion

In our opinion, the financial statements referred to in the first paragraph present fairly, in all material respects, the financial position of the Organization, as of June 30, 20X1, and the changes in its net assets and its cash flows for the year then ended in conformity with accounting principles generally accepted in the United States of America.

[*Signature*]

[*Auditor's city and state*]

September 29, 20X1

The checklists and illustrative financial statements do not include all disclosures and presentation items promulgated.

.03

STEM to STEAM and Beyond, Inc.
Statements of Financial Position
June 30, 20X1

	20X1	20X0[2]
Assets		
Cash and cash equivalents	$978,572	$873,645
Accounts receivable, net	35,752	30,520
Short term investments	1,300,694	
Contributions receivable, net	1,594,053	2,273,761
Prepaid and other assets	151,171	172,712
Note receivable from related party	80,000	
Land, buildings and equipment, net	1,655,368	1,725,538
Endowment and long-term investments	6,457,512	6,402,706
Beneficial interest in trust	2,641,762	2,589,206
Total assets	$14,894,884	$14,068,088
Liabilities and net assets		
Accounts payable	$335,595	258,738
Accrued expenses and other liabilities	594,454	555,238
Asset retirement obligations	148,613	138,811
Obligations under split-interest agreements	337,881	289,734
Notes payable and capital lease obligations	1,513,893	1,512,405
Total liabilities	2,930,436	2,754,926
Net assets:		
Without donor restrictions	1,183,976	1,310,105
With donor restrictions	10,780,472	10,003,057
Total net assets	11,964,448	11,313,162
Total liabilities and net assets	$14,894,884	$14,068,088

The accompanying notes are an integral part of these financial statements.

---

[2] *Note:* Comparative financial information included in the statement of financial position is provided solely to facilitate the reader's understanding of the statement of cash flows. It is not intended to represent a comparative financial statement presentation in accordance with generally accepted accounting principles, nor would it be included in the single-year financial statements illustrated here.

.04

STEM to STEAM and Beyond, Inc.
Statement of Activities
For the Year Ended June 30, 20X1

	Without Donor Restrictions	With Donor Restrictions	Total
Revenues, gains, and other support:			
Support, other than annual showcase:			
Contributions — Science Alliance	$600,000	$1,400,000	$2,000,000
Contributions — gifts in kind	262,440	—	262,440
Contributions — other	701,300	249,600	950,900
Grants from state agencies	215,000	200,000	415,000
Grants from federal agencies	—	500,000	500,000
Total support other than annual showcase	1,778,740	2,349,600	4,128,340
Annual showcase:			
Ticket sales	915,100	—	915,100
Direct benefits to donors	(125,900)	—	(125,900)
Net support from annual showcase	789,200	—	789,200
Program service fees	247,630	—	247,630
Investment return, net	15,768	468,443	484,211
Other revenue	31,100	—	31,100
Other revenues and gains	294,498	468,443	762,941
Support provided by expiring time and purpose restrictions	2,001,385	(2,001,385)	—
Total revenues, gains, and other support	4,863,823	816,658	5,680,481
Expenses			
Program services:			
Curriculum development and class kits	1,891,927	—	1,891,927
Teacher training and awards	1,283,669	—	1,283,669
STEAM Saturdays	621,125	—	621,125
Collaborative activities and other	391,760	—	391,760
Total program services	4,188,481	—	4,188,481
General and administrative	541,765	—	541,765
Fundraising	259,706	—	259,706
Total expenses	4,989,952	—	4,989,952
Change in valuation of split-interest agreements		(39,243)	(39,243)
Change in net assets	($126,129)	$777,415	$651,286

The accompanying notes are an integral part of these financial statements.

© 2020, Association of International Certified Professional Accountants

STEM to STEAM and Beyond, Inc.
Statement of Functional Expenses
Year Ended June 30, 20X1

	Curriculum Development and Class Kits	Teacher Training and Awards	STEAM Saturdays	Collaborative Activities and Other Programs	Program Services	General and Administrative	Fund Raising	Total
Salaries	$730,253	$574,026	$247,126	$146,116	$1,697,521	$201,647	$161,146	$2,060,314
Employee benefits and payroll taxes	202,328	173,280	92,650	42,315	510,573	58,402	47,374	616,349
Total salaries and related expenses	932,581	747,306	339,776	188,431	2,208,094	260,049	208,520	2,676,663
Professional and consultant services	139,807	53,347	24,014	80,847	298,015	125,489	24,205	447,709
Supplies	231,782	3,588	85,424	40,900	361,694	4,952	10,896	377,542
Telephone and internet services	43,363	18,172	3,243	11,016	75,794	1,145	662	77,601
Postage and shipping	2,750	5,365	4,342	785	13,242	2,083	3,243	18,568
Occupancy	57,216	18,769	1,134	10,780	87,899	40,934	18,555	147,388
Equipment rental and maintenance	17,517	2,435	2,614	858	23,424	6,652	934	31,010
Promotion and printing	118,419	12,302	1,786	30,796	163,303	171	49,746	213,220
Travel and meetings expense	186,425	94,672	76,438	12,558	370,093	15,874	45,757	431,724
Teacher awards	—	225,000	—	—	225,000	—	—	225,000
Insurance	12,032	6,107	17,228	2,152	37,519	16,685	2,343	56,547
Interest expense	34,612	23,952	15,578	7,385	81,527	9,479	4,306	95,312
Depreciation and amortization	29,886	20,094	17,327	3,557	70,864	27,577	3,872	102,313
Other	85,537	52,560	32,221	1,695	172,013	30,675	12,567	215,255
Total expenses	$1,891,927	$1,283,669	$621,125	$391,760	$4,188,481	$541,765	385,606	$5,115,852
Direct benefit to donors at showcase							(125,900)	
							$259,706	

The accompanying notes are an integral part of these financial statements.

.05

STEM to STEAM and Beyond, Inc.
Statement of Cash Flows
For the Year Ended June 30, 20X1

Operating activities:

Cash inflows for operations:

Contributions, net of amounts restricted for long-term purposes	$3,588,276
Grants from state and federal agencies	904,379
Ticket sales from annual showcase	915,100
Program service fees	247,630
Investment income and distribution from trust	314,709
Other cash receipts	30,000

Cash outflows for operations:

Payments for salaries, benefits, and payroll taxes	(2,668,839)
Payments to vendors	(1,683,734)
Teacher awards	(225,000)
Interest paid	(94,421)
Net cash provided by operating activities	1,328,100

Investing activities:

Proceeds from sales of investments	380,619
Purchases of investments	(1,540,237)
Note receivable provided to related party	(80,000)
Proceeds from sale of land, buildings, and equipment	49,000
Purchases of land, buildings, and equipment	(5,043)
Net cash used by investing activities	(1,195,661)

Financing activities:

Collections of contributions receivable restricted for long-term investment	20,000
Cash transferred to establish new split-interest agreements	45,000
Payments to beneficiaries of split-interest agreements	(64,000)
Payments of note payable	(23,142)
Payments of capital lease obligations	(5,370)
Net cash used by financing activities	(27,512)

Change in cash and cash equivalents	104,927
Cash and cash equivalents at beginning of year	873,645
Cash and cash equivalents at end of year	$978,572

Supplemental disclosures:

Equipment acquired by capital lease	$30,000
Contribution of equipment	$45,000
Contribution of securities added to endowment	$5,000

The accompanying notes are an integral part of these financial statements.

© 2020, Association of International Certified Professional Accountants

.07

STEM to STEAM and Beyond, Inc.
Notes to Financial Statements
For the Year Ended June 30, 20X1

1. Description of Organization

STEM to STEAM and Beyond, Inc. (the organization) strives to inspire and motivate students to pursue careers in Science, Technology, Engineering, Arts, and Math (STEAM) and to engage educators, families, communities and employers to provide students with opportunities to experience STEAM in an interactive way.

- *Curriculum Development and Class Kits.* The organization has developed over fifty hands-on classroom kits that are coordinated with activities that encourage both teachers and students to build and explore STEAM. These activities are designed to demonstrate unusual or unexpected phenomena, spark curiosity, generate questions, and serve as the starting points for deeper class-room explorations. All classroom kits are provided at a minimal charge to schools thanks to the support of our sponsors.

- *Teacher Training and Awards.* The organization's staff of scientists and veteran science educators leads sessions that help teachers develop their skills as facilitators of inquiry-rich, authentic student learning experiences. Each year, more than three hundred teachers attend programs de-signed to provide opportunities to ask questions as learners, share expertise as practitioners, and develop as leaders. Training takes place via:

    — Daylong conferences, which feature a plenary session, a choice of three hands-on workshops, and a networking wrap-up so teachers can learn from each other, and

    — Summer week-long institutes, in which teachers work alongside staff members of local museums, engineering and science professionals, and expert faculty to learn firsthand how to teach concepts in their classroom and how those concepts are relevant to future technological advances, so they will be better able to share these experiences and knowledge with their own students. Each week-long institute focuses on an area such as applied mathematics, environmental science, or biomedical engineering.

    In addition, the organization seeks out educators who have successfully engaged students in a unique manner and provides monetary awards that allow those teachers to continue their exploration of ways to bring STEAM to the classroom. Many award-winning teachers become trainers at our daylong conferences and summer institutes.

- *STEAM Saturdays.* On weekends, the organization takes its classroom kits on the road, reaching out to children who may not experience STEAM activities in the classroom. We set up in shopping malls, local museums, YMCAs, park districts, and other public places where we will be able to engage elementary-aged children in a workshop setting to explore, design and create. Led by our staff and adult and high-school volunteers, children undertake a wide variety of projects, from constructing zoetropes, kaleidoscopes, catapults, and bridges, to wiring circuits or creating musical instruments to take home with them.

- *Collaborative Activities and Other Programs.* The organization collaborates and cooperates nationally within the STEAM community to share with and learn from others. Due in part to President Bush's "America COMPETES Act" and President Obama's "Educate to Innovate" program, there is a nationwide effort committed to making the improvement of STEM education a national priority. Top universities, companies, philanthropists, scientists, engineers, educators, and the private sector are all involved in the effort.

Management and general activities include the functions necessary to provide support for the organization's program activities. They include activities that provide governance (Board of Directors), oversight, business management, financial recordkeeping, budgeting, legal services, human resource management, and similar functions that ensure an adequate working environment and an equitable employment program.

Fundraising activities include publicizing and conducting fundraising campaigns; maintaining donor lists; conducting special fundraising events; and other activities involved with soliciting contributions from corporations, foundations, individuals, and others.

2. Significant Accounting Policies

The organization prepares its financial statements in accordance with accounting principles generally accepted in the United States of America (U.S. GAAP) for not-for-profit entities. The significant accounting and reporting policies used by the organization are described subsequently to enhance the usefulness and understandability of the financial statements.

Basis of Accounting

The organization prepares its financial statements using the accrual basis of accounting and U.S. GAAP.

Use of Estimates

The preparation of financial statements requires management to make estimates and assumptions that affect the reported amounts of revenues and expenses during the reporting period and the reported amounts of assets and liabilities at the date of the financial statements. On an ongoing basis, the organization's management evaluates the estimates and assumptions based upon historical experience and various other factors and circumstances. The organization's management believes that the estimates and assumptions are reasonable in the circumstances; however, the actual results could differ from those estimates.

Net Assets

The financial statements report net assets and changes in net assets in two classes that are based upon the existence or absence of restrictions on use that are placed by its donors, as follows:

Net Assets Without Donor Restrictions

Net assets without donor restrictions are resources available to support operations. The only limits on the use of these net assets are the broad limits resulting for the nature of the organization, the environment in which it operates, the purposes specified in it corporate documents and its application for tax-exempt status, and any limits resulting from contractual agreements with creditors and others that are entered into in the course of its operations.

Net Assets With Donor Restrictions

Net assets with donor restrictions are resources that are restricted by a donor for use for a particular purpose or in a particular future period. Some donor-imposed restrictions are temporary in nature, and the restriction will expire when the resources are used in accordance with the donor's instructions or when the stipulated time has passed. Other donor-imposed restrictions are perpetual in nature; the organization must continue to use the resources in accordance with the donor's instructions.

The organization's unspent contributions are included in this class if the donor limited their use, as are its donor-restricted endowment funds and its beneficial interest in a perpetual charitable trust held by a bank trustee.

When a donor's restriction is satisfied, either by using the resources in the manner specified by the donor or by the passage of time, the expiration of the restriction is reported in the financial statements by reclassifying the net assets from net assets with donor restrictions to net assets without donor restrictions. Net assets restricted for acquisition of buildings or equipment (or less commonly, the contribution of those assets directly) are reported as net assets with donor restrictions until the specified asset is placed in service by the organization, unless the donor provides more specific directions about the period of its use.

© 2020, Association of International Certified Professional Accountants

Classification of Transactions

All revenues and net gains are reported as increases in net assets without donor restrictions in the statement of activities unless the donor specified the use of the related resources for a particular purpose or in a future period. All expenses and net losses other than losses on endowment investments are reported as decreases in net assets without donor restrictions. Net gains on endowment investments increase net assets with donor restrictions, and net losses on endowment investments reduce that net asset class.

Cash and Cash Equivalents

Cash equivalents are short term, interest bearing, highly liquid investments with original maturities of three months or less, unless the investments are held for meeting restrictions of a capital or endowment nature. The organization maintains cash balances at several financial institutions located in Chicago and its suburbs. Deposit accounts at each bank are insured by the FDIC up to $250,000 per account. The balances occasionally exceed those limits. Cash equivalents, other securities, and limited amounts of cash held in brokerage accounts are protected by the Securities Investor Protection Corporation (SIPC) in the event of broker-dealer failure, up to $500,000 of protection for each brokerage account, with a limit of $250,000 for claims of uninvested cash balances. Additional broker-age insurance — in addition to SIPC protection — is provided through underwriters in London. The SIPC insurance does not protect against market losses on investments.

Accounts Receivable

Accounts receivable are primarily unsecured non-interest-bearing amounts due from grantors on cost reimbursement or performance grants. Management believes that all outstanding accounts receivable are collectible in full, therefore no allowance for uncollectible receivables has been provided.

Short Term Investments

The organization invests cash in excess of its immediate needs in money market funds and U.S Government and Government Agency issues. Short term investments are reported at fair value.

The investment policy specific to these investments is monitored by the Investment Committee of the organization's Board of Directors. The policy requires that investments be readily marketable and nonvolatile. The money market funds must be managed in accordance with Rule 2a-7 of the Securities and Exchange Commission's Investment Company Act of 1940 and have as an objective maintaining a net asset value (NAV) per share of $1.00. The U.S. Department of the Treasury issues must have a maturity of 1 year or less at time of purchase.

Contributions Receivable

Contributions receivable are unconditional promises to give that are recognized as contributions when the promise is received. Contributions receivable that are expected to be collected in less than one year are reported at net realizable value. Contributions receivable that are expected to be collected in more than one year are recorded at fair value at the date of promise. That fair value is computed using a present value technique applied to anticipated cash flows. Amortization of the resulting discount is recognized as additional contribution revenue. The allowance for uncollectible contributions receivable is determined based on management's evaluation of the collectibility of individual promises. Promises that remain uncollected more than one year after their due dates are written off unless the donors indicate that payment is merely postponed.

Prepaid and Other Assets

Prepaid and other assets are primarily classroom kits, which are reported at cost to assemble. Classroom kits are sold at minimal charge to schools because of the support of our contributors, many of whom donate the materials that are included in the kits. Thus, the cost of the kits exceeds the amount that will be realized upon sale, but the utility of the kits on the financial statement date is not impaired.

Land, Buildings, and Equipment

Land, buildings and equipment are reported in the statement of financial position at cost, if purchased, and at fair value at the date of donation, if donated. All land and buildings are capitalized. Equipment is capitalized if it has a cost of $1,000 or more and a useful life when acquired of more than 1 year. Repairs and maintenance that do not significantly increase the useful life of the asset are expensed as incurred. Depreciation and amortization is computed using the straight-line method over the estimated useful lives of the assets, as follows:

Buildings and improvements	40 years
Leasehold improvements	20 years, or remaining lease term, if shorter
Furnishings and equipment	5–10 years
Equipment used under capital leases	5–7 years

Land, buildings and equipment are reviewed for impairment when a significant change in the asset's use or another indicator of possible impairment is present. No impairment losses were recognized in the financial statements in the current period.

Endowment and Long-term Investments

Endowment investments consist of investments purchased with the following resources:

- Donor-restricted perpetual endowments, which are contributions restricted by donors to investment in perpetuity with only investment income and appreciation being used to support the organization's activities.

- Donor-restricted term endowments, which are contributions restricted by donors to investment for the term specified by the donor. During that term, the donor may either require investment income and appreciation to be reinvested in the fund, or may permit the organization to spend those amounts in accordance with the donor's restrictions on use.

- Board-designated endowments, which are resources set aside by the Board of Directors for an indeterminate period to operate in a manner similar to a donor-restricted perpetual endowment. Because a board-designated endowment results from an internal designation, it can be spent upon action of the Board of Directors.

Endowment investments also include investments purchased with unspent investment income and net gains on these resources. Other long-term investments are held under split-interest agreements with donors.

Endowment investments are reported at fair value with changes to fair value reported as investment return in the statement of activities. Purchases and sales of investments are reported on the trade date.

The investment and spending policies for the Endowment Fund are discussed in note 8.

Beneficial Interest in Trust

The organization is the irrevocable beneficiary of a perpetual charitable trust held by a bank trustee. The beneficial interest in the trust is reported at its fair value, which is estimated as the fair value of the underlying trust assets. Distributions of income from the trust assets are restricted to use in the curriculum development program and are reported as investment return increasing net assets with donor restrictions. The value of the beneficial interest in the trust is adjusted annually for the change in its estimated fair value. Those changes in value are also reported as increases in net assets with donor restrictions, because the trust assets will never be distributed to the organization.

Split Interest Agreements

The organization conducts a deferred-giving program that offers gift annuity agreements and irrevocable charitable remainder trusts to donors with the organization serving as trustee. Assets held in the trusts are included in endowment and long-term investments. Contribution revenues are recognized when trusts (or annuity agreements) are established, after recording liabilities for the present value of the estimated future payments to be made to beneficiaries. The liabilities are adjusted annually for changes in the value of assets, accretion of the discount, and other changes in the estimates of future benefits. Additional information about split-interest gifts is found in note 12.

Accounting for Contributions

Contributions, including unconditional promises to give, are recognized when received. All contributions are reported as increases in net assets without donor restrictions unless use of the contributed assets is specifically restricted by the donor. Amounts received that are restricted by the donor to use in future periods or for specific purposes are reported as increases in net assets with donor restrictions. Unconditional promises with payments due in future years have an implied restriction to be used in the year the payment is due, and therefore are reported as restricted until the payment is due, unless the contribution is clearly intended to support activities of the current fiscal year. Conditional promises, such as matching grants, are not recognized until they become unconditional, that is, until all conditions on which they depend are substantially met.

The organization is a beneficiary under several donors' wills. Contributions from bequests are recognized as contributions receivable when the probate court declares that the will is valid and the organization has an irrevocable right to the bequest.

Gifts-in-Kind Contributions

The organization receives contributions in a form other than cash or investments. Most are donated supplies, which are recorded as contributions at the date of gift and as expenses when the donated items are placed into service or distributed. If the organization receives a contribution of land, buildings, or equipment, the contributed asset is recognized as an asset at its estimated fair value at the date of gift, provided that the value of the asset and its estimated useful life meets the organization's capitalization policy. Donated use of facilities is reported as contributions and as expenses at the estimated fair value of similar space for rent under similar conditions. If the use of the space is promised unconditionally for a period greater than one year, the contribution is reported as a contribution and an unconditional promise to give at the date of gift, and the expense is reported over the term of use.

The organization benefits from personal services provided by a substantial number of volunteers. Those volunteers have donated significant amounts of time and services in the organization's program operations and in its fund-raising campaigns. However, the majority of the contributed services do not meet the criteria for recognition in financial statements. GAAP allow recognition of contributed services only if (*a*) the services create or enhance nonfinancial assets or (*b*) the services would have been purchased if not provided by contribution, require specialized skills, and are provided by individuals possessing those skills. Donated services with an estimated fair value of $24,550 met those criteria and are included in in-kind contributions in the statement of activities. Those services were primarily teaching services used in curriculum development and the teacher training classes.

Grant Revenue

Grant revenue is recognized when the qualifying costs are incurred for cost-reimbursement grants or contracts or when a unit of service is provided for performance grants. Grant revenue from federal agencies is subject to independent audit under the Office of Management and Budget's audit requirements for federal awards and review by grantor agencies. The review could result in the disallowance of expenditures under the terms of the grant or reductions of future grant funds. Based on prior experience, the organization's management believes that costs ultimately disallowed, if any, would not materially affect the financial position of the organization.

Expense Recognition and Allocation

The cost of providing the organization's programs and other activities is summarized on a functional basis in the statement of activities and statement of functional expenses. Expenses that can be identified with a specific program or support service are charged directly to that program or support service. Costs common to multiple functions have been allocated among the various functions benefited using a reasonable allocation method that is consistently applied, as follows:

- Salaries and wages, benefits, and payroll taxes are allocated based on activity reports prepared by key personnel.

- Occupancy, depreciation, and amortization, and interest are allocated on a square foot basis dependent on the programs and supporting activities occupying the space.

- Telephone and internet services, insurance, and supplies and miscellaneous expenses that cannot be directly identified are allocated on the basis of employee headcount for each program and supporting activity.

Every three years, or more often when new space or programs are added, the bases on which costs are allocated are evaluated.

General and administrative expenses include those costs that are not directly identifiable with any specific program, but which provide for the overall support and direction of the organization.

Fundraising costs are expensed as incurred, even though they may result in contributions received in future years. The organization generally does not conduct its fundraising activities in conjunction with its other activities. In the few cases in which it does, such as when the annual report or donor acknowledgements contain requests for contributions, joint costs have been allocated between fundraising and general and administrative expenses in accordance with standards for accounting for costs of activities that include fundraising. Additionally, advertising costs are expensed as incurred.

Tax Status

The organization is exempt from federal income taxation under Section 501(c)(3) of the IRC, though it would be subject to tax on income unrelated to its exempt purposes (unless that income is otherwise excluded by the IRC). Contributions to the organization are tax deductible to donors under Section 170 of the IRC. The organization is not classified as a private foundation.

Change in Accounting Principles

The organization implemented FASB Accounting Standards Update (ASU) No. 2016-14, *Not-for-Profit Entities (Topic 958): Presentation of Financial Statements of Not-for-Profit Entities*, in the current year, applying the changes retrospectively. The new standards change the following aspects of the financial statements:

- The temporarily restricted and permanently restricted net asset classes have been combined into a single net asset class called net assets with donor restrictions.

- The unrestricted net asset class has been renamed net assets without donor restrictions.

- The format of the statement of cash flows has changed to the direct method of reporting cash flows from operations, which we believe to be more understandable for the users of our financial statements

- The financial statements include a disclosure about liquidity and availability of resources (note 3)

- At July 1, 20X0, the classification has changed from unrestricted net assets to net assets with donor restrictions for the $13,434 deficit on an endowment fund that had investments with a fair value of $86,566, and an original gift amount of $100,000, and the organization has disclosed how this underwater situation affects spending from the fund (note 8)

The changes have the following effect on net assets at July 1, 20X0:

Net Asset Class	As Originally Presented	After Adoption of ASU No. 2016-14
Unrestricted net assets	$ 1,296,671	
Temporarily restricted net assets	3,613,785	
Permanently restricted net assets	6,402,706	
Net assets without donor restrictions		$ 1,310,105
Net assets with donor restrictions		10,003,057
Total net assets	$11,313,162	$11,313,162

3. Liquidity and Availability

Financial assets available for general expenditure, that is, without donor or other restrictions limiting their use, within one year of June 30, 20X1 are:

Financial assets:	
Cash and cash equivalents	$ 978,572
Accounts receivable, net	35,752
Short-term investments	1,300,694
Contributions receivable, net	1,594,053
Note receivable from related party	80,000
Endowment and long-term investments	6,457,512
Beneficial interest in trust	2,641,762
Total financial assets	13,088,345
Less financial assets held to meet donor-imposed restrictions:	
Purpose-restricted net assets (note 15)	(1,761,418)
Split-interest agreements (note 15)	(516,169)
Donor-restricted endowment funds (note 15)	(5,277,070)
Beneficial interest in trust (note 9)	(2,641,762)
Less financial assets not available within one year:	
Contributions receivable (note 6)	(118,940)
Note receivable (note 18)	(80,000)
Less board-designated endowment fund (note 8)	(371,326)
Amount available for general expenditures within one year	$ 2,321,660

The preceding table reflects donor-restricted and board-designated endowment funds as unavailable because it is the organization's intention to invest those resources for the long-term support of the organization. However, in the case of need, the Board of Directors could appropriate resources from either the donor-restricted funds available for general use ($3,388,819, of which $2,450,000 is the original gift) or from its board-designated endowment fund ($371,326). Note 8 provides more information about those funds and about the spending policies for all endowment funds.

As part of our liquidity management plan, we invest cash in excess of daily requirements in short-term investments (note 5). The organization maintains a revolving line of credit of $175,000 to cover short-term cash needs (note 10).

4. Fair Value Measurements

The organization reports fair value measures of its assets and liabilities using a three-level hierarchy that prioritizes the inputs used to measure fair value. This hierarchy, established by GAAP, requires that entities maximize the use of observable inputs and minimize the use of unobservable inputs when measuring fair value. The asset or liability's measurement within the fair value hierarchy is based on the lowest level of input that is significant to the measurement. The three levels of inputs used to measure fair value are as follows:

- *Level 1.* Quoted prices for identical assets or liabilities in active markets to which the organization has access at the measurement date.

- *Level 2.* Inputs other than quoted prices included in level 1 that are observable for the asset or liability, either directly or indirectly. Level 2 inputs include

  — quoted prices for similar assets or liabilities in active markets;

  — quoted prices for identical or similar assets in markets that are not active;

  — observable inputs other than quoted prices for the asset or liability (for example, interest rates and yield curves); and

  — inputs derived principally from, or corroborated by, observable market data by correlation or by other means.

- *Level 3.* Unobservable inputs for the asset or liability. Unobservable inputs should be used to measure the fair value if observable inputs are not available.

When available, the organization measures fair value using level 1 inputs because they generally provide the most reliable evidence of fair value. However, level 1 inputs are not available for many of the assets and liabilities that the organization is required to measure at fair value (for example, unconditional promises to give and in-kind contributions).

The primary uses of fair value measures in the organization's financial statements are

- initial measurement of noncash gifts, including gifts of investment assets and unconditional promises to give.

- recurring measurement of short term investments (note 5).

- recurring measurement of endowment and long-term investments (note 5).

- recurring measurement of beneficial interests in trusts (note 9).

5. Investments

Investments consist of the following at June 30, 20X1:

	Fair Value
Short-term investments:	
Money market funds	$302,240
U.S. treasury obligations	998,454
Total short term investments	1,300,694
Endowment and long-term investments:	
U.S. corporate bonds	460,450
U.S. common stocks	
Consumer goods	557,146
Technology	418,000
Other	289,733
Mutual funds — fixed income	1,162,350
Mutual funds — large cap value	802,250
Mutual funds — large cap growth	762,709
Mutual funds — small cap	232,778
Mutual funds — international	818,592
Exchange-traded funds	780,622
Real-estate partnership fund	172,882
Total endowment and long-term investments	6,457,512
Total investments	$7,758,206

The real-estate partnership fund invests primarily in office, industrial, and retail properties in the United States. This investment cannot be redeemed at will with the fund manager. Instead, distributions will be received from the fund manager as the underlying properties are sold. It is estimated that the underlying properties would be fully liquidated over the next 5–7 years. The organization is committed to a future investment of $150,000 in January 20X2.

As discussed in note 4 to these financial statements, the organization is required to report its fair value measurements in one of three levels, which are based on the ability to observe in the marketplace the inputs to the organization's valuation techniques. Level 1, the most observable level of inputs, is for investments measured at quoted prices in active markets for identical investments as of the June 30, 20X1, including investments measured at NAV if the NAV is determined as the fair value per share (unit) is published, and is the basis for current transactions. Level 2 is for investments measured using inputs such as quoted prices for similar assets or quoted prices for the identical asset in inactive markets. Level 3 is for investments measured using inputs that are unobservable, and is used in situations for which there is little, if any, market activity for the investment.

The organization uses the following ways to determine the fair value of its investments:

Money market funds: Determined by the published NAV per unit at the end of the last trading day of the year, which is the basis for transactions at that date.

U.S. Department of Treasury obligations: Determined using contractual cash flows and the interest rate determined by the closing bid price on the last business day of the fiscal year if the same or an obligation with a similar maturity is actively traded.

Equity securities traded on national securities exchanges: Determined by the closing price on the last business day of the fiscal year.

Equity securities traded on the over-the-counter market: Determined by the last reported bid price, if actively traded.

Open-end mutual funds: Determined by the published NAV per unit at the end of the last trading day of the fiscal year, which is the basis for transactions at that date.

Exchange-traded funds: Determined by the published closing price on the last business day of the fiscal year.

Real estate partnership fund: Determined by the NAV per share, as a practical expedient for a fair value measurement, because the underlying general partner's calculation of NAV is fair value based, and the NAV has been calculated by the fund manager as of the organization's fiscal year end date. NAV is determined based on appraisals of properties held and are conducted by third party appraisers retained by the general partner. NAVs provided by the general partner are evaluated by the organization's investment committee and are believed to present a reasonable estimate of fair value.

For investments that are not actively traded at June 30, 20X1, the organization uses a pricing service. The service employs a proprietary market approach method that uses as inputs observed interest rates and yield curves, prices in active markets for similar assets, and prices for identical assets in inactive markets that have been adjusted by observable indexes (level 2).

The following table summarizes the levels in the fair value hierarchy of the organization's investments at June 30, 20X1:

	Total	Level 1	Level 2
Money market funds	$ 302,240	$ 302,240	
U.S. treasury obligations	998,454		998,454
U.S. corporate bonds	460,450	80,459	379,991
U.S. common stocks	1,264,879	1,006,439	258,440
Mutual funds — fixed income	1,162,350	1,162,350	
Mutual funds — large cap value	802,250	802,250	
Mutual funds — large cap growth	762,709	762,709	
Mutual funds — small cap	232,778	232,778	
Mutual funds — international	818,592	818,592	
Exchange-traded funds	780,622	780,622	
	$7,585,324	$5,948,439	$1,636,885
Measured using NAV as a practical expedient	172,882		
Total investments	$7,758,206		

                    © 2020, Association of International Certified Professional Accountants

6. Contributions and Grants Receivable

Contributions and grants receivable at June 30, 20X1, are due as follows:

Currently due	$1,010,000
Less than 1 year	485,950
1 year to 5 years	129,950
	1,625,900
Less:	
Allowance for uncollectible contributions receivable	(20,837)
Unamortized discount, at rates ranging from 2.55% to 4.45%	(11,010)
	$1,594,053

At June 30, 20X1, the organization is attempting to raise $125,000 to create a space in the County Library's teen area. If the organization is able to do so before January 1, 20X2, those funds will be matched by a corporate donor, so that $250,000 would be available for the program. At June 30, 20X1, donors have promised $25,000 toward this goal, of which $10,000 has been collected.

7. Land, Buildings and Equipment

Land, buildings and equipment at June 30, 20X1, are as follows:

Land and land improvements	$209,205
Buildings and improvements	2,431,807
Leasehold improvements	238,631
Furnishings and equipment	457,660
Equipment acquired by capital lease	79,197
	3,416,500
Accumulated depreciation and amortization	(1,761,132)
Total land, buildings, and equipment, net	**$1,655,368**

8. Accounting for Endowments

The organization's endowment consists of 12 individual funds established either by donors (referred to as *donor-restricted endowment funds*) and or by resources set aside by the Board of Directors to function as endowments (*referred to as board-designated endowment funds*). Donor-restricted endowment funds are further divided into those that provide a perpetual source of support for the organization's activities (referred to as *perpetual endowments*) and those that are restricted by donors to investment for a specified term (referred to as *term endowments*). As required by GAAP, net assets associated with endowment funds are classified and reported based on the existence or absence of donor-imposed restrictions.

Included in the organization's endowment is a perpetual charitable trust held by a bank trustee (note 9). The trust's management, including investment policies and distribution policies, are determined by the donor's trust agreement with the bank trustee. The following discussion describes only the endowment funds that are under the organization's management.

The state of Illinois enacted the Uniform Prudent Management of Institutional Funds Act (UPMIFA) effective June 30, 2009. UPMIFA establishes law for the management and investment of donor-restricted endowment funds. Donor-restricted endowment funds are subject to a time restriction imposed by UPMIFA until amounts are appropriated for expenditure by the organization. In addition, most donor restricted endowment funds are subject to restrictions on the use of the appropriated amounts. Note 15 describes the purposes for which donor-restricted endowment may be used. As a result, donor-restricted endowment funds are classified as net assets with donor restrictions.

UPMIFA permits the organization to appropriate for expenditure or accumulate so much of a donor-restricted endowment fund as it determines is prudent for the uses, benefits, purposes, and duration for which the endowment fund is established. In making its determination to appropriate or accumulate, the organization must act in good faith, with the care that an ordinarily prudent person in a like position would exercise under similar circumstances, and it must consider, if relevant, the following factors:

- The duration and preservation of the endowment fund

- The purposes of the organization and the donor-restricted endowment fund

- General economic conditions

- The possible effect of inflation and deflation

- The expected total return from income and the appreciation of investments

- Other resources of the organization

- The investment policy of the organization

The net asset composition of the endowment as of June 30, 20X1, is as follows:

	Without Donor Restrictions	With Donor Restrictions	Total
Type of Endowment Fund			
Donor-restricted funds			
Perpetual endowment		$5,233,000	$5,233,000
Term endowment		44,070	44,070
Perpetual charitable trust		2,641,762	2,641,762
Board-designated endowment	$371,326	—	371,326
Total	$371,326	$7,918,832	$8,290,158

One donor-restricted perpetual endowment fund, created in 20Y8, currently has a value of $91,665, which is less than the amount of the original gift ($100,000). The deficiency of $8,335 at June 30, 20X1, is reported in net assets with donor restrictions.

Investment and Spending Policies

The organization has an investment policy specific to its Endowment Fund, which is monitored by the Investment Committee of its Board of Directors. The investment policy describes the objective for the fund and sets ranges for asset allocation. The objective of the Endowment Fund is to earn the highest possible total return consistent with a level of risk suitable for these assets. At a minimum, long term rates of return should be equal to an amount sufficient to maintain the purchasing power of the Endowment Fund assets, to provide necessary capital to fund the spending policy, and to cover the costs of managing the Endowment Fund investments. The desired minimum rate of return is equal to the Consumer Price Index plus 500 basis points on an annualized basis. Actual returns in any given year may vary from this amount. In light of this return requirement, the portfolio is constructed using a total return approach with a significant portion of the funds invested to seek growth of principal over time. The assets are invested for the long term, and a higher short term volatility in these assets is to be expected and accepted. The organization limits its investments in so-called alternative investments — investments in the form of limited partnerships, limited liability companies, or joint ventures, which might commit the organization to future investments or have legal restrictions that prevent the sale or redemption of the investment for more than a year.

The following is a summary of the asset allocation guidelines, with allowable ranges for each asset type.

Asset Category	Target	Minimum	Maximum
Cash	0%	0%	10%
Domestic fixed income	10%	5%	15%
Equity — Mutual funds	60%	55%	75%
Fixed income	20%	10%	30%
Domestic large cap	20%	10%	30%
Large cap growth	10%	5%	20%
Large cap value	10%	5%	20%
Domestic small cap	5%	0%	20%
International	15%	5%	20%
Exchange-traded funds	15%	0%	20%
Domestic common stock	10%	0%	20%
Alternative investments	5%	0%	10%

The organization uses an endowment spending formula based on total return of the investments for determining the amount to spend from the Endowment Fund each year. The appropriation is 5% of the average fair value of the Endowment Fund investments for the prior 12 quarters calculated at March 31 of each year. In establishing this policy, the organization considered the long term expected return on its Endowment Fund investments and set the rate with the objective of maintaining the purchasing power of its donor-restricted perpetual endowment funds over time.

The Board of Directors of the organization has interpreted UPMIFA as requiring the preservation of the fair value of the original gift as of the gift date of the donor-restricted endowment funds unless there are explicit donor stipulations to the contrary. The original gift is defined by the organization as (a) the original value of gifts donated to all donor-restricted endowments, (b) the original value of any subsequent gifts to donor-restricted endowments, and (c) the original value of accumulations to donor-restricted endowments made in accordance with the direction of the applicable donor gift instrument at the time the accumulation is added to the fund. As a result of this interpretation. if the value of a donor-restricted endowment fund falls below 75% of its original gift, the Board of Directors will cease applying the spending rate to the fund until its value exceeds the original gift.

The changes in endowment net assets for the year ended June 30, 20X1, are as follows:

	Without Donor Restrictions	With Donor Restrictions	Total
Endowment net assets, July 1, 20X0	$452,129	$7,683,572	$8,135,701
Investment return:			
Investment return	10,368	295,543	305,911
Perpetual trust return		172,900	172,900
Total investment return	10,368	468,443	478,811
Contributions		5,000	5,000
Appropriation of endowment assets for expenditure — spending rate	(11,171)	(238,183)	(249,354)
Appropriation of endowment assets from board-designated endowment for note receivable to related party	(80,000)		(80,000)
Endowment net assets, June 30, 20X1	$371,326	$7,918,832	$8,290,158

© 2020, Association of International Certified Professional Accountants

9. Beneficial Interest in Trust

The organization is the irrevocable beneficiary of a perpetual charitable trust held by a bank trustee. These resources are neither in the possession of, nor under the control of, the organization. The terms of the trust provide that the organization is to receive an annual distribution from the trust, the amount of which is at the discretion of the trustee, but will not be less than 3% or more than 7% of the trust assets at the beginning of the trust's fiscal year. The beneficial interest in the trust is reported at its fair value, which is estimated as the fair value of the underlying trust assets. As discussed in note 4, because there are no observable market transactions for assets similar to the beneficial interest in the trust and because the trust cannot be redeemed, the valuation technique used by the organization is a level 3 fair value measure.

Beneficial interest in trust, beginning of year	$2,589,206
Investment return earned by trustee	172,900
Amount distributed to the organization	(120,344)
Beneficial interest in trust, end of year	$2,641,762

The distributions from the trust are available for the teacher training program and are included investment return increasing net assets with donor restrictions in the statement of activities. The change in the fair value of the beneficial interest in the trust is recognized as an increase in net assets with donor restrictions in the statement of activities.

10. Note Payable and Capital Lease Obligations

Note payable and capital lease obligations at June 30, 20X1, are as follows:

Note payable to First Main Bank of Chicago in the original principal amount of $1,650,000, due on December 1, 20Z9. Fixed interest rate of 6.125%, payable in monthly principal and interest payments of $10,757.41, beginning January 1, 2005. The bonds are secured by the organization's buildings in Ottawa, Illinois and Davenport, Illinois.	$1,463,993
Various capital leases for equipment that may be purchased for a nominal amount at expiration of the leases. The interest rate implicit in these leases are 6% to 7.5%. Monthly payments at June 30, 20X1, are $1,767 and leases expire at varying dates through May 1, 20X6. Secured by equipment with an original purchase price of $79,197 and accumulated amortization of $40,687.	49,900
Total note payable and capital lease obligation	$1,513,893

	Note Payable	Capital Lease
Year ending June 30,		
20X2	$40,540	$21,200
20X3	43,093	13,200
20X4	45,808	11,050
20X5	48,693	6,750
20X6	51,762	6,350
Thereafter	1,234,097	—
Total payments	1,463,993	58,550
Less portion representing interest		(8,650)
Note payable or capital lease obligation	$1,463,993	$49,900

In addition, the organization has a $175,000 unsecured revolving line of credit with a local bank, which has an expiration date of June 24, 20X2. As of June 30, 20X1, there are no amounts outstanding under the line.

Interest expense incurred during 20X1, was $480 on borrowings under this line of credit. Interest is based on the beginning of month Secured Overnight Financing Rate, plus 125 basis points. At June 30, 20X1, that rate was 0.54%.

11. Asset Retirement Obligation

The organization has legal obligations to perform certain activities upon the renovation of certain buildings that contain asbestos or upon the abandonment of certain leasehold improvements. The obligations (referred to as asset retirement obligations) were initially recorded at fair values, which were estimated as the present values of the estimated costs of remediation or removal. Concurrent with the recognition of the obligation, the costs of the corresponding long-lived assets were increased. The capitalized costs are being depreciated over the remaining useful life of the assets. Annually, the obligation is adjusted for the time value of money and for new information, if any, about the future costs of remediation or removal. The changes in the obligation, which were $9,802 for the year ended June 30, 20X1, are reported as part of occupancy costs and allocated to the programs and management and general activities that benefit from the use of those buildings and leasehold improvements.

12. Split-interest Agreements

The organization conducts a deferred-giving program in which a donor makes an irrevocable transfer of assets to the organization. In exchange, the donor (or a beneficiary named by the donor) receives periodic payments for his or her lifetime. The payments to the individuals are fixed amounts (annuities) or are a percentage of the fair value of the trust assets (charitable remainder unitrusts). The obligations to the individuals are determined using present value techniques, mortality information in the 2012 Individual Annuity Reserving Table, and interest rates of 2%–4% (dependent upon market rates when the agreement was signed). The obligations are adjusted annually for changes in mortality, investment returns, and the time value of money, and the adjustment is reported in the statement of activities as the change in the value of split-interest agreements.

At June 30, 20X1, the organization held investments of $854,050 relating to split-interest agreements with obligations of $337,881. The remainder interests of $516,169 are classified as net assets with donor restrictions because they are unavailable for spending until the deaths of the donors or other beneficiaries.

There was the following activity in the split-interest obligation during the year ended June 30, 20X1:

Split-interest obligations, June 30, 20X0	$289,734
New agreements signed, gift portion of $22,332	22,668
Investment return	50,236
Payments to beneficiaries	(64,000)
Change in valuation of split-interest agreements	39,243
Split-interest obligations, June 30, 20X1	$337,881

13. Operating Lease Commitments

The organization has various operating leases for several meeting room facilities. The following is a schedule of future minimum rental payments:

Year ending June 30:	
20X2	$19,200
20X3	19,200
20X4	12,000
20X5	12,000
20X6	6,000
Total future minimum rental payments	$68,400

© 2020, Association of International Certified Professional Accountants

Rent expense for meeting rooms, which is included in occupancy costs in the statement of functional expenses, was $24,000 for the year ended June 30, 20X1.

14. Retirement Plan

The organization participates in a defined contribution, individual account, money purchase, retirement plan that covers substantially all of its full-time employees. This plan is available for the benefit of all full-time employees of the organization who have completed one year of service to the organization.

In accordance with the plan agreement, the organization makes contributions to the plan, which are determined based on a percentage of the participating employee's salary and the amount of an employee's elective contributions. The organization's contributions, which are included in employee benefits in the statement of functional expenses, were $98,100 for the year ended June 30, 20X1.

15. Net Assets With Donor Restrictions

At June 30, 20X1, net assets with donor restrictions are available for the following purposes or periods:

Purpose restrictions, available for spending:	
Curriculum development	$756,680
Teacher training	583,275
Teacher awards	175,000
STEAM Saturdays	236,463
Maker space in County Library	10,000
Total purpose-restricted net assets	1,761,418
Time restrictions:	
Contributions receivable, which are unavailable for spending until due, some of which are also subject to purpose restrictions	584,053
Split-interest agreements, which are unavailable for spending until the deaths of the beneficiaries	516,169
Endowment Funds, which must be appropriated by the Board of Directors before use:	
Donors specified for the general use of the organization, time restricted until appropriated (original gift $2,450,000)	3,388,819
Donors restricted to the following purposes:	
Curriculum development (original gift $850,000)	1,179,525
Teacher training (original gift $518,500)	708,726
Total Endowment Funds managed by the organization	5,277,070
Beneficial interest in trust for curriculum development	2,641,762
Total net assets with donor restrictions	$10,780,472

16. Commitments and Contingencies

The organization has entered into contracts with the Greater Midwest Convention Center for its 20X1 and 20X2 Showcases. These contracts contain cancelation penalties determined on a scale based on the number of days prior to the scheduled event, with the penalty increasing as the time period decreases. The penalties for cancellation under these contracts would be:

	As of June 30, 20X1	Maximum Penalty
20X1 Showcase	$90,000	$100,000
20X2 Showcase	$25,000	$100,000

17. Concentrations of Risk

A significant portion, approximately 35%, of the organization's annual funding comes from the Science Alliance of Metropolitan Chicago. At June 20, 20X1, $510,000 is receivable from Science Alliance.

The majority of the organization's contributions and grants are received from corporations, foundations, and individuals located in the greater Chicago metropolitan area and from agencies of the state of Illinois. As such, the organization's ability to generate resources via contributions and grants is dependent upon the economic health of that area and of the state of Illinois.

The organization's investments are subject to various risks, such as interest rate, credit, and overall market volatility risks. Further, because of the significance of the investments to the organization's financial position and the level of risk inherent in most investments, it is reasonably possible that changes in the values of these investments could occur in the near term and such changes could materially affect the amounts reported in the financial statements. Management is of the opinion that the diversification of its invested assets among the various asset classes (see notes 5 and 8) should mitigate the impact of changes in any one class.

18. Related-Party Transactions

In January 20X1, the organization advanced $80,000 to Chicago STEAM Outpost, a newly established 501(c)(3) organization that will blend the Girl and Boy Scouts' time-tested character-building qualities with hands-on STEAM modules. STEAM Scouts will involve boys and girls in elementary, middle, and high schools. A member of the organization's board of trustees is also a member of the Chicago STEAM Outpost's governing body. The note, which bears interest at 6% per year payable quarterly, is due on December 31, 20X3, in a lump-sum payment. Management believes the note to be fully collectible; therefore, no allowance for uncollectible amounts is recorded.

In 20X0, the organization entered into a three-year lease agreement for meeting rooms in a building owned by a member of the board of trustees. Rent is for $10,000 per year. That lease agreement expires on June 30, 20X3. The lease agreement was approved by the organization's board of trustees; the board member who owns the building recused herself from the discussion and vote.

At June 30, 20X1, contributions receivable included $75,000 (present value of promised cash flows $71,355) from members of the organization's board of trustees.

19. Subsequent Events

Subsequent events have been evaluated through September 29, 20X1, which is the date the financial statements were available to be issued. Events occurring after that date have not been evaluated to determine whether a change in the financial statements would be required.